EFFECTIV
COMMUNICATION
SKILLS

for Scientific and
Technical Professionals

Other Books by Harry E. Chambers

Getting Promoted: Real Strategies for Advancing Your Career

The Bad Attitude Survival Guide: Essential Tools for Managers

No-Fear Management: Rebuilding Trust, Performance and Commitment in the New American Workplace
(coauthored with Dr. Robert Craft)

EFFECTIVE COMMUNICATION SKILLS

for Scientific and Technical Professionals

HARRY E. CHAMBERS

PERSEUS PUBLISHING
Cambridge, Massachusetts

Many of the designations used by manufacturers and sellers to distinguish their products are claimed as trademarks. Where those designations appear in this book and Perseus Publishing was aware of a trademark claim, the designations have been printed in initial capital letters.

Cataloging-in-Publication Data for this book is available from the Library of Congress
ISBN 0–7382-0287-8

Perseus Publishing is a member of the Perseus Books Group.

Find us on the World Wide Web at http://www.perseuspublishing.com

Perseus Publishing books are available at special discounts for bulk purchases in the U.S. by corporations, institutions, and other organizations. For more information, please contact the Special Markets Department at HarperCollins Publishers, 10 East 53rd Street, New York, NY 10022, or call 1–212–207–7528.

Text design by Jeff Williams
Set in 10.5-point Janson by Perseus Publishing Services

First printing, November 2000
1 2 3 4 5 6 7 8 9 10—03 02 01 00

As always:
To Chris, Shari, Michael, and Patrick.

In memory of:
Earl John Chambers, 1913–1999
Richard C. Kern, 1917–1999

CONTENTS

ACKNOWLEDGMENTS

This book was written during a time of great emotional turmoil for my family and me. My father passed away at the age of eighty-six after a relatively brief illness. One week after his funeral, our son Michael was married to Sandra Falteau, and within seven days, my wife, Chris, and I experienced both life's great sadness and a parent's joy. Six weeks later, Chris's father passed away, finally succumbing to a long bout with cancer. Through it all, our youngest son, Patrick, was like a rock and helped everyone in the family to deal with the cascade of events and the ebb and flow of emotions. He demonstrated a maturity far beyond his twelve years. Since that time, our daughter, Shari, and her husband, Eddie, have announced that our first grandchild is on the way, and with great excitement we await that new life. The circle of life continues: as members of the family depart, new life begins in the eternal experience of continuation.

Also during this time, Perseus editor Nick Philipson and his wife, Ruth, celebrated the birth of their first child, Rachel Grace, and Nick tells us that she is the most beautiful of God's creations. Mickey Beatty, who has assisted in the development of this book, as she did with my three previous publications, celebrated the wedding of her son, Sean, to Beth Lamborn, and learned that she and her husband, Mike, will soon be welcoming their second grandchild. This manuscript was created during a tumultuous time, one that included great joy.

Chris was very helpful in the writing of this book. She is evolving into a true coauthor. And her editing efforts were invaluable. I owe great thanks to her and our son, Patrick, for their patience and support during this project.

Once again, Mickey Beatty worked her magic, and I continue to be amazed at her ability to transform my chaotic thoughts into a coherent manuscript. She plays a very big role in our overall business, and I can't imagine writing books without her help.

My gratitude goes to Nick Philipson of Perseus Books for the opportunity to continue writing and I am thankful for all his help. I truly appreciate his understanding of and patience with this project. I was extremely fortunate to work again with Julie Stillman, who provided her usual exceptional editorial guidance. It is a privilege and a pleasure to work with such competent people.

I would like to thank the many people who provided background information as well as actual content for this manuscript: Ken Edwards and Bob Stander of the International Brotherhood of Electrical Workers; Tim Green and Ted Lehne, Delta Air Lines; Elizabeth Haggerty, Carrier Corporation; Ken Hodina, Otis Elevator Corporation; Michael Ostack, IT consultant, MCSE (Microsoft Certified Systems Engineer), Net/X Solutions; Carol Price, Unlimited Dimensions and Training, Inc.; Sandra Skinner, Lear Corporation; Dr. Mitchell Springer, Raytheon Systems Company; Hank Szumowski, Connecticut Hospital Association; Jeff Treiber, Pratt & Whitney; Shari Harper, Analytical Services, Inc.; Richard Cox, Magaro and Associates.

I appreciate their willingness to help and their openness in sharing their thoughts and experience.

And finally, my thanks to you, the reader. I appreciate you most of all!

EFFECTIVE COMMUNICATION
Skills

for Scientific and
Technical Professionals

1

Today's Communication Realities

Communication is an art, not a science. It encompasses inconsistencies, interpretations, and emotional variables, and is greatly influenced by every individual's unique frame of reference and life experience. All communication, whether delivered or received, is processed through our internal belief system, a mechanism that is commonly called our "filter." Communication is always influenced by the overwhelming internal belief of being *right:*

"The things I say are truthful and accurate. I am *right.*"
"The things I do are correct, fair, and justifiable. I am *right.*"
"The conclusions I draw are intellectually sound. I am *right.*"

Conversely, those who say, think, or do things differently are typically judged to be *wrong.*

This self-righteous perception of always being right, moral, accurate, more knowledgeable, and so on distorts the communication process and creates potentially damaging disconnects in the delivery and reception of the message.

The negative impact of poor communication is everywhere.

What is the number one challenge facing every organization in today's economy?
Effective Communication

What is the number one challenge facing every marriage or significant relationship in today's world?
Effective Communication

What is the number one challenge facing every parent-child relationship in today's families?
Effective Communication

What is the number one challenge you face in your career?
Effective Communication

Becoming a highly skilled communicator is not easy. The good news is that the skills of effective communication are learned. Though some of us are inherently better communicators than others, we all can learn. However, it takes both a willing student and a competent teacher to lead the process. Improving your communication skills is a particularly unique endeavor. Most people, especially those from a professional background, are convinced of their own communication superiority, harboring beliefs such as these:

"I am a good communicator . . . it's everyone else who has a problem."
"My boss doesn't communicate well, but I do."
"My peers have problems in communicating, but not me."
"People in other departments are bad communicators; they certainly do not do it as well as I."
"It's not my communication delivery that is the problem; they just don't listen well."
"It's not my listening skills that are the problem; they don't know how to deliver communication effectively."

Blaming everyone else for communication problems seems to have become an American pastime.

The truth is, we all demonstrate various strengths and weaknesses in all aspects of our communication. There is not one person on planet Earth who does not need to increase the effectiveness of his or her communication skills. Effective communication is the eternal and universal challenge facing us all.

Do scientific and technical professionals experience more communication problems than those in other professions? Absolutely not, yet by the very nature of your training, experience, and evolving responsibilities, you face unique communication challenges that are much more complex than those impacting other professionals.

The communication challenges you face today cannot be successfully addressed with generalized one-size-fits-all recommendations. The issues demand specific targeted responses.

Let's begin to take a closer look at the complexity of the communication challenges facing today's scientific and technical professionals.

Who Are Today's Scientific and Technical Professionals?

You are probably very intelligent and make your living by inventing, designing, improving, or fixing things, and have a penchant for problem solving and creativity. Typically, your inventory of skills is knowledge-based and your activities and accomplishments are intellectually driven. Highly trained in math, the sciences, and computer technology, you more than likely have shown less interest in the study of psychology, sociology, or political science, and see most of those subjects as "touchy-feely" time wasters. You probably have highly evolved organizational skills and manage your time efficiently. Your job titles have included various engineering specialties, chemist, metallurgist, physicist, designer, and a wide spectrum of specialized science disciplines such as technician, researcher, information specialist, and technical editor. You are labeled a "techie," and the earlier negative stereotypical description of you as a "pocket protector–wearing pencil-necked geek" has been obliterated by your successes and accomplishments. You are a member of one of the fastest-growing segments of our economy and enjoy some of the most rapidly accelerating compensation scales in today's ever-changing organizations. Your educational qualifications may range from Ph.D.s and master's degrees to specialized certifications from various technical institutions. People like you are employed in every major industry, including aerospace, automotive, electronics, energy, finance, information, manufacturing, marine, medicine, petrochemical, publishing, oil, software, telecommunications, and transportation. Though some of you work in relative obscurity, most find your visibility increasing every day and your value to your organization escalating at an unparalleled rate.

The monumental contributions of scientific and technical professionals and their ever-increasing influence on today's world, workplace, and economy cannot possibly be overstated. Your numbers and influence are growing rapidly in every organization in the United States today. Technology alone has added more than one million jobs to the economy since 1994, and according to the Bureau of Labor Statistics, computer-related jobs are the fastest-growing occupational category in the U.S. economy.[1] As our economy speeds away from domination by manufacturing and toward more knowledge-based intellectual and service capabilities, scientific and technical professionals are truly becoming the big fish in a very big pond. Consider the impact that scientific and technically oriented corporations have on our economy. This reality was acknowledged formally by the stock market with the addition of Intel and Microsoft to the thirty stocks that make up the Dow Jones Industrial Average. A bad day for science and technology stocks means a bad day for Wall Street. Advances in science and technology are creating more wealth than any other economic category. In the past, the barons of manufacturing and banking were the most highly visible economic giants. Today, the economic giants are Bill Gates and his breed of innovators who captain the ships of scientific and technological commerce. Today the "best and the brightest" are drawn to the challenges and opportunities of the scientific and technical workplace.

Your Impact and Contributions

These contributions are only a few of the gifts you have given to the world . . . and you have only just begun. When cancer is cured and men and women live and travel to outer space, it will be because of the efforts of scientific and technical professionals such as you.

You are at the forefront of driving change.

Though you are fiercely protective of your past contributions and achievements, the pursuit of improvement—finding new ways to increase speed, quality, and efficiency—lies at the core of your motivation. The challenge of creating new processes and finding new alternatives and applications is the very lifeblood of your efforts. Never being satisfied with the status quo, you are relentlessly driven to achieve the next level and create the next significant breakthrough. Yours is a constant quest to invent, discover, adapt, modify, combine, substitute, eliminate, reduce, and rearrange. As the true "change agents" of the world's economy, you are continually influencing not only what we do, but how, why, and when we do it. Behind every headline, news report, or business development exists an underlying contribution of the scientific and technical community.

As a scientific and technical professional, you have given us:

- The explosion of information technology that has created the Information Age
- Today's telecommunications capabilities
- The speed and safety of our transportation
- Exploration of the moon, planets, and the stars
- The enchantment and creativity of virtual and real entertainment
- The miracles of medical breakthroughs: curing illness, easing pain, and extending life
- The capabilities of computer science to influence our business, professional, and private lives
- The technology to maintain our physical comfort and personal health, freeing us from the drudgery, inconvenience, and the discomfort of the past
- The ability to transform the learning and training process by providing educational presentations in alternative formats, such as enhanced audiovisual presentations and online interactive learning
- Weapons to defend our nation and ensure the increased safety and welfare of the civilian population as well as the men and women in our armed forces

Increased Visibility and Influence Creates Complex Communication Challenges

Because of your rapidly escalating importance, prominence, visibility, and contributions, you are facing far more personal and organizational communication challenges today than ever before in our economic history. You are being asked to assume duties previously performed by managers or other specialists. No longer do you labor in isolation. Your work is being done in environments demanding high levels of collaboration and extensive interaction with others. You find yourself working in close partnership with both internal and external customers. You are thrust into interactive team environments and called upon to coordinate your efforts with nontechnical peers. The amount of critical interaction between you and managers from different backgrounds, disciplines, and experiences has increased dramatically.

In the past, many scientific and technical professionals worked independently with little interaction or collaboration with others. You could be the

Lone Ranger, and you probably preferred it that way. You would likely have been an individual performer, not necessarily oriented toward being a team player. Today's environment, with its heavy emphasis on speed, cost, and quality, renders this old model of detached contribution obsolete. The days of succeeding as an isolated specialist or by playing corporate "solitaire" are over.

In today's restructured, reengineered, and downsized workplace, many of you find yourselves responsible to supervisors, managers, and department heads who do not share your technical background and training.

One of your most critical challenges is having to justify your efforts and results to various funding sources and to the people responsible for other critical resources. The bottom line counts as never before, and you may have to fight for support of your research, creations, ideas, and theories on an ongoing basis. The scientific and technical community has become extremely competitive, and increased communication skills elevate your ability to compete.

As ever-increasing amounts of information are being received and delivered, the importance of effective communication escalates daily. The risks and potential downsides of miscommunication compound almost by the minute, and the speed at which we can make mistakes and flirt with disaster is increasing. Among the root causes of today's most visible and impacting problems and failures is poor communication. Perhaps no greater example exists than the disaster NASA experienced with the Mars Climate Orbiter, which was lost in September of 1999.[2] The $125 million dollar spacecraft malfunctioned and was destroyed because of a basic and catastrophic miscommunication. NASA navigators assumed a contractor was using metric measurements when in fact English units had been used. NASA converted to the metric system in 1996, and apparently this change of standard was not effectively communicated to every person and organization involved in this mission. With no intention here to assign blame, it is nonetheless irrefutable that this monumental miscommunication resulted in a huge financial loss, the waste of countless hours of valuable effort, and the loss of critical data the mission was intended to generate. The results may be irreparable.

The scientific and technical community is not untouched by the escalation of workplace violence that is occurring in the United States today. Frequently, violent acts have issues of miscommunication in their origin. Many of the most painful experiences of life could be averted by early, successful communication intervention.

The responsibility for communicating well with people of differing functions, personalities, authority, and influence demands that scientific and technical professionals continually improve their communication skills—skills that in the past were not necessarily held in high regard, for yesterday's successful scientific and technical professionals were not called upon to be beacons of communication. This does not mean that the responsibility for effective communication lies solely on your shoulders. On the contrary; *everyone* has the obligation to increase his or her communication skills. However, the painful truth is, "You can only influence that which you have influence over." You cannot compel others to be better communicators. You can only compel and control yourself. As you sharpen your communication abilities, hopefully others will follow suit, yet there is no guarantee. Avoid at all costs the self-justification trap of believing, "Nobody else is doing it . . . why should I?" or "No one else cares about how they communicate with me . . . why should I be concerned about how I communicate with them?" Hold yourself to a higher professional standard: pursue maximum communication efficiency.

The first step in any correction or development is to diagnose and assess the current state of your communication skills. For medical practitioners, prescription without diagnosis is considered malpractice. For you and your communication skills, correction without self-assessment and diagnosis is an inefficient waste of time!

Six Critical Communication Realities for Scientific and Technical Professionals

Throughout this text you will be invited to self-assess a number of very specific communication issues. In doing so, you will confront the critical communication realities that are facing every scientific and technical professional in today's workplace. Here you will be asked to rate on a scale of 1 to 10 your effectiveness in meeting six of the most significant communication challenges that you face. This rating is obviously very subjective, and you may be tempted to rate yourself higher than a more objective observer would. I urge you not to fall into that self-serving rating trap. It is easy to perceive yourself as a great communicator and that it is everyone else who needs to change. It is harder to deal with reality and be brutally honest with yourself. You will do yourself a big favor if you are accurate in your self-assessment. Identify any true areas of weakness and realize that growth begins with an acknowledgment of the necessity for improvement and development. You have many professional strengths. Celebrate them and be willing to seize opportunities for improvement. Denial is not your friend!

1. You Are More Task-Oriented Than People-Oriented

Typically, your training, education, and thought processes concentrate on technical development and focus more on tasks and less on interpersonal issues. Though this preparation develops your exceptional technical capabilities, it generally leads to challenges when you are working and communicating interactively with nontechnical peers or in team environments.

Signs and Symptoms

- *Weak "Soft" Skills*

The precision of your training, skill, and operating style cannot always be readily transferred when dealing with people. Such interaction calls for weighing many considerations, some of which may not be easily quantifiable or are often rooted in abstract influences. You consider yourself to be a person rooted in "exactness" in an "inexact" world. You probably experience this frequently in dealing with peoples' varying degrees of emotion, differing perceptions, and shifting priorities. Gray areas in personal interactions are not easily addressed with black and white decisiveness.

"Soft" skills such as communication, conflict resolution, customer service, dealing with difficult people, and effective listening are common components of the educational curriculum and training programs for many types of professionals, yet not necessarily for technical professionals. These skills are given much less emphasis in the training and development of the scientific and technical disciplines. Thus, you may not have been exposed to all of the education and skill development necessary for success in today's ever-changing business environment. This potentially puts you at a disadvantage in competing with others for career growth.

An example of this disadvantage frequently occurs when you are promoted into leadership positions. You possess great intellect and mastery of your discipline, which is why you have been promoted, but you have not been trained in the skills of leadership and management, which have been defined as "getting the job done with and through others." You quickly find that your performance is no longer dependent on your exceptional technical knowledge and ability. Your success depends on your ability to impart knowledge and develop the skills of others while increasing overall group, team, or departmental productivity. People in this situation commonly experience high rates of frustration and confusion because they lack appropriate soft skills training, including leadership. You cannot be expected to perform well in areas where you have not been trained in the skills that define success. When scientific and technical professionals experience difficulty in managing others, it is not usually the result of their incompetence as technical professionals. It is probably rooted in the absence of training and development in leadership skills, and chief among these is effective communication.

Real-World Commentary
Elizabeth Haggerty is the program manager for business and manufacturing-process improvements at the Carrier Corporation, in Hartford, Connecticut. She has bachelor's and master's degrees in metallurgical engineering, and after seven years of practical experience in research and development, she received her MBA. Liz commented on the imbalance in the training that scientific and technical professionals receive:

> In engineering school you take technical courses. Many times even your electives are in technical areas. You are often not required to take soft skill classes. I think a lot of what is taught in MBA programs should be required in undergrad and engineering schools. The path of being an engineer/scientist and spending the rest of your life as an individual contributor does not really exist anymore. You need to have the skill base to understand how an organization works to be able to move upward through that organization. If you really want to get promoted, get salary increases, and be recognized for your contributions, you need to have these skills. In the past, effectiveness was based purely on technical competency, and that just isn't the case anymore. We are finding that we need more people with a science or technology background who also understand the total business environment. Many graduates of engineering and technology schools do not understand organizational dynamics, organizational change, or how to be effective in multifaceted organizations that are both business- and technology-driven. Basic communication and presentation skills are also often lacking. I do not know how many times I have watched technical people get up and give a presentation and at the end you are asking yourself, "What in the world were they just talking

about?" They need the skills to understand their audience and how to build a presentation to fit the group. The scientific and technology environment has changed, and good communication skills are necessary. You can't survive without them.

Soft-Skills Training Assessment
On a scale of 1–10 (1 being extremely low/never; 10 being extremely high/frequently), rate the level and effectiveness of the training and education you have received in the critical areas of soft skills, including:

- Effective listening
- Communication
- Customer service strategies
- Successful conflict resolution
- Dealing with diverse personalities
- Functioning in a multiculturally diverse work environment
- Working interactively in a collaborative team environment

2. You Are Highly Committed and Dedicated to the Work You Do

Most of you identified very early what you wanted your life's work to be. It is as if you popped out of the womb knowing you wanted a career in engineering, science, information technology, and so on. Your first real toy was probably a chemistry or Erector set. The vast majority of people in other professions and functions do not share a similar identification of interest or specific dedication of purpose. Scientific and technical professionals truly are unique. Because of this commitment and dedication, two developments often occur.

Signs and Symptoms

- *"Us Against Them"*

Because you place such a high value on what you do, there may be a tendency to devalue the importance of other organizational functions.

You may (perhaps unintentionally) dismiss the contributions of others whose jobs are not technically oriented as being unimportant or nonessential. The perception "If it's not technical, it doesn't matter" may exist to a significant degree. High incidence of "us-against-them" cultural mind-sets often occurs between scientific and technical groups and other departments, such as operations, manufacturing, sales, marketing, and human resources. This often results in ineffective communication between these groups, which can then become the root cause of animosities and internal organizational conflict.

Real-World Commentary

This mind-set of discounting other types of work is not limited just to technical-versus-nontechnical groups. Hierarchies often exist within particular functions as well. Dr. Mitchell Springer is the director of training and employee development for the Communications Systems Division of Raytheon Systems Company in Fort Wayne, Indiana. He is the author of *Program Planning: A Real Life Quantitative Approach* (Purdue University Press, 1998). Raytheon Systems Company is a defense-oriented division of the parent company, Raytheon. Dr. Springer pointed out:

> Within engineering itself as a discipline, there is a recognized hierarchy, and I was floored when I first began to see this evolve about ten years ago. But it certainly has been exhibited, at least in our industry. Let's take engineers. We have software engineers, systems engineers, electrical engineers, and mechanical engineers. . . . Software engineers tend to be in the greatest demand and have the highest place in the engineering discipline. Next are systems engineers, which is a little ironic because systems engineers frequently look at things from an operational perspective, from the outside. . . . The existence of these internal hierarchies can contribute to communication problems and a type of unspoken warfare.

Assessing "Us Against Them"

On a scale of 1 to 10 (1 being extremely low/never; 10 being extremely high/frequently), rate the level of your personal involvement with the "us-against-them" mind-set. You may also want to rate the overall opinion of your department, team, or intimate work group separately. What is your tendency to devalue the importance of other organizational functions or to dismiss the individual contributions of those whose jobs are not technically oriented? Do you frequently have negative communications with others from different technical backgrounds?

1____ ____ ____ ____ ____ ____ ____ ____ ____ ____10

Difficulty Accepting Criticism

Your passionate identification with your work sometimes blurs the line between professional performance and personal identity.

This "I am what I do" mind-set can make it very difficult to objectively evaluate your own work or accept criticism from others. Critical comments about your work can appear as personal attacks.

Real-World Commentary

Liz Haggerty of Carrier shared this observation: "Accepting criticism is a hard thing for people with high intellect. In a technical environment your work becomes almost like your child. My work is a product of my intellect. It is extremely hard to accept that possibly what you have produced is not what someone else was looking for in terms of what they asked you to do or what they expected."

Interestingly, this perceived lack of willingness or ability to accept comments critical of your work, no matter how positively stated or well intended, is one of the most frequent criticisms leveled at you and your scientific and technical peers by others within the organization. Their perception is "You can't take it but you sure can dish it out."

Assessing the Ability to Accept Criticism

When someone rejects your work or offers suggestions for improvement, how do you respond?

On a scale of 1 to 10 (1 being extremely low/never; 10 being extremely high/frequently), rate your ability to accept the criticism or critiquing of your work. Higher ratings would indicate a high willingness and ability to accept critical comment. Be wary here of giving yourself an unrealistic, self-serving rating.

1___ ___ ___ ___ ___ ___ ___ ___ ___ ___10

3. You Are Highly Motivated to Pursue Exceptional Quality and Perfection in Your Profession

This reality is a double-edged sword. The good news is, it drives scientific and technical professionals such as you to great achievement and is the primary motivator of your exceptional performance. Humanity owes a great debt to this scientific and technical pursuit of excellence. The bad news is, pursuing perfection can lead to a stress on quality at the expense of other critically important considerations such as budget and time constraints. The perception "If only we had more time and money, we could achieve perfection" often contributes to deadline failures and expensive cost overruns. Misunderstandings and problems occur, which are the result of ineffective communication and failure to grasp or appreciate the complete picture. The primary root cause is the inability or unwillingness to listen effectively and give equal value to the issues and concerns of others.

Signs and Symptoms

- *Overengineering, or overbuilding*

Internal or external customers want a Chevrolet, but the scientific and technical professionals choose to build a Rolls Royce. The technical professional pursues perfection, even though it is not required. It is difficult to accept that the overall goal is not the pursuit of exceptional quality (of which you are capable), but, rather, to limit your performance to meet the requirements of those who are driving the task or project. Scientific and technical creativity frequently disregard the real-world boundaries of cost, time, and customer requirement constraints.

Real-World Commentary

Dr. Mitchell Springer has said,

> As an engineer you want to do the right thing, or certainly what you perceive to be the right thing. As an example, we design hardware and software electronic systems, and we don't want to design something with a technology that's obsolete. In today's environment, where technology becomes obsolete so quickly, it's hard to go through a two-year design and development cycle where that technology is not obsolete by the time you are completed. So from an engineering perspective, we begin by asking what is the best we can buy at this point in time to make this product the best it can be two years from now? So we buy the cutting-edge stuff and design cutting-edge hardware and software, knowing there are no guarantees that two years from now it's not going to be antiquated. As a result, however, of buying the most state-of-the-art hardware or software or trying to design it, we take on inherent risks that we may be producing more capability than is necessary and increasing the likelihood of a schedule or cost problem.

"Design greed" and "project scope" are common problems that can be eliminated by effective communication. These occur when tasks and projects grow in magnitude and intensity as you begin to pursue the limits of quality capability and lose sight of the original agreements and actual parameters of performance. When what *you* want to do takes precedence over what *they* want you to do, you are in big trouble!

- **Pursuing interests and challenges beyond necessity.**

Often, obscure or secondary aspects of a task or project can become an intense focal point of activity because they are interesting, or professionally and intellectually challenging. The truly critical aspects of the primary task can be relegated to the back burner, which leads to conflicts with managers and customers who are adamant about getting things back on track.

Information service technicians, whose task it is to make sure the computer and related systems function properly, often make this mistake. They may become intensely involved in troubleshooting a problem and invest much more time than the problem is actually worth. Perhaps they take three hours to analyze and correct a printing problem, whereas the client would have been happy if they had made the more expedient decision to just go around the problem and redirect the work to another printer. The three-hour tinkering results in a higher bill. To the technical professional, the customer's desired outcome (the customer can be internal or external) may become secondary to the lure of meeting a unique challenge or solving an intricate problem. Your effort and focus must be aligned with the expectations of those who will actually benefit from the result. The temptation to solve the riddle or become the puzzle buster is strong and must be overcome.

Real-World Commentary
Ken Hodina is the coordinator of the A.C.E. (Achieving Competitive Excellence) Program for the manufacturing division of Otis Elevator Company in Bloomington, Indiana. Otis Elevator is a 150-year-old elevator manufacturing and installation company. Ken shared this observation:

> Overengineering a product, or so greatly exceeding the customer's demand that we drive ourselves out of cost competitiveness or speed of delivery, is a fairly typical potential problem. Overengineering, or hesitating on finishing a project while adding features beyond the customer's requirements, can be a trap. Trying to deliver more features than are required just because we are capable of doing it is not being responsive to the customer. We must provide a trouble-free, safe product within the customer's time and cost requirements that meets their predetermined expectation to eliminate any such problems.

We use "agreed terms of reference," which clearly identifies the customer's requirements, performance characteristics, cost, and time demands. Marketing, manufacturing, and engineering all sign off on this document. This ensures that marketing knows exactly what we are providing the customer, manufacturing knows exactly what they are required to build, and engineering is confident that quality and safety requirements are always being met. One of the results of this is defeating "feature creep," and making sure we do not overlook essential customer requirements or add unnecessary features.

Assessing Overengineering and Getting Sidetracked
On a scale of 1 to 10 (1 being extremely low/never; 10 being extremely high/frequently), rate your tendency or ability to overcome the temptation of pursuing perfection. Rating this issue low would indicate frequent experiences of providing clients or management with more than they are actually asking for, or perhaps being unresponsive to the importance of time and budget constraints. Typically, this would result in frequent incidents of conflict, criticism, or complaint.

1____ ____ ____ ____ ____ ____ ____ ____ ____ ____10

4. Obsolescence of Past Successful Strategies

The strategies, techniques, and behaviors that generated success for scientific and technical professionals in the past have become obsolete. In fact, many of these past practices are actually counterproductive in today's redefined, reengineered workplace. They can lead to performance problems and career failures. There are many examples of this shift of strategies, techniques, and behaviors; those discussed below are perhaps the most significant.

Signs and Symptoms

- *Information Hoarding*

The refusal to share information, the desire to play things close to the vest, are no longer acceptable. With the exception of confidential or highly proprietary data, today's scientific and technical professionals are required to keep others informed on project status, developments, delays, changes, and so on. This is especially true in the areas of direct managerial reporting and developing successful internal and external customer relationships. In the past, scientific and technical professionals found it beneficial to establish and maintain themselves as subject matter experts. It was an effective strategy to raise their value to the organization, which they did by establishing their uniqueness and becoming the sole holders of specific, critical knowledge. Today, organizations are holding you responsible for a totally redesigned information flow. You are required to effectively disseminate information, not collect or hoard it. The speed and accuracy with which information is moved to others and the ability to help people with diverse backgrounds and experience to understand technically challenging data define the greatness of today's scientific and technical professional. This is a complete reversal from past practice.

As an example, IT professionals serving as internal computer support are sharing as much specific technical information as possible to reduce the number of times they are called upon to correct software problems. One IT support person said,

> I am not necessarily judged on how effectively I solve problems, but rather on how effectively I teach others to solve problems. I am expected to teach others to avoid and correct the problem themselves. When I receive calls for routine or relatively minor problems, it may be an indication that I did not do a good job in providing people with enough information about the system. I am doing a great job when other departments can fix things themselves and do not have to call me.

Assessing Your Hoarding Behavior
On a scale of 1 to 10 (1 being "extremely low/never"; 10 being "extremely high/frequently"), rate your ability to defeat the tendency to hoard information.

1____ ____ ____ ____ ____ ____ ____ ____ ____ ____10

- **"Turfism"**

"Turfism" means protecting personal boundaries or territory by refusing to allow others to make contributions or participate in ongoing tasks and projects. Today's workplace calls for cooperation and collaboration. You are expected to obliterate boundaries. Seeking input, encouraging involvement, and increasing the skill inventory of others is highly valued and encouraged in today's organizational culture. The demand to work in interactive teams is extremely high. Instead of working independently and protecting their turf, today's scientific and technical professionals are required to focus on incorporating others effectively into their ongoing activities. There exists an interdependency in today's workplace where everyone relies on the actions, productivity, and effectiveness of others. *There is no "I" in team!* Today you are required to perform at a high level of efficiency, be willing to contribute to increased productivity and performance of the people around you, and invite input on problem solving and creativity from others.

One research chemist said that a formal part of her team meetings is for all team members to share any specific challenges they are facing so they can receive suggestions and ideas from the group for addressing the problem. "At first it was very uncomfortable. It felt like being forced to admit you were having problems or couldn't handle something. Now it is one of the most productive parts of our meetings and it is not uncommon to spend most of the time actually brainstorming one person's problem to generate solutions and alternatives. While not all suggestions are worthwhile, we have saved significant time and resources by opening up the process."

Assessing Turfism
On a scale of 1 to 10 (1 extremely low/never; 10 extremely high/frequently), rate your tendency and ability to avoid turfism. Once again, be wary of a self-serving high rating.

1____ ____ ____ ____ ____ ____ ____ ____ ____ ____10

- **Lack of Involvement in Internal Politics**

In the past, staying above the fray of organizational politics and refusing to become involved was frequently a source of pride and a trademark behavior of scientific and technical professionals. Being aloof was a point of honor. It is naïve to assume that this luxury still exists today. Building effective relationships and being responsive to the political climate of the moment are as critical to scientific and technical success as to any other professional or organizational function. Refusing to become involved in the corporate political culture while continuing to expect all the benefits, such as increased funding, increased compensation, promotions, high visibility, and attractive projects, is an absurd inconsistency. You cannot expect the payoffs if you are not willing to participate.

Organizational politics are generally driven by subjective factors that are not quantifiably or objectively measured. The political issues of the moment often change dramatically and rapidly owing to obscure or seemingly insignificant developments. Often these nuances are misunderstood or remain undetected by scientific and technical professionals. The reality is, you may not have a clue about the internal political issues of the moment. You and some of your peers may be totally oblivious! Internal politics are an anathema to the consistent, measurable, predictable world of science and technology, yet political awareness is critical to success today.

For example, a company that designs and manufactures medical diagnostic equipment has three facilities across the United States. Resource allocations to the various facilities are controlled by the home office and are influenced by the results of internal efficiency surveys. Employees are regularly surveyed to assess the effectiveness of management, fluctuations in morale, and how well the various internal departments cooperate and support each other. In each of the facilities, particular emphasis is placed on how the quality assurance people rate their relationship to design and manufacturing. Scientific and technical professionals in both of those departments have learned to put extra effort into their responsiveness when interacting with the quality assurance staff. One person said, "At times I resent the emphasis placed on the quality assurance function. Their people are undoubtedly the favored children around here. I have also learned that when we keep them happy, we have less pressure on us. When they are satisfied with us, we are given much more autonomy and flexibility in running our department. We have all learned to play the game, perhaps reluctantly, but well."

Assessing Political Astuteness
On a scale of 1 to 10 (1 being extremely low; 10 being extremely high), rate your ability to participate, understand, and benefit from the internal politics of your organization.

1___ ___ ___ ___ ___ ___ ___ ___ ___ ___10

• The Escalation of Time Demands

The pace of organizational life for scientific and technical professionals has risen tremendously. In the past, a quasi-academic culture dominated by collegial relationships was the norm in research and development divisions.

This has been replaced by the accelerated pace of an intensely competitive, market-driven environment. The importance of reducing response time is ever increasing, and the speed at which poor decisions, mistakes, or miscommunications are exposed is much greater than ever before. You are experiencing greater pressure and vulnerability owing to the accelerated speed of possible negative exposure. This potential risk by its very nature demands increased effectiveness in your communication.

Real-World Commentary
Ken Hodina, of Otis Elevator, has said:

> There is an extreme pressure to shrink schedules. The time from the initial contract engineered package to the purchase of material through the drawings and the specs being released to the shop floor must be greatly reduced. Also, the time it takes to execute engineering changes is being accelerated. We have very little time to react to correcting problems or even executing changes to the customer's desires. Now the typical engineering-to-manufacturing communication takes place much faster and with much more data than ever before. There's greater volume coming through the pipeline at a faster rate, so if there's something wrong in it, you get the negative effect more quickly and it is more pronounced.

Assessing Sluggishness of Response
On a scale of 1 to 10 (1 being extremely low; 10 being extremely high), rate your ability to successfully address the issues of the demand for speed of response.

        1____ ____ ____ ____ ____ ____ ____ ____ ____ ____10

5. Your Logical and Linear Thought Patterns Can Contribute to Miscommunication

Your normal black-and-white, open-and-shut, "no frills" mind-set—typical of technology- and science-oriented professionals—may lead to a communication style that comes across as abrasive or confusing. This may negatively affect your general communication and becomes especially evident when you are conveying critical comment, negative feedback, or bad news to others.

Signs and Symptoms

• Negative Delivery Style

Many scientific and technical professionals are incredibly surprised and dismayed when they discover that others perceive them to be arrogant or self-absorbed. Perhaps you have received similar feedback from others and probably could not understand where they got that idea. When this perception occurs, it is usually because the communication focus is centered on the actual message or content to be delivered without considering the impact on the recipient. Little or no thought is given to how the recipient will react or the possible short- and long-term consequences of the message. Focusing so heavily on your content and not considering the recipient and his issues can contribute to perceptions of a brusque, insensitive communication style.

• Overly Complex Information

Disconnects between you as a communicator and your audience also occur as a result of the frustrations inherent in communicating complex information to those who are not trained in or capable of understanding it. Finding effective methods to be sure you are understood can be very challenging and time-consuming, and may seem like a waste of time. Your listeners may sense your frustration and be put off by what they believe to be an unwarranted negative stance.

The depth and volume of information you communicate can be overwhelming to others. Your command of extensive knowledge and your intricate understanding of complex concepts and data also contribute to the appearance of arrogance, which negatively impresses the recipient. If delivered in a style that demonstrates intolerance, frustration, superiority, or lack of concern for the impact on the recipient, your message will surely be rejected, and you will have ongoing communication problems as you continue to generate negative perceptions and emotions. Your challenge is usually not *what* you say, but *how* you say it. It is not productive to focus exclusively on the content of your message; you must maintain awareness of its potential impact on the recipient.

Interestingly, this is generally not the case with communication *among* scientific and technical professionals. You enjoy engaging your peers in spirited conversation and debate and communicate very effectively. You revel in the intellectual challenge and earn and extend respect on the basis of the quality and content of your positions and rebuttals. The give-and-take of ongoing challenge and response is both interesting and beneficial. You benefit from the intellectual stimulation, especially in areas of particular interest to you. Communicating with others who do not offer the same stimulation, or who you assume to have difficulty in comprehending your message, results in a negative delivery style readily observed by the recipient. It probably does not happen with your scientific and technical peers, so do not make the mistake of assuming it does not happen with others, especially those from different professional backgrounds.

Assessing Your Delivery Style
On a scale of 1 to 10 (1 being extremely low; 10 being extremely high), rate your effectiveness in presenting information in a style that takes into account the impact of the message on the receiver. Do you avoid sending negative messages of judgment, intolerance, or frustration to those perceived to be slow in grasping the complexity of the information? Once again, be wary of an inappropriately high rating.

1____ ____ ____ ____ ____ ____ ____ ____ ____ ____10

6. Communicating with an Expanded Constituent Base

Due to shifts in organizational culture and responsibilities, activities previously done by others now involve you in high-level communication with customers as well as internal and external funding sources. These emerging responsibilities demand better communication skills on your part, especially in establishing expectations and summarizing results. Expanded competencies are required in determining needs, aligning those needs with actual capabilities, and determining the criteria to be used for measuring success or acceptability. Today it is not enough simply to establish and meet the customer's needs. Customers must know their needs and requirements are being met by receiving clear, concise, and timely feedback. This requires exceptional communication skills.

Signs and Symptoms
- **Poor Customer Service**

The skills of internal and external customer service, previously the domain of service, marketing, and sales departments, are becoming a core responsibility for you. Undoubtedly you have much more contact today with internal and external customers than you did even a few short years ago. The buck of customer-service responsibility now stops directly with you, the scientific and technical professional. It is of critical importance not only to discover expectations but also to develop successful strategies for identifying what, how, and when to provide ongoing feedback to the customer. Learning how to check for mutual agreement and reemphasizing previously negotiated deliverables and outcomes is an important part of the customer-service process.

• Inefficiency in Securing Resources

Securing funding and other additional resources has become extremely competitive. Others are seeking those same dollars and resources in competition with you and they value their tasks, projects, and achievements as much as you value your own. Poor communication efforts result in the denial of requests and reluctance or refusal to collaborate on future efforts.

Your responsibilities for customer service and funding-source relationships are expanding, and the necessary training to meet those expectations is probably nonexistent.

You are also finding yourself called upon to sell your ideas and programs to others. This is especially true when you are competing for internal resources. This emerging sales role is one you may find discomforting. It requires the specific skills of communicating through resistance, helping others to listen and set aside their preconceived or competitive positions. This is extremely difficult for those who would rather have the merits of their ideas and efforts stand on their own. In the past, that was possible; today it is not. Though many resent this sales aspect, it is critical that it be executed well when you are competing for resources and funding.

Assessing Customer-Service and Funding-Source Communication Effectiveness
Give thoughtful consideration to past outcomes, especially those where miscommunications or conflicts may have occurred. Regardless of the outcome, past experiences are valuable indicators of weaknesses and opportunities for growth in this area.

On a scale of 1 to 10 (1 being extremely low; 10 being extremely high), rate your ability to communicate effectively with internal and external customers, as well as with those responsible for the funding of your activities.

1____ ____ ____ ____ ____ ____ ____ ____ ____ ____10

In Conclusion

Liz Haggerty shared this poignant observation:

> Scientific and technical professionals need to understand business. We all need to be cognizant of the fact that there are many aspects of business, finance, and marketing that have an impact on what we are doing in our chosen field. We must understand that many people think differently than we do, and we must expose ourselves to different types of training that will help us to communicate more effectively, do a better job of accepting and receiving criticism, and giving feedback to others. We must help scientific and technical professionals see how they fit into the big picture. Training on understanding others and increasing communication effectiveness can be very helpful in broadening the skills of those of us in these professional areas. This is especially critical for those who have ambitions to move up in the organization.

In Chapter 2 we will begin to discuss communication as an overall process and identify many of the specific procedures you can implement to upgrade your communication skills.

2

Building the Bridge of Effective Communication

Picture, if you will, the First Brands Corporation, which distributes under its "STP" label a line of automotive maintenance and performance-related products designed to improve automobile performance by increasing engine and transmission efficiency, reducing friction, and minimizing damage from heat and pressure. Mastering the fundamental skills of communication is very much like producing this line of high-performance products. These skills will increase your efficiency, reduce friction and conflict, and minimize the damage to productivity, relationships, and individuals that can be caused by poor, ineffective communication. Throughout this book, let's use the acronym STP to refer to you, the high-performance scientific and technical professional, as you develop these critical communication skills.

Henceforth, the term "STP" will be used to refer to you, the scientific and technical professional.

The Two Critical Components of Effective Communication

In his book *The Seven Habits of Highly Effective People*, Dr. Stephen R. Covey lists as habit number five "Seek first to understand, then to be understood." This lofty goal to first understand requires us to view the entire communication process.

Every communication involves two critical components:

1. *The content of the delivered message.* Message content is generally perceived by the sender to be objective, accurate, necessary, and meaningful. The challenge occurs when the receiver does not share the same perception of the message and its meaning.

2. *The emotional impact of the message on the receiver.* Emotional impact is the result of the message on the person or people on the receiving end of the information. It includes their overall reaction to the communication and whether they interpret it as positive or negative.

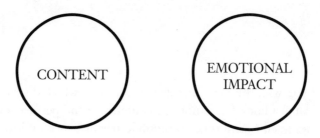

Typically, we tend to assume that everyone has the same understanding of our messages that we do and we expect our communications to be judged solely by the content as we perceive it. Though this perception is very common, it is inaccurate and is, in fact, an incomplete and unrealistic expectation. Major communication problems occur when we automatically assume this identical interpretation of the message.

Effective communication takes place only when a bridge is built between content and emotional impact, connecting the two components and assuring that both are given equal consideration.

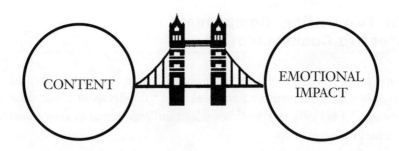

Communication disconnects take place when there is no bridge or connection between content and emotional impact. Almost certainly you have had the experience of being on the receiving end of a communication that was 100 percent content-driven and little or no consideration was given for the impact on you, the receiver. You have probably also experienced impact-only communication, which was primarily intended to provoke an emotional response in you where little or no consideration was given to the actual content. Any one-dimensional communication focusing on only one of these components is incomplete and ineffective. One-dimensional messages are usually rejected, listening breaks down, negative emotions escalate, and miscommunications create future problems. The key is for you to maintain a consistent, multidimensional balance of both message and impact.

Often, STPs judge communication that is not content-focused to be shallow, unimportant, and based in fluff. Communication that is not rich in content is a waste of your time. You must realize that others frequently view content-only communication to be arrogant, overbearing, and ego-driven. Being unaware of or dismissing the importance of this reality contributes to the negative perceptions that others may form about your communication style.

In most communication events, STPs such as you are in command of the content. When disconnects occur, it's usually because the emotional impact is neither considered nor addressed. For most of you these disconnects are unintentional and are usually the result of a lack of awareness of the importance of the emotional impact. Rarely is there an intentional dismissal or blatant disregard for the receiver. You are probably completely unaware that the message you are so intent on delivering could possibly have an undesirable or negative impact. When these reactions occur, the misunderstandings and negative reactions are very confusing. You have a difficult time understanding them. While some STPs may demonstrate complete disdain for or total rejection of the importance of the emotional impact of their communication, the overwhelming majority certainly does not. These communication problems are unintended and unwanted, and the good news is, they can be reduced and even eliminated.

Building an Effective Communication Bridge

Effective bridges must be designed for structural integrity, longevity, stability, and usefulness. Communication bridges between the content and emotional impact of the message are very much the same. They do not occur by accident. They are constructed by starting with a solid foundation and must be consistently maintained to ensure their continued success. Three factors combine to create strength, stability, and effectiveness in your communication bridges.

1. Choice of Information

You command a wealth of knowledge and information. Your challenge is to determine exactly what information should be communicated to others and the level, depth, and complexity of the content. The criteria for determining what to communicate varies from organization to organization and from discipline to discipline. Reporting requirements, job descriptions, and the knowledge base of the receiver play significant roles. When breakdowns occur involving information distribution, they are usually the result of some common, predictable communication mistakes. To avoid these mistakes, always communicate beginnings and endings; changes; developing needs; priorities and deadlines; and the impact of your activities on others.

Beginnings and Endings.   As you begin or complete tasks, assignments, projects, etc., it is always important to let the appropriate people know the status of your activities. Do not assume that others have a crystal ball which accurately updates them on the nature of your progress. In the absence of timely communication from you, they probably make inaccurate assumptions concerning your achievements or lack of accomplishments. They may assume you have completed a task when in fact you have not, or they may be stewing because you have not even started, when you are actually already done. Obviously, such assumptions can be very detrimental. Keeping people informed of beginnings and endings eliminates misunderstandings and false assumptions, and allows them to draw accurate perceptions about the quality and timeliness of your work.

Changes.   Changes and developments can be either positive (shortcuts, eliminated steps, securing resources, etc.) or negative (delays, failures, loss of revenue or resources, etc.). Regardless of their nature, it is imperative that changes be communicated to all key people as quickly as possible. Early communication is effective communication. Especially in the event of bad news, it is extremely important that people hear it from you directly and not be informed by the informal communication highway of rumor, gossip, and the grapevine. If they do hear rumors prior to hearing any bad news from you, they will probably already have formed negative opinions and conclusions that are not in your best interest.

Throughout this book you will find a series of "Specific Procedures for Effective Communication" (SPECs), designed to reinforce key messages and help you develop a personal action plan for communication skill improvements, identifying awareness of both *what* to do and *how* to do it. They will appear in this format:

SPEC

Key message—a specific technique or strategy to enhance communication effectiveness.

Developing Needs.   Do you anticipate any changes in the things you will need to complete your current tasks, assignments, or projects? These needs may include more time, additional resources (including assistance and support from others), more funding, and additional or unanticipated approvals.

Developing needs must be identified and articulated as early in the communication process as possible. The earlier you communicate your needs, the less disruption and the greater your chances of getting what you need. Many crises are created because developing needs were not anticipated and communicated early enough to allow for proper planning and availability.

It is also critical to your success to raise awareness of developing needs prior to your attempts to gather additional resources or seek help. Others may be quick to assume that you are going behind their backs or undermining their authority if you have not notified them of your developing needs. When you do request assistance or additions, communicate *why* you are making the request. If the need is clearly understood, it has a much greater chance of being supported. It may be necessary to document your developing needs and requests with supporting data. Requests for additional help or resources that are not supported with appropriate explanations and documentation are frequently rejected or judged harshly.

Priorities and Deadlines.   Keeping others informed of your priorities and deadlines accomplishes a number of things. It raises their comfort level that you are on top of your responsibilities (especially important with your manager and other key people above you in the organization who are aware of or monitor your activities). It also limits the additional demands others may place upon you. When they are aware of your workload, they will be less likely to call on you for assistance or overload you with additional assignments. When they are unaware of your current workload, they may assume you are under-utilized and their demands upon you may escalate. If you are being consistently overloaded, the cause may be poor communication on your part and not necessarily callous disregard for you on theirs.

As their confidence in your command of your activities and responsibilities increases, their need to closely monitor you decreases. By providing priority and deadline information willingly, you eliminate or reduce their need to come looking for it. You create additional breathing space for yourself by being ahead of the curve in communicating priority and deadline awareness. Effective communication proves to them they do *not* have to monitor you so closely.

How Your Current Activities May Impact Others in the Future.   As you learned in chemistry class, for every action there is an equal and opposite reaction. You may be working on a task or instituting a change today that may somehow impact someone else's work in the near or distant future. Anticipating these circumstances and raising awareness of pending events early in the process prepares others for the developments to come. The best surprise is no surprise! If they are blindsided by something as a result of your activities that they did not expect, you undoubtedly will create an adversary. Give others time to anticipate and plan for future impact.

2. Identifying Whom to Share Information With

This is the second factor in building in creating strength, stability, and effectiveness in your communication bridges.

Identifying Your Critical Communication Points.   It is important to thoughtfully identify the people who constitute your critical communication points, those with whom you share important data or information that impacts performance, either yours or someone else's. This information may establish current or future expectations. It may contain either positive or critical comments and the evaluation of past activities. Critical communication points include all of the people directly or indirectly involved in your professional activity; those who generate tasks, assignments, or projects, as well as anyone else who benefits from the outcome of your actions, efforts, and decisions. They include the individuals, departments, teams, or groups who may precede you in the process and upon whom you are dependent for the quality of their work. You rely on them to do a good job so that you in turn can perform well at your point in the process. Those who influence funding or future assignments are especially important as critical communication points.

Consistent communication breakdowns can occur when the critical communication points are not accurately and completely identified. Frequently omitted are those who are indirectly involved or somewhat removed from your immediate activities. They exist on the perimeter, and it is, unfortunately, a common communication mistake to leave them out of the loop. It is in your best interest to broaden the depth of your communication network and share information as broadly and deeply as possible. Keep in mind, your actions will create a ripple affect. Any changes you recommend or actions you take are going to affect others beyond your immediate intimate group. They may be affected rather quickly or perhaps in the near future, and sharing information broadly with as many people as possible avoids creating adversarial reactions and responses. Exercise extreme caution and err by including people in the loop no matter how insignificant their input or need to know may appear. Even if you do not require their immediate support or effort, failing to share information creates someone who may be predisposed against your efforts. When people are not included in the normal communication flow, negative reactions are common and predictable. Typically, these responses are knee-jerk emotional reactions and not necessarily rational. These emotions may lead to their actually working against you or withholding support for your efforts. Consider your own response when you are left out of the loop or find yourself saying "nobody told me." Being excluded from communication commonly results in the assumption of adversarial positions.

SPEC

Make your communication network as inclusive as possible and avoid becoming exclusive.

Avoid this typical communication problem. Many STPs limit the distribution of information to those whose approval they are required to seek or whose assistance is required. They may say, "Why should I communicate with them? I don't need their approval and they don't need to know what I'm doing." This response indicates an unwillingness to communicate to a broad network and results in the limited or exclusive distribution of information. Do not limit your communication to circumstances of approval, requests for assistance, or formalized reporting. Broaden your distribution network to include as many people as necessary and increase the depth of their ongoing and future support.

The following exercise is an opportunity to use the guidelines outlined in this chapter.

Communication Action Step

On a separate sheet of paper, list the names of all of the critical communication points in your workplace. Keep this list with you for the next ten days and add additional names as they occur to you. At the end of this time, you will have an accurate inventory of the people you must include in your telephone messages, e-mails, faxes, and as CCs on written communication.

Rumors, antagonism, and resistance flourish in information vacuums. You will find more willing support and less overt or covert resistance from those in other areas of the organization, as well as your own peer group, if you are willing to share appropriate information. It is better to communicate with too many people than not enough.

If people believe you are giving them too much information or information they do not need, they will tell you. It is a nice problem to have because you will be seen as a communication conduit, not an information hoarder.

Selection of Language/Vocabulary/Jargon.   Whom you are communicating with determines the words and terminology you will use. It is necessary to put information in the language of the *receiver*. As an STP you frequently use references, terms, and nomenclature well known and accurately understood within your discipline or intimate work group, and it can be meaningless or intimidating to others. This use of specialized insider language or codes is another major contributor to the misconception that STPs are arrogant or intimidating in their communication with others.

Do not assume that others have an accurate comprehension of your discipline or specialty. When people do not understand, they will not ask . . . they do not want to appear stupid. Instead, they will react negatively to your intimidation or self-perceived superiority.

SPEC

Avoid jargon, acronyms, and code phrases in communications outside your team, department, or intimate work group.

Real-World Commentary

Dr. Mitchell Springer offered this suggestion:

I would recommend limiting the use of jargon to those who understand it. It's difficult to do because there's so much technical jargon out there, especially associated with computers. As an example, coming from a software engineering background, we have a word called "default." The default value of a number might be zero—references like that. When I was building a home a number of years ago, I asked them the default stove that they used. The builder looked at me, obviously taking it in a negative way. "What do you mean by a default stove? All of our products are quality products." I really didn't understand his reaction, couldn't figure out why it was that he had come back with such a strong voice. Then it dawned on me that the word "default" had a very different meaning for him. I think he understood me to say "defect." "Default" had no meaning or value to him. To be effective communicators, I think we need to speak to people in a language they understand.

Communication Assessment

1. Am I aware of the importance of both content and emotional impact in my communication? *yes* ☐ *no* ☐

2. Do I consistently communicate:

   On a timely and effective basis? *yes* ☐ *no* ☐

   The beginnings and endings of my tasks and projects? *yes* ☐ *no* ☐
   The developing needs for additional resources, funding, assistance, or support? *yes* ☐ *no* ☐

3. Do I accurately communicate the current status of my activities and projects:

   Emphasizing increasing momentum? *yes* ☐ *no* ☐

   Explaining the shifting status of priorities and deadlines *yes* ☐ *no* ☐

   The future impact of my activities? *yes* ☐ *no* ☐

4. Have I accurately analyzed and identified my network of critical communication points?   *yes* ☐   *no* ☐

5. Do I consistently share complete and appropriate information with all critical communication points?   *yes* ☐   *no* ☐

6. Do I consistently ensure that no one who is even remotely impacted by my activity is left out of the loop?   *yes* ☐   *no* ☐

7. Do I adjust my vocabulary to avoid language, jargon, or codes unfamiliar to others?   *yes* ☐   *no* ☐

Any *no*-responses identify opportunities to improve your communication effectiveness.

3. How the Information Is Delivered

The third factor in creating your effective communication bridge is how you actually deliver your message. According to the work of Dr. Albert Mehrabian, words are only 7 percent of the actual message we communicate. Tone of voice or voice inflection accounts for 38 percent of our message, and nonverbal communication is by far the most important aspect, making up 55 percent of the actual meaning of the communication. Obviously, what counts is not *what* you say but *how* you say it. Words primarily address the *content* of your message. All three combined, words, tone of voice, and nonverbal communication, convey the *emotional impact* of the message.

Words.   Communication is heavily dependent upon words; you choose them very carefully, and the selection is based on accuracy and relevance. As an STP, you are accustomed to using very specific language; your words have clear unequivocal meanings to you. If everyone has the same understanding of the words, terms, and phrases, an effective transfer of content probably takes place. However, the risk of miscommunication is huge if your listeners have different understandings of the specific words and your tone of voice and nonverbal messages are not aligned. Telling someone to "reboot the computer" would probably send two very different messages to an IT professional and a rugby player!

The English language is full of words that have different meanings. If you use the word "crazy" to describe someone's behavior, it can be a compliment or a serious, perhaps libelous, statement. In a social context, describing someone as crazy typically means they are lots of fun, unpredictable, and a joy to be around. In a clinical context, describing someone as crazy implies impairment of mental ability, mental illness, or perhaps lack of emotional control. It is of paramount importance to always remember that the meaning of any message is determined solely by the *receiver*, not the deliverer of the communication. You lose total control over message meaning once it has been delivered. It is not the actual content of your message that matters, it is what the receiver thinks you said that matters. At this point, be aware that words are the least influential part of your communication. To assume that your words alone define your message is a dangerous assumption.

In Chapter 3 we will discuss your role in ensuring the receiver's accurate comprehension of your message.

Tone of Voice.   STPs such as you are typically so focused on the selection of words, terms, and phrases in your communication that much less attention is paid to tone of voice. This may be a significant cause of communication disconnects between you and others, and it is one of the most easily corrected. While appreciating the importance of tone of voice in everyone else's communication, we commonly overlook our own. We assume that our communication is composed entirely of the specific words we use. We select our language carefully, delivering a very clear and concise message, and expect it to be received exactly as we intended. Conversely, we are very aware of the negative impact the tone of voice has on us when we receive it from others.

The reality is, we don't hear ourselves as others hear us. What is your first response when you hear your voice on tape?

"That's not me."

"Those are my words, but that's not my voice."

"That's my (mother, father, sister, brother, grandmother, grandfather), not me."

"An alien took over my voice box!"

We know how others sound to us and have little or no realization of how we sound to them.

For example, if you are reacting negatively or perhaps resenting someone's inability to grasp the complexity of your information, they clearly sense your emotion and it inhibits the communication process. If you feel compelled to patronize them by simplifying the communication so their lesser minds can absorb it, it is certainly not necessary for you to vocalize those feelings. The receiver gets the message loud and clear, not by *what* you say, but *how* you say it! Your message has a negative emotional impact on the receivers. Their listening efforts shut down automatically, and they are predictably resistant to your message and contentious in discussing your input. Their reaction is no different than yours when you are on the receiving end of such negative voice-tone communications. You know when someone is frustrated or being judgmental toward you, and you do not react well to it. Neither do others when they are subjected to the same messages from you. Again, we are aware of it in others, unaware or perhaps unwilling to see it in ourselves.

Consider these guidelines for vocal presentation:

- A low-pitched, well-modulated voice conveys strength and confidence.
- A high-pitched voice indicates excitement, lack of control, and perhaps panic.
- Speaking too softly conveys lack of confidence and fails to engage the listener.
- Speaking too loudly signals aggressiveness, intolerance, or lack of patience.
- Varied pace and tone indicates excitement and importance.
- Pausing adds emphasis to the last statement. Pausing also allows the receiver time to process the message.
- Raising, lowering, and altering the tone of voice overcomes a monotone delivery.
- Emphasize points by raising or lowering your voice (whispering can be very effective).
- Avoid vocal distractions, including the repeated use of words and phrases such as, "you know," "uh," "okay," "um's," and "er's" (they distract the listener from concentrating on your message).

SPEC

Emphasizing or stressing a word indicates importance and frequently impacts the meaning of the entire message!

To demonstrate the importance of stress and voice inflection, consider the very simple statement "I did not say he stole the money." Read this statement out loud six times, inflecting on or emphasizing the *italicized* word or phrase. You will see that the statement takes on six entirely different meanings without making any word changes.

I did not say he stole the money.
I *did not* say he stole the money.
I did not *say* he stole the money.
I did not say *he* stole the money.
I did not say he *stole* the money.
I did not say he stole the *money*.

Six very different messages are conveyed merely by varying the stress and inflection of the voice. Take great care to ensure that your voice inflection accurately conveys your intended message.

Tone of Voice Effectiveness.   The quality of your tone and vocal presentation obviously impacts the success of your communication. While you may not possess the melodious voice tones of entertainers, orators, or television personalities, you certainly can use your individual vocal capabilities to your greatest advantage.

Pace.   Another technique that impacts how the communication is delivered is the pace of your speech. It is a good idea to match your pace with that of the person with whom you are communicating. If they speak very fast, you probably want to increase your rate of delivery. If they speak more slowly than you, slow your delivery to match theirs. But be wary. There is the potential to be perceived as mimicking or mocking, which creates a very negative reaction in the receiver.

You can also use this technique to influence the communication pace of others. If you are talking with someone whose pace is so fast or slow that it detracts from the quality of the communication, you can help her to modify her delivery by specifically adapting an opposite strategy. If they are talking too quickly, slow your delivery slightly. If they are talking too slowly, a slight increase in your delivery may encourage them, perhaps subconsciously, to match your pace. If they are too loud, talk slightly softer; if they are too soft, increase your volume to once again encourage them to match you.

Nonverbal Communication.   In addition to being unaware of how we sound to others, we are also often unaware of how we look to others while we speak. We are acutely and sometimes painfully aware of the impact the nonverbal messages of others have on us, yet we do not realize that we are doing this same thing to them. In reality, we are all delivering (usually unintentionally) as many negative nonverbal messages as we receive, if not more! You look as bad to them as they look to you, you just are not aware of what they see.

While you may not realize it, left unchecked or uncorrected, body language betrays your true emotion. If you are talking to someone you do not want to talk to, or are in a circumstance you do not want to be in, or perhaps are doing something that you really do not want to do, it is not necessary for you to say a word. Your nonverbal actions (with a probable assist from your tone of voice) convey a very clear message to everyone around you. Even though you do not say what's really on your mind and you work hard to clean up your communication for "human consumption," it is a very serious communication error to think that your true thoughts are not being very clearly transmitted to the receiver. While you may refrain from actually vocalizing what you are thinking, the receiver absorbs a very clear message and he or she does not need a psychic hotline to figure out what it means.

Let's address three specific aspects of your nonverbal communication: eye contact, physical distance, and body language.

Eye Contact. It is important to maintain appropriate eye contact with your communication partners. Consistent, intermittent eye contact is the most effective. Not making eye contact results in your sending some significant unintended negative messages: lack of confidence, untruthfulness, arrogance, and condescension. Avoid allowing your eyes to focus downward or up above the receiver. Effective eye contact is usually maintained for a count of three with a brief look away, and then reestablishing the connection. Staring is not effective eye contact. It can signal flagrant disrespect, intimidation, or insubordination. With members of the opposite sex, it can send a message you have no intention of sending. Maintaining appropriate eye contact may be a challenge for you. When deep in thought or pondering questions or responses, it is not uncommon for many STPs to unconsciously allow their eyes to wander. Doing so while silent is fine; starting or maintaining a conversation without effective eye contact is not. You may be sending very negative messages with inappropriate eye contact without even realizing it.

Physical Spacing. The physical distance you establish and maintain has as much impact as the type of eye contact you use. During a business communication, maintain a distance of eighteen to thirty-six inches between yourself and the receiver. Getting closer than eighteen inches can be extremely intimidating and may be interpreted as a violation of personal space. Most people tend to react negatively when they feel crowded. More than thirty-six inches creates a natural disconnect in workplace communication, requiring both parties to raise their voices to an uncomfortable level to be heard.

It is also important for you to be aware that eye contact and physical spacing distances are culturally defined. Different cultures attach different degrees of importance to both. Some cultures review eye contact as disrespectful and it sends a very negative message, especially if the receiver is older than you or ranks above you in the organization. Some cultures have a much tighter physical spacing zone and may feel comfortable at distances of ten to twelve inches. You are at a disadvantage if you do not have at least a general understanding of the various cultural interpretations of physical spacing.

SPEC

The explosion of cultural diversity in the scientific and technical professions means you must be proactive in becoming familiar with cultural variations and avoiding unintended offenses or miscommunications.

Body Language. This is a very complex subject. Understanding the messages of body language is not a science; it is an incomplete art at best. Many people believe themselves to be experts at reading other people's body language or nonverbal messages. It really is an area subject to misinterpretation and misunderstanding. Subjective interpretation is rampant. Do not fall prey to assuming that you can be sure what someone else's body language is expressing. Everyone has had their nonverbal messages misunderstood and we all have misunderstood the messages of others.

In observing the body language of others, it is important to focus on changes in their position and their physical reactions to specific observations or comments. Such reactions indicate some sort of response. Don't assume you know precisely what their exact response means. You don't! It is the equivalent of your phone ringing: you know someone is calling. You don't know who it is or what the call is about until you answer the phone and find out.

For example, when people cross their arms in response to something that is said, it is generally assumed to be a negative reaction—a rejection of the message or a sign of closed-mindedness. And that may be exactly what they are thinking. On the other hand, their response could also mean that they are cold, or that they are merely assuming a more comfortable posture. The action may have nothing to do with your message at all. It is very easy to jump to conclusions, which results in the explosion of miscommunication and inappropriate reaction.

SPEC

What you **intend** *to say with your nonverbal language really doesn't matter. It's what the receiver interprets that counts.*

It is extremely important not only to avoid making assumptions concerning the meaning of the nonverbal communication of others, it is also important to become aware of the assumptions others may make about your body language and nonverbal messages. Common assumptions are attached to specific nonverbal gestures; the following chart lists some body language messages and the meaning or interpretation that is typically attached.

Typical Positively Interpreted Body Language Gesture	Interpretation
Nodding head	"I see" or "I understand."
Stroking chin	Serious evaluation or deep consideration or thought
Palms open, hands extended forward at chest height	Seriousness, emphasis of importance
One hand above head	Emphasizing a point

(*continued*)

Both hands above head	Triumph (this can be a negative message if conveyed at the wrong time or at someone else's expense)
Counting things off on your fingers	Confidence and logic
Leaning forward or facing speaker directly	Intensity and interest
Arms and legs in an open position	Openness to ideas and suggestions
Steepling of fingers	Extreme self-confidence

Typical Negatively Interpreted Body Language Gesture	**Interpretation**
Rolling eyes	"That was a stupid remark."
Rubbing eyes	Suspicion or rejection
Clearing throat	Nervousness
Open palms below chest level	Helplessness, plea to be understood
Hands or fingers in front of mouth	Reluctance to talk, nervousness or embarrassment
Wagging finger back and forth	"You are wrong."
Pointing	Aggressiveness
Hands clasped behind back	"I'm in charge"; generally interpreted as negative assertion of authority
Chewing a pencil or other object	Nervousness and uncertainty
Crossing arms over chest	"I don't agree"; resistance or rejection of message
Leaning back in chair or turning body away from speaker	Pulling away from involvement or creating distance or detachment

---

(continued)

Deep sighing	Impatience or boredom
Smirking	Self-superiority and condescension

Whether you like it or not, these are the common assumptions people make about your nonverbal and body language messages.

Preparing Yourself to Communicate

When preparing for important communications, you probably spend an agonizing amount of time preparing the data and selecting the exact words, phrases, and terminology to ensure an accurate delivery of your message. Little if any time is spent considering the voice tone and inflection or nonverbal aspects of the communication. Your attention and preparation are focused on what will be said, not how it will be heard or what will be seen. If you have experienced the agony of sitting through a scientific or technical presentation that was so boring you were challenged to remain upright and awake, it may not have been the data or content that put you to sleep (on the contrary, you probably found it very interesting), it was the presenter's lack of attention to the emotional impact of her tone, body language, delivery style, etc.

Pay twice as much attention to your tone/inflection of voice and body language as you do to your selection of words.

This may appear to be overkill. However, it is a deadly communication mistake to dismiss the importance of the total communication package. Creating antagonism, resentment, or hurt feelings in the receiver because

SPEC

Always take time to focus not only on what you will say, but how you will say it. What will the receiver see and hear?

This may appear to be overkill. However, it is a deadly communication mistake to dismiss the importance of the total communication package. Creating antagonism, resentment, or hurt feelings in the receiver because your tone of voice and nonverbal messages are not consistently aligned with your words is unnecessary and easily eliminated by raising your awareness and preparing appropriately.

Consistently ask yourself:

SPEC

Prior to delivering an important message (to either individuals or groups), practice your delivery in front of a mirror. If at all possible, have your presentation videotaped for review and evaluation.

What nonverbal and voice messages am I sending?
How do I *really* look and sound?

If videotaping is not possible, you can also use a small hand-held tape recorder to tape your voice tone and quality. Practicing with a recorder or actually audiotaping a presentation is very helpful in letting you hear yourself as others hear you. Your initial response will probably be one of embarrassment. Once you get past it, you will find it to be a valuable listening experience. You already practice your words, why not practice your voice quality, tone, and inflection?

Communication Assessment

1. Am I aware of how words, tone of voice, and nonverbal messages interact to influence the emotional impact of my communication?
   yes ☐ *no* ☐
2. Am I aware of the true impact my voice quality has on others?
   yes ☐ *no* ☐
3. Am I aware of the power and influence of tone of voice and voice inflection? *yes* ☐ *no* ☐
4. Is the pace of my communication always appropriate to meet the needs of the receiver? *yes* ☐ *no* ☐

5. Do I maintain an effective physical presence during important communication?   *yes* ☐ *no* ☐

6. Am I consistently aware of the physical spacing between myself and the receiver?   *yes* ☐ *no* ☐

7. Do I avoid making reactive assumptions on the meanings of the nonverbal messages of others?   *yes* ☐   *no* ☐

8. Am I consistently aware of the nonverbal and body language messages I send?   *yes* ☐   *no* ☐

9. Do I effectively avoid sending unintended negative nonverbal messages?   *yes* ☐   *no* ☐

Any no-responses identify opportunities to improve your communication effectiveness.

If you answered yes to the last two questions . . . please get a second opinion!

In Chapter 3, we will discuss your role in influencing the receptiveness of the receiver to your message.

3

Influencing How Your Communication Is Received

An effective communication bridge between content and emotional impact must also focus on the importance of the correct reception of your message by the receiver. What can you do to increase the probability that your message will be received exactly as you intend and that the receiver will react in a positive manner and take the action you desire? This goal is a high, yet scalable, mountain!

The quality of communication is judged by the accuracy of the information transferred to individuals or groups of people. Communication is ineffective if the message is not accurately comprehended by all receivers. Accurate comprehension should not be confused with *agreement*. Communication effectiveness ensures that everyone is dealing with equal and consistent information. Communication effectiveness encompasses mutual understanding, it does not necessarily result in mutual agreement.

In addition to the deliverer's skill in presenting the message, three major factors influence the accurate transfer of information.

1. The receiver's *ability* to process the message
2. The receiver's *willingness* to process the information
3. The receiver's accurate *comprehension* of the message

1. The Receiver's Ability

Ability includes the receiver's listening skills, overall knowledge, relevant experience, intellect, and possession of a realistic frame of reference. In truth, you actually have very little influence over the receiver's ability to process your message. Though you can help to educate him or recommend meaningful resources to increase his knowledge, you cannot compel him to listen or absorb your message correctly. In fact, listening skills are among the least practiced skills in America today, and your audience may indeed be deficient in this respect. It has frequently been said, that "most of us truly do not listen; we just wait to talk." Though you exercise total control over your own listening patterns, someone else's ability to listen to your message is totally under their control.

Despite the fact that your ability to influence the listening of others is virtually nonexistent, there are some very specific things you can do to make your communications more "receiver-friendly." Your method of delivery, managing the physical environment, and giving consideration to relevant time pressures all encourage others to actively engage and process your message accurately.

Method of Delivery

It is generally accepted that people process or absorb information in three primary ways.

- Visually: by what they see
- Auditorily: by what they hear
- Kinesthetically: by what they do or are actively involved in

Everyone absorbs information differently, and it is important to expand your communication skills to address all three of these factors. Do not limit your presentation of information to only one method of delivery.

One of the typical communication traps STPs fall into is making the faulty assumption that everyone processes information the same way. It is a very common mistake to assume that everyone processes information exactly the same way. Perhaps things would be much easier if that were true. We all sometimes believe that the world would be a better place if everyone were just like us. The reality is, that is not how it is! You must realize that everyone is different.

As an example, most STPs are exceptionally good at processing visual information. The written word or visual presentations dominate your educational curriculum, training programs, and everyday communication. Tables, graphs, schematics, flowcharts, etc., are examples of information presented in your preferred fashion, visually. Communication problems are inevitable if you assume everyone absorbs information the same visual way. If you are communicating with your manager, customers, people in other areas of the organization, and even with other STPs, you may be attempting to transfer information in a method that may be highly efficient for you, not for them. Auditory communicators may not absorb written information easily or efficiently. Visuals can be confusing to them; such people need to hear information. Visual communicators may not possess the strong auditory or listening skills they need to do the math, take the notes, or conduct the research to truly understand all of the information. Some may need to be actively involved in processing your message. Even those oriented toward the visual absorption of information may not always be able to wade through highly complex visual presentations. Some people blend all three of these methods in their unique way of absorbing information. Even among STPs, communication styles may vary significantly.

SPEC

When it comes to style of communication, one size does not fit all. Never assume that everyone processes information in exactly the same way.

How an individual processes information has nothing to do with his or her intellect or overall ability to perform. It is not an indicator of IQ. Some people are at a great disadvantage because they may not be able to process information as it is generally presented. Many bright people have struggled in school because educational information and teaching methods were not aligned with their absorption style. For you, being aware of and developing flexible communication presentation styles are two of the most important things you can do to strengthen your communication effectiveness.

SPEC

It is **not** *the receivers' responsibility to process information the way you present it . . . it is your responsibility to deliver information in a method compatible with their ability to process it.*

How can you incorporate all three communication styles, visual, auditory, and kinesthetic, into your message delivery? Implement this three-step strategy SPEC for any important communication:

1. *Tell them* what you want them to know.
2. *Show them* the information.
3. *Involve them* in the assimilation.

For example:

1. Tell receivers the information face to face, or with an auditory delivery through voice mail. (They hear it.)
2. In writing, by fax, or e-mail, present the information visually, either in its entirety or a brief summarization. (They see it.)
3. In either face-to-face or telephone discussion, ask receivers to make highlights, margin notes, or personalized summaries of the most important aspects of your message. (This involves them in the process.)

Obviously, this strategy of tell them, show them, and involve them requires an increased commitment on your part. You are probably thinking that you do not have the time to communicate in this manner. You are right. You do not have the time! Unfortunately, the real-world truth is, if you want to increase your communication effectiveness, you must make the time. If your current communication efforts are working fine, then there is no reason for you to change. (If they are . . . why are you reading this book?) If they are not as effective as you want them to be, it is necessary for you to commit to changing your communication strategies. You cannot continue to do it the same old way and expect better results.

Your communication is worth doing right the first time. Do not cheapen or lessen the value of your information by continuing to communicate in an inefficient style. You deserve a better outcome! Think of the time you spend fixing problems resulting from ineffective communications. This includes repeating tasks, excess meetings, and the time spent stewing and venting over misunderstandings. It always takes more time to fix the fallout from poor communication than it does to do it right the first time.

In any important communication, especially those involving: the transfer of important data, addressing performance issues (yours or theirs), customer-centered discussions, information concerning problems or outcomes, or issues that are politically sensitive, you must be willing to dedicate the time to communicate effectively. Communication shortcuts in these critical areas can shorten careers! Investing the time to tell them, show them, and involve them is time well spent. If you are involved in casual conversation about a new movie, a sporting event, or your kid's newest adventure . . . who cares? If it is important communication . . . do it right.

How can you determine in which form someone prefers to have information presented? Use a revolutionary technique: ask them! Pose this question to the people who are your critical communication points (especially if they evaluate or somehow impact your performance).

Memo, e-mail, verbally, voice mail, in face-to-face discussion, or a combination of any of these? Do you want it visually, auditorily, or do you want to be actively involved in the transfer of information? (You may be very surprised by their response. Their preference may be different from yours!)

This will help you to identify the most productive way to establish a communication partnership, and is a strong indicator of your desire to increase the quality of your communication. (This is also a great exercise to use with the important people in your personal life.) You may assume people want information in one form and then discover they actually prefer it

SPEC

"When I have important information to communicate to you, how would you like me to present it?"

to be presented differently. Projects have failed, careers have been shattered, and marriages have dissolved because those involved were communicating in methods that were not mutually efficient.

Determining the preferred communication method is especially critical in communicating with your boss, a topic discussed in Chapter 5.

This technique works in both directions. Just as you will inquire of others how they want you to deliver information, you must also communicate your preferred style of reception. Let them know your preferences. If someone has very important information to share with you, how do you want him to present it? Do those who constitute your critical communication points know how you best absorb information? If you have consistent communication problems with certain individuals, the miscommunication may actually be rooted in the method of delivery (either yours or theirs). Addressing this factor alone can help clear up a significant portion of your communication problems.

The Importance of Repetition.　Comprehension is enhanced by repetition. Individuals must be exposed to information a minimum of three times before an accurate and permanent comprehension can take place. Minimal exposure to information merely raises awareness. Multiple exposure increases overall command and comprehension. Many STPs are quick studies, able to grasp information at an accelerated rate, especially if it falls into their area of expertise. Others may not have that ability. New or particularly complex information must be presented many times to ensure complete understanding. Repetition is an integral part of the absorption process. When you utilize the technique of tell them, show them, involve them, you are taking advantage of repetition in a simple yet direct way to help increase your communication effectiveness.

External Factors

There are additional factors that affect a receiver's ability to absorb information that you can at least influence, if not totally control. They include the physical environment and some of the receiver's internal issues.

Physical Environment.　When planning any significant communication, give careful consideration to the location where the discussion or presentation will take place. Where you communicate with someone has impact on the quality of the transfer of information. Is this location or environment conducive to helping the receivers absorb your message? Are there barriers that will impede their ability to get it? The worst place for you to have a meaningful conversation with anyone is probably in his office or his primary area of responsibility. Why? Very simply, that's exactly the area where this person's stress is highest, the potential for disruption or interruption is greatest, and the individual's preoccupation with other subjects is overwhelming. The second worst place for you to have a meaningful communication is in your office or your area of primary responsibility. Why? For precisely the same reasons.

Granted, you do not always have complete control over where your important communications take place. However, it is important to control as much as you can. You will find that you have greater influence if you consider the location before the communication takes place. You could suggest meeting at a neutral location, taking a walk, having a private discussion over coffee in an isolated area of the building. All are better than attempting to communicate in more distracting environments.

SPEC

An effective way to influence the choice of environment is to establish the ground rules.

"We really have some important information to discuss. It will probably take less time, and we will communicate more effectively if we go to a conference room or the cafeteria for a cup of coffee. Which would be best for you?"

You can also exert influence by stating, "This is important information. Let's meet in the (name the location) to discuss it."

The importance of the physical environment will be discussed further in Chapters 7 and 8.

Timing. Timing is always a factor in effective communication. Deciding when to initiate a communication is an extremely important factor that is often overlooked. Determine the best time for your communication partner to receive your message and plan accordingly. This can be accomplished in a number of ways.

The Productivity Cycle

Observe the productivity cycle of those who constitute your critical communication points. It is best to engage them when they are at their highest energy point. Are they "morning" people, or do they tend to be more energetic or productive during the second half of the day? Most everyone has a predictable energy cycle, times when they are at their best, and times when their energy is typically low. Communicating with people during their down time obviously increases the risk of miscommunication. They are less focused and their concentration is probably weak. Whenever possible, plan your communication for a time when they are most likely to be in a state of high energy. This is when concentration is highest, listening is least impeded, and intellect and creativity can best be targeted on your message.

The optimum communication time may not be the receiver's high-energy time of day. Suppose you want to make people aware of your information, yet you don't really want their immediate feedback, input, or creativity. In that case, plan to deliver the message when they are in their low-energy trough. They will be more likely to agree, less likely to contest, and reluctant to invest the energy to add their creativity or spin to your message.

For example, if you want to get your boss's approval on something without her looking too closely at the details of your proposal, present it during her low-energy period. She is more likely to wave you off with a terse comment like "Whatever you want to do is fine with me." If she objects to your actions later, you can legitimately point out that she gave you the approval to use your own judgment. This can be a very effective strategy.

Discuss Timing with the Receiver

Invite receivers' input when scheduling communication sessions. They will probably avoid scheduling discussions during their worst times and will appreciate your partnering with them by your asking for their input as to

SPEC

Say: "We could meet around ten or immediately after lunch. Which would be best for you?" If your suggested times are not good for them, they will offer alternatives.

when the discussion should take place. They will be more willing to process your information. They will be at their best and that is exactly what you deserve.

Be aware that some people may try to consistently schedule you when they don't have anything better to do. They will actually be denying you access to them during their peak productivity times. If they are using you to fill their "down time" you will probably experience a lower quality of interaction, and this is generally an indication they do not place a high value on what you do or what you have to say. It could also indicate they do not find communications with you to be especially productive, perhaps because of time investment or quality of delivery issues. Structuring your communication to be more concise and focused could pay dividends. Helping them to understand more clearly the importance and priority of your work will probably yield an improvement in your overall joint communication. Your challenge may lie first in establishing that you are worth listening to before you can transfer your information effectively.

When possible, avoid scheduling important communication during your predictable lowest-energy periods. Though you may not always be able to control the timing, merely being aware of your own peak communication times will help you to be more effective.

Who deserves more consideration, you, the deliverer, or the receiver, when it comes to peak communication times? The receiver. Proper planning and preparation on your part help you overcome your depleted energy, and few things are more critical than having a focused receiver.

Be Responsive to Circumstances.   If you are attempting to communicate and the receiver does not appear to be effectively engaged (you know how that looks; the lights are on and nobody is home!), it is probably in your best interest to acknowledge the distraction or inattention (acknowledge, do not attack). Offering to reschedule is in everyone's best interest. "I'm sensing this may not be a good time for us to have this discussion.

SPEC

Give careful consideration to your own optimum communication times.

Would it be better if we scheduled it for later today?" Usually the response is one of instant recovery, your listener probably saying something like, "No, this is a good time, my mind was just wandering." Generally the receiver will then focus more intently on the discussion. Occasionally, he may opt to reschedule. Though this may be a disappointment to you, it actually works to your advantage. You will find a more committed and focused receiver when you reconvene.

Avoid aggressive statements such as *"You* are obviously not listening to me" *"You* are not paying attention." Such accusations are not helpful to the communication process. They put the receiver on the defensive, and your message will not transfer accurately.

SPEC

It is always to your advantage to delay important communication to a time of greater receptivity. Do not attempt to force your message on a preoccupied or uninterested receiver.

Communication Assessment

1. Do I plan and present my important communications to facilitate the receiver's ability to accurately comprehend my message?
   yes ☐   no ☐

2. Do I assume that everyone absorbs information exactly as I do?
   yes ☐   no ☐

3. Do I always allow the receiver to absorb my message visually, auditorily, and kinesthetically?   yes ☐   no ☐

4. Do I deliver my communication just once, failing to incorporate repetition into my communication process?   yes ☐   no ☐

5. Do I always tell them, show them, and involve them?
   yes ☐   no ☐

6. Does the physical environment interfere with the effectiveness of my communication?   yes ☐   no ☐

7. Do I know the optimum communication time for my critical communication points?   yes ☐   no ☐

8. Do I attempt to schedule communication when it is best for me?
   yes ☐   no ☐

9. Do I willingly reschedule communication if the receiver appears distracted or inattentive?   yes ☐   no ☐

Any *no*-responses to the odd-numbered questions (1, 3, 5, 7, 9) and *yes*-responses to the even-numbered questions (2, 4, 6, 8) indicate opportunities to increase your communication effectiveness.

2. The Receiver's Willingness

The willingness of the receiver to accept, process, and comprehend your message is an area over which you can wield considerable influence. All communication is a consensual activity. No one can be forced to listen, communicate, or absorb information as it was intended. Every individual is in total control of his or her own willingness to listen, and the STPs who are the most effective communicators strive to encourage and cultivate the willingness of their communication partners.

There are at least two strategies you can implement to impact the receiver's willingness, and while they are few in number, they are powerful in their impact.

Use an Assertive Communication Style

This is the most compelling strategy available to have a positive impact on the reception of your messages by others. The style of your communication, or the package in which it is presented, can make or break your communication partner's willingness to receive your message. To increase your communication success, learn to use assertive communication patterns.

Assertive communication patterns are identified by *I*- or *we*-based messages. They reduce the negative emotional impact that results when making *you*-statements, encourage receivers to listen, and increase their willingness to process your message.

Aggressive communication patterns utilize harsh *you*-based messages. They increase the negative emotional impact on receivers, shut down their listening activity, and severely reduce or eliminate their willingness to give any objective consideration to your communication. Ineffective communicators use aggressive patterns that tear down the bridges that you are striving to erect! If your message is delivered offensively or with any hint of intimidation by threat or blame, the receiver becomes focused on protecting and defending himself.

While the difference between aggressive and assertive communication may seem like a subtle nuance, it is a major factor in determining the effectiveness of your communication. Most STPs do not intend to sound ag-

SPEC

With the exception of messages of high praise, you-statements are offensive and attacking, and imply negative accountability. They shift responsibility to your communication partner and translate into establishing blame.

gressive when they use *you*-based communication. The reactions created by such communications are confusing because the deliverer of the message usually has no intention of sending an aggressive or offensive message. Regardless of intent, aggressive messages result in significant communication breakdowns.

Assertive versus Aggressive Communication.   How do you react when someone says "You are wrong" as opposed to "I am not sure I agree"? Which phrase creates a more positive response in you? We all understand the negative impact such aggressive messages have on us, yet we frequently fail to understand the impact our aggressive messages have on others.

The use of an aggressive communication style may be the single greatest contributor to communication disconnects and misunderstandings in our workplace today, and this communication flaw is by no means limited to the scientific and technical community. It is often the dominant communication style for all segments of our society. Usually aggressive communication patterns are learned very early in life, which adds to the difficulty of changing them. It will not be easy for you to abandon your aggressive patterns and embrace assertive ones. If you are successful, you will significantly increase your communication effectiveness.

Here are some examples of aggressive and assertive messages:

Aggressive: "Your conclusion or recommendation is wrong." (Sends the message that the receiver is stupid and you are superior.)
Assertive: "I disagree with the conclusion or recommendation and I'd like to explain why." (Invites discussion or dialogue on the content.)

Aggressive: "Because of your lack of performance, we are going to fail on this project." (Communicates negative judgment and heavy blame.)

Assertive: "I'm afraid this continued performance problem could lead to failure if we don't react quickly." (Implies a solution to a problem.)

Aggressive: "Tell me why your report is late." (Invites a negative defensive reaction.)
Assertive: "Help me understand why the report wasn't submitted on time." (Asks for explanation.)

Aggressive: "Because of your background and lack of knowledge, you probably don't understand the complexity of this information." (Implies ignorance and blames the receiver for any potential inaccuracy or miscommunication.)
Assertive: "I want to do everything I can to make this complex information clear and understandable." (Allows the deliverer to take responsibility and implies a strong commitment to communicating effectively.)

STPs may have more significant challenges with aggressive communication patterns than most because of their extensive command of the content, passion for their message, and tendency to view things in terms of absolutes. Have you noticed a high rate of defensiveness in others when you communicate with them? You may actually be creating this response without realizing it. It is a significant challenge for most STPs to shift to an assertive style. Are you up to the task?

Avoid Provoking Phrases and Words

There are certain common phrases and words that provoke a negative reaction in receivers and instantly turn off their willingness to process your message. These phrases and words are bridge destroyers, and using them is guaranteed to create a disconnect between content and emotional impact. Perhaps chief among them is the word *but*. *But* is a very negative word that delivers an emotional wallop in any communication. It cancels the statement the other person just made and announces that a contentious statement is about to follow. When used as a response to someone else's comments, it sends a clear message of dismissing or devaluing the other party's statements. Even if you basically agree with your communication partner, if you interject *but*, it diminishes the impact of your statements of agreement.

Consider these examples:

"I agree with you to a point, *but* there are other important things to consider." (The *but* means I disagree and here is what I think is much more important.)

"I appreciate the information you sent me, *but* it is incomplete." (The *but* means I really do not appreciate your efforts, dummy!)

Here are some effective alternatives:

"I agree with you *and* there are some additional things to consider."

"I appreciate the information you sent *and* there are some additional things I need."

SPEC

In every case where you could say **but** *you can substitute the word* **and**— *unless you are describing a body part!*

Additional provocative words and phrases—and alternatives to them—include the following:

Provocative	Alternative
Can't	Can
Sorry	Thank-you
I don't know	I'll find out
You should have	I understand why you didn't
Why didn't you	I can see why you didn't
The only thing we can do is	I think the best option is
However	And (*however* is nothing but a dressed up *but!*)

You must eliminate these ten statements from your communications.

1. "That's not a bad idea, but . . . "
2. "The problem with what you said is . . . "
3. "Your idea sounds good in theory but it won't work in practice because . . . "
4. "There's no way that will work here."
5. "What you are recommending is impossible under our current system."
6. "We've never done it that way before. Why should we start now?"
7. "We've been doing it the same way for ten years; why should we change to your idea now?"
8. "That's the dumbest thing I've ever heard."
9. "You probably don't want to hear this, but . . . "
10. "You need to listen to what I have to say."

Some Thoughts About Body Language

Discussed extensively in Chapter 2, your body language and nonverbal messages have a huge impact on receivers' willingness to process your message. Listeners may decide to reject your information and may begin reacting negatively even before you open your mouth if your nonverbals project a judgmental, intimidating, or threatening message.

Communication Assessment

1. Do my communication patterns contribute to the unwillingness of the receiver to absorb my message? *yes* ☐ *no* ☐
2. Do I always implement an assertive communication pattern and avoid an aggressive style? *yes* ☐ *no* ☐
3. Does my communication ever convey intimidation, threat, or blame? *yes* ☐ *no* ☐
4. Do I always use *you*-based statements when delivering messages of high praise? *yes* ☐ *no* ☐
5. Do I experience a high rate of defensiveness in others when I communicate with them? *yes* ☐ *no* ☐
6. Am I willing to change my tendency to use an aggressive communication pattern? *yes* ☐ *no* ☐
7. Do I have a tendency to use provoking phases without realizing it? *yes* ☐ *no* ☐

8. Do I avoid using the words *but* and *however*?   yes ☐   no ☐
9. Do my body language and nonverbal communications contribute to a low receptivity in the people I communicate with? (If your answer is *no*, please seek a second, third, and fourth opinion!)
yes ☐   no ☐

Any *yes*-responses to the odd-numbered questions (1, 3, 5, 7, 9) and *no*-responses to the even-numbered questions (2, 4, 6, 8) indicate opportunities to increase your communication effectiveness. Please pay close attention to your responses to questions 1, 2, 5, and 9.

SPEC

The result of an effective communication is not necessarily agreement, it is the consistent understanding of a message by all parties.

3. The Receiver's Accurate Comprehension

The third major factor that influences the transfer of information is the receiver's accurate comprehension of your message. You have communicated effectively if the receiver has correctly understood the intended meaning of your message.

Barriers to Accurate Comprehension

There are many things that can impact receivers' comprehension of your message. Even when their ability and willingness to process the message are very high, the information must run the gauntlet of multiple comprehension barriers.

To illustrate, we use the image of a funnel.

Your communication is poured into the funnel and flows through the comprehension barriers, which act as filters. The meaning of the message can become distorted at any point during this passage through the funnel. The impact and intensity of the barriers and the degree of the distortion

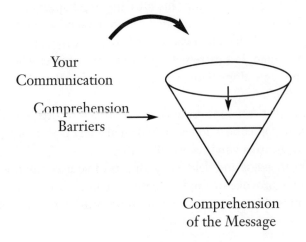

Your
Communication

Comprehension
Barriers

Comprehension
of the Message

will vary from individual to individual, and you must consistently evaluate the barriers' effects.

Education and Experience.   Is your message appropriate to your receivers' level of education and experience with the subject matter? Do their training and experience offer reference points that will help them understand what you are saying, or are they significantly different from yours? Perhaps you stress issues of quality, whereas they give greater value to cost or time. Do they have a different set of filters in their funnels? Where you see opportunities do they see problems? Do you see options where they perceive there are only absolutes? It has been said that "mankind is the sum total of its individual experience." Is their experience different from yours in ways that influence how they receive your message? Your saying "We could be in trouble with this project" could have an unintended devastating meaning to someone who was recently downsized from her previous job.

If your communication consists of information above their level of education or experience, your receiver could become intimidated or overwhelmed. If it is below their level, they may become angry or resentful at your perceived condescension.

Age.   Age is a significant factor for communicating in today's science- and technology-driven workplace. The Baby Boomers (born 1946 to 1964) and Generation X-ers (born 1965 to 1976) have very different perceptions of their profession, activities, and quality of life. Undeniably, generational barriers exist. Negative intergenerational judgments contribute to preconceptions (addressed in greater depth in subsequent chapters). Baby Boomers may question the work ethic and dedication of Generation X-ers, who may for their part see their more experienced colleagues as set in their ways and resistant to change. It is extremely important to consider whether the context of your message, along with any references and analogies, is appropriate for the receiver's age.

For example, saying that someone "sounds like a broken record" has absolutely no relevance to someone who has only owned a CD player, or perhaps has never seen or heard a vinyl record album!

It is also important to assess and delete any aspects of your communication that may somehow provoke or imply negative judgments of members of different age groups. Your communication must convey a consistent blend of wisdom and openness to others.

Culture.   Cultural values vary considerably. Your message may take on an entirely different meaning to your receiver when there are cultural differences between you. Though the United States and other Western cultures stress individualism, the majority of the world's cultures embrace collectivism and interdependence. The laws and customs in most cultures are designed to protect the society or greater good at the possible expense of the individual. In the United States, the laws and customs are designed to protect and promote the individual at the possible expense of the society. Do you think such cultural differences could lead to occasional miscommunications?

Words and gestures can have vastly different meanings and create varied reactions when used in cross-cultural contexts. Nonverbal aspects of communication such as eye contact and even physical positioning can also be barriers to the accurate transmission and reception of your message.

The scientific and technological professions are among the most culturally diverse groups in America today. It is going to be increasingly important for you to broaden your cultural awareness. It will be necessary for you to take the initiative to learn as much as you can about the backgrounds of the people you communicate with to ensure that miscommunications are minimal. This is an issue of escalating importance for STPs.

It is beyond the scope of this book to address the multitude of significant cross-cultural communication issues. Such important information may be available to you through organizational training/awareness initiatives, programs provided through your professional societies and associations, and the offerings of local colleges and universities. Be proactive and seek the information.

Gender. Men and women are very different in their patterns of communication. This is a topic that is very popular in today's publication market, especially concerning successful personal relationships. If you have an interest in exploring this topic further, you will have no trouble finding some excellent resources.

When it comes to communication in the workplace, men often interpret situations to reflect a more competitive and formally hierarchical point of view, whereas women may perceive the same situation from a more collegial and participative perspective. Men are more single task–focused and women regularly flourish in multitask environments. For example, men typically focus on a single factor in decision making; women consider a greater number of factors when making decisions.

Other gender communication differences occur in the following contexts:

Apologies

1. *Men:* Tend not to apologize, assuming that apologies are unnecessary if communication or interaction continues. Men often see an apology as a sign of vulnerability or self-deprecation. They may also see apologies as an acknowledgment of a subordinate position, a lack of power.
2. *Women:* Tend to apologize more than men. Frequently, women use apologies to express concern over disruptions of interaction, and their apologies may be misinterpreted as excessive admissions of guilt or wrongdoing. They may actually be expressions of concern or sympathy and not admissions of error.

Content

1. *Men:* Communication tends to focus on sharing information objectively, emphasizing the transmission of facts, observations, experiences, or events.
2. *Women:* Developing interaction or rapport is often given equal weight to imparting information as the reason for their communication. This involves a greater tendency to discuss feelings, share thoughts, or validate emotion.

Intent

1. *Men:* Communication is often intended to establish uniqueness or perhaps primacy. They communicate to establish themselves as an

independent entity, not part of the group. Communication is often designed to set them apart.

2. *Women:* Communication is often intended to promote inclusion or participation. They communicate to be an active and important part of a collective. Frequently the intention is to make a contribution to a group effort.

Silence

1. *Men:* Silence is frequently used for emphasis, to demonstrate power, or assert pressure and control.
2. *Women:* Often use silence introspectively to preconsider statements or assess the messages they have received. Women's use of silence is sometimes misunderstood as an indication of weakness, uncertainty, or lack of power.

Physical Positioning

1. *Men:* Prefer to sit side by side for communication. Frontal positioning can be interpreted as either confrontational or intimate, both of which can cause significant miscommunication.
2. *Women:* Prefer to sit face to face with their communication partner to enhance interaction and connectedness. Positioning is designed to enhance partnering.

To be an effective communicator you must consider any and all potential gender-related barriers to comprehension. Alter your message to neutralize the potential for misunderstanding.

Language

Language is another area in which you should be aware of gender-related pitfalls. Use gender-nonspecific language like the following:

Salesperson, not *salesman.*
Spouse, not *husband/wife.*
Police officer, not *policeman.*
Leader/manager/owner/businessperson, not *businessman.*
Use *Ms.* when unsure of preference of *Miss* or *Mrs.*
Avoid using *boy* or *girl* in organizational communication ("the *men* in the shipping department," not "the *boys* in the shipping department"; "the *women* in the office," not "the *girls* in the office)".

SPEC

It is important to make your communication gender-nonspecific.

Communication Assessment

1. Do I consider my communication partner's education and related experience when planning my communication? *yes* ☐ *no* ☐
2. Do I consider potential age-related barriers to comprehension in planning my communication? *yes* ☐ *no* ☐
3. Do I refrain from using terms, analogies, or references that may have little or no meaning to people of different age groups? *yes* ☐ *no* ☐
4. Am I aware of possible cultural barriers in my communication with others? *yes* ☐ *no* ☐
5. Have I taken specific action to learn about and overcome cultural communication barriers? *yes* ☐ *no* ☐
6. Am I aware of the general differences between men's and women's communication styles? *yes* ☐ *no* ☐

Any *no*-responses indicate opportunities for improving your communication effectiveness.

Personal Action Plan
Identify the individuals with whom you experience your most obvious communication challenges.

- Are there possible barriers to accurate comprehension related to education, experience, age, culture, or gender?
- What specific strategies can you implement to reduce or eliminate the impact of those barriers?
- What can you do to acquire more in-depth knowledge about those barriers?

Checking for Comprehension of Communication with Individuals

Once your communication has been delivered, the most effective way to determine whether you have achieved accurate comprehension is to ask the receivers to summarize their understanding of your message. If the receiver can correctly restate the message as you intended it, then you have communicated effectively. If the receivers cannot restate accurately, it is a clear indicator that a communication breakdown has occurred. In reality, discovering that the receiver did not accurately comprehend your message is a very positive thing. It gives you the opportunity to repair the communication and avoid any problems resulting from the miscommunication before they develop. Discovering miscommunication early is the proverbial "dodging the bullet."

Though most STPs are aware of the idea of checking for comprehension, few implement it effectively. Why? Perhaps its importance is underestimated. Maybe little or no training has been offered for successful implementation, or more likely, previous attempts to use the technique have failed miserably.

Problems Associated with Checking for Comprehension

For all STPs there are at least three problems to confront in implementing this strategy of accurately checking for comprehension:

1. Assuming success
2. Negative past experience
3. Inaccurate verification

1. Assuming Success.   STPs assume the message has been comprehended with complete accuracy and make no formal effort at verification.

You deliver the message and walk away confidently, thinking "He knows exactly what I want him to do" or "She understands exactly what I said." The receiver, in stark contrast, may be mumbling, "I have no clue what he just said." Such assumptions of accurate comprehension are not only arrogant, they can be extremely costly. When communication problems do occur, it is easy to heap blame upon the receiver. It would be much more effective to avoid the problem entirely by not making your assumptions and effectively checking for accurate comprehension.

2. Negative Past Experiences.   In the past you may have had a negative response when you attempted to get a communication partner to summarize their understanding. Some communication partners may take offense at being treated like a child or resent having their intelligence questioned. Angry and defensive responses are very common.

In light of these negative experiences, you probably refrain from implementing the strategy. This avoidance results in allowing communication problems to continue.

3. Inaccurate Verification. Perhaps you have not questioned the receiver correctly when attempting to verify the accuracy of the received message. Inappropriate phrases such as the following are often used:

> "Did you understand what I just said?" (Frequently accompanied with a subconscious affirmative nodding of the head.)
> "You don't have any questions, do you?" (Frequently accompanied with a subconscious negative nodding of the head.)
> "Are you with me?"
> "You're getting all of this, aren't you?"

The receiver responds by saying, "Oh sure, I understand" or "No, it was very clear, I don't have any questions." When confronted in this manner people will rarely acknowledge that they did not understand or that they do have questions. Many factors encourage this inaccurate response. They probably wish to avoid embarrassment that would result if they admitted that they really did not understand. Doing so could make them appear or feel stupid. The receiver may also want to avoid a negative reaction from you. Feigning understanding eliminates any perceived negative judgment on your part. It is possible the receiver may be attempting to end the communication. She could be under time pressures or might simply want to remove you from her presence! The best way to do that is to imply agreement and understanding and quickly bring the communication to a conclusion. Quick agreement ends communications. Posing questions or offering dialogue prolongs them.

Only in relationships with very high trust are people willing to acknowledge any lack of understanding. Otherwise, it is easier to pretend they have understood than risk a negative reaction. Although it is a short-sighted behavior, it is much more common to cover up a lack of comprehension than it is to acknowledge it and seek clarification.

Successfully Asking Receivers to Summarize Their Understanding

When problems occur with verification, it is usually because the comprehension check was done *aggressively* and not *assertively*. The aggressive implementation is to be avoided:

A great way to provoke a *negative* reaction in your communication partners is to use *you*-based messages, such as this: "I want to be sure that *you* understood what I just said. Would *you* repeat back to me in *your* words what *you* think the message was?"

This aggressive tone implies the receiver is responsible for proving he is bright enough to comprehend your message. (Guilty until proven innocent!) It also places total responsibility for the communication squarely on the shoulders of the receiver. If there is a problem, it must be his fault. This is a very arrogant challenge and it is not a good method for checking comprehension. It leaves receivers feeling they have been treated with condescension and guarantees a negative reaction and a disruption in the communication process. Do *not* use any aggressive phrases.

What is the successful alternative? A statement like this:

SPEC

"I want to be certain that I have done a good job of communication. Help check me out. Please summarize what was said."

This assertive style, totally devoid of the word *you*, invites receivers to critique you as the deliverer of the message. It creates a safe opportunity for them to acknowledge any lack of understanding and it puts the responsibility for the communication squarely on your shoulders. Instead of challenging them, you invite them to evaluate your message and, in the process, discover their level of comprehension.

It is far better to discover any miscommunication or distortion of comprehension early than to deal with the wreckage later when problems arise. Most communication problems are avoidable.

If your past attempts to check for comprehension have not been successful, it is probably because you inadvertently used an aggressive approach.

The Receivers' Restatement Must Be in Their Own Words. It is important to remember that the summary by receivers must be in their own words, not yours. You do not want them merely to parrot back the exact words you used. A reasonably intelligent bird is capable of exact restatement! If you say "Good morning" to a parrot, the bird will respond by saying "Good morning." This certainly does not imply the bird understands what "Good morning" means! When receivers summarize in their own words, you can readily determine the level of comprehension.

If receivers are not able to restate or summarize correctly, you have the opportunity to repeat your message until you are confident an accurate transfer of information has taken place.

If the Restatement Is Inaccurate. How you structure your response is extremely important. If you react negatively by snapping, "That's not what I said. I'll repeat the message again, but please pay attention this time," you are obviously not creating high receptivity in the receiver. Any negative response on your part will either provoke or intimidate your communication partner and further erode your efforts.

The appropriate response would be: "Obviously, *I* did not do a good job of communicating. Thank you for helping me discover that. *I* am really glad we found this out now rather than later. Let *me* try the communication again."

This response allows the responsibility to fall to you and protects receivers from embarrassment or negative judgment. It encourages them to focus on your message. Reacting positively takes the pain out of communicating with you!

Change Your Communication Approach. If subsequent restatements are not successful, it could be an indicator that the receiver does not have strong auditory or listening skills. You may be communicating with someone who has a more visual or kinesthetic orientation. Continued attempts to put across your information verbally will only contribute to frustration for both of you. It is probably in everyone's best interest for you to vary your communication approach. Perhaps you can encourage the receiver to take notes, or you may choose to summarize the communication in writing prior to delivering it. This would allow them to review written communication rather than relying solely on a verbal presentation. Do not continue attempts to communicate in a method that is obviously counterproductive.

When Restatement Becomes a Communication Habit.   When you routinely implement the assertive technique for comprehension checking, you will find that the receiver's summary is offered quickly and easily. The more you use the technique, the more comfortable everyone becomes. When others realize you are not checking their IQ but are checking the transfer of information, they will participate enthusiastically. Take the threat out of this technique and you will soon reach the point where the receiver offers his summary automatically or in response to a short statement from you like "Now, give it back to me" or "Let's summarize." As communication trust increases, the transition from message delivery to comprehension verification becomes seamless. The way to establish that trust is through repetitively using the technique and avoiding aggressive phrasing.

Checking for Comprehension of Communication with Groups

Most STPs such as you are experiencing greater opportunity for communication in groups. Very likely a few of the communication circumstances you are facing involve internal teams, presentations to customers, or providing formal programs to management. It is important to ensure that your group communications are as accurately comprehended as your individual discussions. When you are in a position of presenting information to any group, use the following techniques.

Written Summaries.   Ask the individuals in the group to summarize in writing (outline form encouraged) the most important points they heard. An excellent way to approach this is to ask them to follow a 3–2–1 model. Ask them to. . .

   . . . list the *three* most important things that were covered in this presentation.
   . . . list *two* things they would have liked more in-depth information on.
   . . . identify *one* thing they would like to discuss in follow-up meetings.

This strategy allows you to illicit a very specific summary and will help you determine whether your message was received accurately. It is important to use the 3–2–1 structure. The actual wording of the questions is up to you. The 3–2–1 format ensures specific feedback. Even though individuals' responses will differ, you will quickly be able to determine whether you got your primary message across to the group.

Group Summary.   At the conclusion of your presentation, ask for a volunteer from the group to lead a group summary of what was discussed. The role of the volunteer is to record the group's responses on a flip chart or large piece of paper. It is not her responsibility to perform a solo debriefing. She is a facilitator, not an individual responder. Generally you would ask the participants to do this summary without the benefits of any notes or reference material. As you observe this activity, listen for the most significant points you presented to be summarized. Specific responses mean your message was accurately transferred. Overly general responses indicate miscommunication.

This exercise allows you to test the group without the threat or possible embarrassment that individual testing could bring.

Conduct a Verbal Debriefing.   Ask the participants to write down on a sheet of paper the single most important thing they learned or that you presented, and two things they will actually do as a result of the information that was transferred. Have each individual share with the group the responses he or she wrote down. Once again, listen carefully for specific responses.

You know the message was received accurately if the responses are specific, for example: "I learned how important it is to test the samples within one hour after the process is completed."

You are in trouble if most of the responses are very general, for example: "I learned this is important stuff." If one person in the group responds that way, it is probably an individual communication issue. If the majority of the group responds that way, it is probably a result of your communication!

This strategy will help you to find out whether or not the message you intended to communicate was received accurately.

Communication Assessment

1. Do I frequently experience negative or defensive reactions from others when I attempt to verify their understanding of my message? *yes* ☐   *no* ☐
2. Do I assume that my communications are always received exactly as I intended to deliver them?   *yes* ☐   *no* ☐
3. Do I tend to use aggressive or provoking phrases when I check for comprehension?   *yes* ☐   *no* ☐
4. Do I expect others to be able to repeat back to me exactly what I said?   *yes* ☐   *no* ☐
5. Do I use assertive *I*- and *we*-messages to reduce any negative reactions when I check for comprehension?   *yes* ☐   *no* ☐

6. Does my communication style encourage others to speak up when they have questions or do not completely understand my message? *yes* ☐ *no* ☐

7. Do I routinely check for comprehension when I present information to groups? *yes* ☐   *no* ☐

8. Do I use effective techniques to encourage the individuals in a group to provide specific information on what they learned by asking: What was most important? What will you actually do with the information I presented? *yes* ☐   *no* ☐

Any *yes*-responses to questions 1, 2, 3, or 4 and *no*-responses to questions 5, 6, 7, or 8 indicate opportunities to increase your communication effectiveness.

In Chapter 4 you will learn to deal with one of the most common communication problems facing STPs in today's organizational environment: the challenges of giving and receiving criticism or negative feedback.

4

Giving and Receiving Criticism

In normal day-to-day activities, STPs find themselves in circumstances requiring them to give corrective feedback or constructive criticism to others, or to receive similar messages concerning their own work. These circumstances always create communication challenges. Though giving critical feedback certainly is easier than receiving it, most STPs find dealing with people's reactions to their comments frustrating at best. The ability to deliver critical messages appropriately demands exceptional communication skill, and once again, it is a skill in which people rarely get any training. Even more difficult is accepting negative comments, constructive criticisms, or critical judgments about one's work; this is difficult for everyone and especially so for STPs like you, who take such great pride in their work and make such a high personal investment in what they do. Recall that in our communication model, communication has two components: content of the message and emotional impact of the communication. Giving and receiving critical comment has the potential to trigger a nega-

CONTENT   EMOTIONAL
                 IMPACT

tive emotional response in the receiver. When delivering these messages, you must maintain a keen awareness of the possible impact your communication will have on the receiver. You may have to adjust your delivery to neutralize or minimize the negative reaction. Skillful and effective adjustment on your part increases the probability that the receiver will process the information in a positive, constructive way. By the same token, when you are on the receiving end of this type of critical feedback, it is important that you control your own internal emotional reaction and minimize any impulsive negative or defensive responses. This is certainly easier said than done, but you can learn and implement the skills if your commitment to succeed is high.

You may downplay or dismiss the negative reaction your criticisms create in others. At times you are probably quick to suggest that people should "deal with it" or "get over it" and "just accept what I'm telling you and move on." For most of you, it is relatively easy to see negative reactions in others as signs of emotionalism, fragility, and weakness. While you may be quick to judge others, you probably react just as emotionally when someone else's critical comments are directed at you. Perhaps it's part of human nature to believe that when we offer critical comment and constructive criticisms to others, we are right in doing so, yet when they offer them to us, they are unreasonable, unfair, and misguided. When I do it to you . . . it's okay. When you do it to me, it's not!

You are probably very frustrated when others react negatively to your comments. You expect your communication to be judged by the *intent* of your message, which you of course perceive to be totally fair, necessary, positive, and only intended to increase knowledge and performance. By being focused on the intent, you absolve yourself of responsibility for any negative reaction your message may create in the receiver. You may actually feel, "It's what I intend to communicate that matters, not what was actually said." How often do you hear people defend themselves with statements similar to, "Well, that's not what I meant to say . . . it's not my fault if you took it the wrong way"? It's as if these people expect others to read their minds and decipher their intended message and disregard what they actually said. Instead of listening with your ears, they want you to listen with your "psychic powers." Conversely, when on the receiving end of critical messages, these same people are quick to judge the impact of the messages on themselves and not the intent of the deliverer. Isn't it interesting how we all seem to want it both ways! This inconsistency, while understandable, obviously does not contribute to overall effective communication.

Packaging Your Criticisms Effectively

Despite the temptation to dismiss the importance of the emotional impact your critical messages have on others, in reality you are responsible for delivering these messages with tact and understanding. Receivers' reactions are just as intense and justified as your reaction is when you are the receiver of the critical comment.

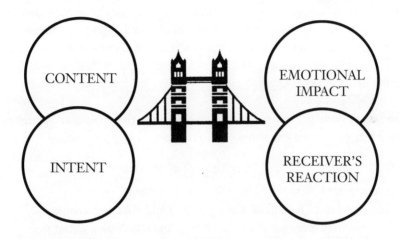

This requires us to add an additional layer to our communication model: Effective communication demands the building of an additional bridge between message intent and the receiver's reaction. Expecting receivers to judge the message strictly on the basis of what you intended to say and to disregard their own reaction is making the assumption that others can read your mind!

CASE STUDY 1

Sandra is an IT quality assurance engineer for a company that designs patient information and diagnostic software for hospitals. When the program designers are confident that their products are ready to be released to customers, Sandra challenges and evaluates the system prior to its being approved for distribution to the end user. Her primary area of responsibility is to test beta software, software not yet ready to put on the market, for both ease of use and the existence of any bugs within the program. Her job is literally to find flaws in the work of others.

When weaknesses in the system are found she is responsible for communicating her findings back to the program design department and working closely with them to correct the problems she has identified.

This process requires that she deliver critical comments to others while continuing to maintain a close working relationship. She says, "That is the toughest part of my job. I have to point out mistakes to people who don't think they make mistakes and then help to fix the problems without their seeing me as an intrusion on their authority or expertise."

In the past, she has experienced some significant communication problems, and one design programmer actually resigned because she thought Sandra's criticisms were unfair. Sandra sought help in dealing with her communication challenges.

First, let's consider some general assumptions that you and Sandra can make when giving critical comment to others:

- They probably don't want to hear it!
- They won't necessarily like what you tell them.
- They will want to defend their position and challenge yours.
- It is not necessary for them to agree with your message, but it certainly is necessary that they accurately comprehend its content.
- Some people have a greater ability and willingness to accept critical messages and learn from them than others.
- Factors such as maturity, experience, and realistic self-assessment dramatically affect this communication process.

Even though Sandra is only doing her job when she discovers problems and provides feedback, she is still responsible for doing so in a way that is not offensive to the receiver. What can be done to successfully deliver critical comment? Here are six recommendations.

1. Be Tactful

Do not become so focused on the content and intention of your message that you dismiss the importance of the emotional impact it will have on the receiver. No matter how much you believe someone deserves to be criticized or how frustrated you may be with the person's lack of performance,

SPEC

Dignity and respect must be maintained at all times.

cooperation, or faulty conclusions and assumptions, you are not absolved of the responsibility to use tactful communication.

You do not have the right to be undignified or disrespectful just because you believe it is warranted. This is especially important if you have an emotional involvement with the message you are delivering. Some of you take great pride in perceiving yourselves to be just "honest, straightforward people who tell it like it is." Critical comments are frequently prefaced by qualifying statements such as: "The only way I know how to say it is to lay it right on the line and tell you the truth" or "I'm going to tell you this for your own good." If Sandra's critical comments were delivered in this style, the message that followed may have been received as searing and painful criticism. It may have been perceived as a personal attack or indictment with no apparent regard for the emotional impact on the receiver (some STPs actually intend to create a negative reaction). By pre-qualifying statements when delivering your critical comments, there is a self-serving assumption that it is no longer necessary to use tact and show respect. This demonstrates a perception of "It's okay for me to treat you unmercifully and have no regard for your well-being whatsoever as long as I issue a disclaimer first!" There are many mean-spirited, hurtful people who enjoy delivering painful messages under the guise of "truth." What's really interesting is that these same individuals scream the loudest when others do it to them. It is quite a consistent phenomenon that "the attack dog usually has very thin skin."

One of the primary aspects of showing tact is to plan the location of where you will deliver any critical comments to someone. Such communication should always be delivered in a private, nonthreatening, neutral location. Never subject people to public embarrassment by confronting them in the presence of others. Your message will be meaningless as they react to defend themselves and lash out in retaliation. Regardless of the accuracy of

SPEC

Never structure communication to cause anyone to lose face.

your critical message, it is extremely difficult, or perhaps impossible, for them to agree in front of others.

Willingly subjecting anyone to public embarrassment is considered abusive behavior in today's workplace and demonstrates a clear lack of respect and selfish disregard of others.

2. Use Assertive, Not Aggressive, Communication

As discussed earlier, *you*-statements increase negative emotion and reduce the willingness of the receiver to absorb your message. Communicating critical comment aggressively shuts down the receiver's listening process and creates an inevitable defensive response. If you experience a high rate of defensiveness in others when you offer feedback or criticism, such as apparently was happening with Sandra, carefully check whether you have been using an aggressive communication style. You may be creating their reaction unknowingly and unintentionally.

Some examples:

SPEC

Always avoid **you**-*based messages when delivering critical comment. Use assertive* **I**- *and* **we**-*based messages.*

Unacceptable	*Acceptable*
"You're wrong."	"I don't agree."
"I saw what you did, you violated our policy."	"Tell me what it means when our policies are disregarded."
"Why did you do this? You didn't give me what I asked for."	"Help me understand why it was done this way" or "Help me understand what happened."

Receiving criticism or negative comment always takes people down. Listening becomes less efficient and perceptions of being picked on, treated unfairly, or persecuted escalate. Defensiveness sets in and people become contentious, aggressively justifying their actions, and trying hard to prove you wrong. When these negative emotions and behaviors manifest themselves, any possible positive outcome of your critical comment is lost.

3. Identify the Positive

To avoid generating defensiveness in others, you must blend critical comments with very clear positive statements. It's a good model or guideline to make two positive statements before delivering the critical comment (one positive comment is the *absolute* bare minimum; two should be the norm), and to conclude with an additional positive observation. The positioning of positive comments first accomplishes a number of things with your receivers:

- They are not subjected to criticism only.
- It establishes the fact that you have a balanced view of them and their work.
- It encourages them to listen more actively. When people say positive things to you, the intensity of your listening increases and you pay greater attention to the content of their messages.

Concluding with a positive observation ends the communication on a high note and encourages an overall positive reaction. Ending with a negative or critical statement results in the receiver having a prolonged negative reaction, which tends to fester.

When Sandra presents her feedback to the program designers, she should point out all of the positive aspects of the software they have created. If she only identifies the flaws, there will be a negative reaction.

SPEC

Critical comment must always be positioned between positive statements. Stand-alone negative messages create a predictable and understandably defensive response in the receiver.

Incorporating positive messages can be difficult, especially when you have an emotional investment in the problem or critical comment you are about to deliver. As difficult as it may be, you must not eliminate or fail to point out the positive. At times you may have to struggle to find positive things to say. Never use a shortage of time as an excuse for delivering negative-only messages. Your time constraints will not make their reaction any less damaging.

Regardless of how bad you perceive people to be or how big the problem they have created, there is something good in them somewhere. They breathe just fine! They drink water well! They walk upright with great ability! It's easy to focus on the negative; identifying positive comments takes talent and creativity.

The positive observations must be specific statements (not generalized) and should be related to the topic you are going to discuss. Once the tone has been set by the positive input, the critical comment follows.

Here is an example of what Sandra might say: "Jim, you have worked very hard on this software project and it appears that with your help we are going to build it right and complete it on time. You have done so many things right, and there are a couple of things we need to discuss. I have found this problem . . . " (*or* "Help me understand. . . " *or* "We need to do further work on this. . . ").

Once the critical comment has been delivered and the information discussed, conclude the communication with an additional positive statement: "Another thing I've been impressed with is . . . and I'm very sure that we're going to be able to fix this and move on."

Please note, there is no *but* to cancel any positive statements!

Concluding with positive observations and optimistic statements helps to neutralize any negative emotional impact and discourages any tendency on the receiver's part toward prolonged anger or grudge holding. Negative reactions or emotions do not linger if you have concluded on a positive note. This technique also reaffirms the overall positive message that the good outweighs the bad; the receiver will be more accepting of your message and committed to making corrections or behavior changes. Without positive follow-up statements, the communication concludes on a down note and negative reactions fester. Keep in mind, it takes no talent to deliver critical messages; it takes great talent to be able to deliver a critical message and have the receiver comprehend it, accept it, and demonstrate his or her willingness to respond in a positive way.

SPEC

Increase the number of stand-alone positive messages to your peers, boss, subordinates, and all others with whom you maintain consistent, ongoing, significant communication. Critical comments are more effective when they are the exception, not the norm.

If the only time the program design people hear from Sandra is when there is a problem, they will react negatively to everything she says. When negative-only messages are delivered consistently, receivers learn to shut down their listening activity and erect a communication barrier as soon as they see you coming. When they see you approaching, they probably say, "Here we go again. She never has anything good to say. All she ever wants to do is criticize." Your message is rejected before you even begin to deliver it. History is an excellent teacher, and if your history teaches others to consistently expect a negative message, you have lost the communication battle before it's begun.

Negative messages should not stand alone; positive messages, however, certainly can and must. The more positive messages people hear from you, the more meaningful your feedback and constructive criticisms. People are more willing to accept occasional negative communication when you have demonstrated a pattern of delivering a majority of positive messages.

You can easily identify the people in your working environment who only have contact or communication with you when there is a negative or critical message. You may have developed that same predictable reaction to them without realizing it. Is it possible people could currently have the same perceptions about you? Obviously, any such pattern is unintentional on your part and you are probably unaware that it has occurred. Again, we judge harshly in others behaviors we often commit ourselves. A careful self-assessment of these possible negative communication patterns would be very beneficial. The good news is, they can be successfully reversed and repaired.

For example, consider how you react when a negatively patterned communicator approaches. You do everything possible to avoid engaging this person. If the communication is unavoidable, you really do not listen and process the message. You are planning your escape! Are there any signs that other people may be responding to you in a similar manner?

4. Depersonalize the Message

When preparing to deliver critical comments, assess your own emotional control at the moment. It may be wise to delay your communications to be sure you are not making mountains out of mole hills. Diffuse the negative impact of your critical comments by first examining the true intent of your message. If your message is emotionally influenced and truly intended to punish, threaten, intimidate, or emphasize your brilliance or expose the receiver's stupidity, then you are not prepared to have an effective communication. Chances are great that you will probably have something to apologize for when your emotions ebb. If so, the true relevance of your comments will be lost in your apology and emotionalism. Wait until you are ready to deliver a positive message focused on correction and not a critical message of negative judgment before you begin to communicate. Use time as a communication tool.

Avoid any comments that may be received as personal. Fix problems; do not assign blame. Focus on what happened, not on who did it. Structure your message to describe behavior, events, standards, procedures, expectations, and advantages.

SPEC

When delivering constructive criticism or recommending corrective action, depersonalize the message by focusing on what has happened or what you want them to do differently.

5. Provide Suggestions for Corrective Action

It's not enough to tell people what they have done wrong. Offer suggestions for corrective action. Merely pointing out their failures, or exposing faulty conclusions and assumptions, no matter how legitimate your comments may be, is shallow and incomplete communication. It does not take a lot of talent to be a problem identifier; it is much more helpful to be a problem solver. Ideas or advice for corrective action must be presented in tandem with critical comment.

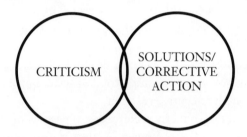

Combining specific recommendations or identifying corrective options, along with critical comments, creates an inclusive, complete communication and contributes to creating a positive outcome. Failing to do so creates negative, exclusive communication, which is generally perceived as blaming, ridicule, or intimidation.

This communication tandem of criticism and solution is especially important in group discussions or team meetings. Disagreeing or occasionally playing the devil's advocate is fine as long as you also demonstrate your willingness to make positive contributions by offering solution-oriented communication.

You are not helpful if you just identify problems. Become an asset by identifying and providing solutions.

6. Don't Dwell on the Past

Critical comment or constructive criticisms should focus only on the present and the future. Avoid engaging in emotional discussions of past negative events. The past is past. It is gone, do not try to resurrect it. Do not harbor grudges. Be sure your communications always address current events, not history lessons. If negative events have happened in the past, structure your current comments to focus on avoiding any repeats in the future.

SPEC

Do not allow your critical comments to lapse into history lessons.

Practice the 90/10 critical communication rule: Critical comment or constructive criticisms should focus 90 percent on fixing future behavior, or what we will do differently next time, and only 10 percent on what has already taken place.

If Sandra's feedback to the program designers contained comments on past flaws or somehow kept a running total of system problems, she should not be surprised at any negative reaction.

Unnecessary and unproductive references to past events only serve to increase the negative emotional impact on the receiver and decreases their ability and willingness to process your message.

Communication Assessment

1. Am I aware of the emotional impact my critical comments may have on the receiver of my message? (It is extremely beneficial to seek input from others to align your perceived awareness with their communication reality.) *yes* ☐   *no* ☐
2. Do I give equal importance to the emotional impact and content of my messages? *yes* ☐   *no* ☐
3. Do I realize the effectiveness of my communication lies in the receiver's actual reaction to the message and not in what I intended to say? *yes* ☐   *no* ☐
4. Do I avoid an aggressive use of the word *you* in delivering critical comment? *yes* ☐   *no* ☐
5. Do I use appropriate positive messages when delivering critical comments? *yes* ☐   *no* ☐
6. Do I consistently deliver stand-alone positive messages to my peers, boss, and other critical communication points? *yes* ☐   *no* ☐
7. Do I examine the true intent of my message before delivering critical comments? *yes* ☐   *no* ☐

8. Do I consciously depersonalize negative messages?
   yes ☐   *no* ☐
9. Do I avoid offering critical comment in public or other potentially embarrassing situations?   *yes* ☐   *no* ☐
10. Do I always keep my comments current and avoid any negative historical references in my critical comments?   *yes* ☐   *no* ☐

Any *no*-responses identify an opportunity to improve your communication effectiveness.

CASE STUDY 2

Ken is a design programmer with Sandra's company. He expressed great frustration and resentment toward Sandra. "She never has anything good to say about my work. She is always finding fault. I work very hard and I am very good at what I do. I'm tired of her always harping about flaws in the programs I design. She is never satisfied. I am not the only one who has problems with Sandra. Another designer, Beth, quit last month because of Sandra's constant criticism of her work and I don't blame her. Sandra was always picking on Beth and me; now it's just me. She thinks she is so much smarter than everyone else. The problems she finds are usually very small and easily corrected. But she makes a big deal out of them and lets everybody else know that 'Ken screwed up.' The other five designers seem to do okay with Sandra, but she sure has it in for me. They are afraid of her. I'm the only one who will stand up to her around here and I'm not going to do it much longer. When I see her coming, I find somewhere else to go. I don't even want to talk to her."

Receiving Criticism

Receiving critical comments or negative feedback concerning our performance, behaviors, conclusions, or decisions is never a pleasant experience. Emotionally healthy, mature people can generally accept feedback that is unflattering as long as it is well intended and effectively delivered; however, no one truly relishes the experience. Developing this communication skill will contribute to improved performance, better working relationships, and establish you as an exceptional STP! The better you are at accepting and processing criticism, the more you stand out from the group.

This requires you to take some measure of responsibility for your own emotional response. Learn to manage yourself and do not allow others to exercise control over you by making it easy for them to push your buttons.

From Sandra and Ken's description of the communication problems they encounter, it is difficult to determine any single source of responsibility. Undoubtedly, there is opportunity for communication improvements on all sides. It is interesting that Sandra acknowledges the problem and is seeking help. Ken merely blames Sandra and apparently perceives that his communication skills are not an issue. Unfortunately, this is not an uncommon scenario for many STPs when they are on the receiving end of information they do not want to hear.

Obviously, Sandra must assess her communication skills and increase her effectiveness in using tact, avoiding an aggressive or provoking style, and emphasizing the positive aspects as well as her points of criticism. She must also concentrate on depersonalizing her message and keep her comments focused on the project or the work and not the person. By the nature of what she does, working with the design programmers to fix the flaws, she is probably doing a good job of providing corrective action. It is extremely important that her corrective recommendations be presented in a spirit of collaboration, not self-perceived superiority. Sandra must also avoid any tendency to dwell on past events.

Regardless of where the responsibility for the miscommunication lies, you can see the disturbing results. Sandra feels hindered in her ability to do her job, the collaborative interaction between her and the program designers has deteriorated, and a valuable employee has apparently resigned, at least in part because of the negative emotional impact Sandra's communication had on her. Current productivity is suffering and negative emotions and reactions are prevalent, especially anger, resentment, and perceptions of being picked on or singled out for criticism. Improvements in communication are obviously necessary.

Let's now turn our attention to Ken. There are a number of things he must consider about his role in this communication process. First and foremost, he must develop a mature understanding of the importance of critical comment, appreciate the value of having his work reviewed, and overcome the tendency to take criticism very personally.

The Value of Seeking Honest Feedback

As difficult and frustrating as receiving critical comment from others can be, it is also some of the most valuable information you can ever receive.

Ken obviously has not yet achieved this awareness. Seeking out and accepting honest, critical feedback has an unparalleled positive impact on your performance and career growth. In reality, feedback from others is truly a gift they offer if we are willing to receive it. It is a wise and mature professional who can recognize the value of this gift. It not only helps us to grow, it provides valuable insight into how we are perceived by others. Though we may not like it, it is truly good for us. It is utterly naïve and an example of professional denial for you to perceive that everything you do is perfect and leaves no room for growth or improvement. Such self-perceived perfection only serves to reduce the quality of work, inhibit growth, and stall careers. Intellectually, most of you acknowledge the importance of receiving occasional critical comment or constructive criticism about your work, yet the reality of hearing these messages and dealing with the negative impact on your own emotions can be a challenge. We all have personal strengths and weaknesses and experience peaks and valleys in our overall performance.

Reacting negatively to critical comment or constructive criticism is interpreted by others as immaturity and perceived to be hard evidence that you are unwilling or incapable of evaluating your work objectively. You damage others' positive perceptions of you, or perhaps reinforce existing negative ones, by your inappropriate responses to constructive feedback. When you read Ken's comments, you probably find yourself reacting negatively to his perceptions.

It is in your best interest not only to learn to accept and process critical comments effectively, but also to seek out opportunities to obtain honest feedback. This will be the cornerstone, along with your own self-awareness, for future growth and increased competence.

There are seven specific areas in which to consistently seek evaluation and constructive critical comment from peers, your boss, and others who constitute your critical communication points:

SPEC

Consistently provide others the opportunity to offer constructive criticisms of your efforts.

1. The overall quality of your work
2. Your ability to control costs and address budget concerns and constraints
3. Your ability to consistently meet deadlines
4. Your overall skills in critical thinking and problem solving
5. The quality of your decision making
6. The depth of your creativity
7. Your skill levels in personal organization; people skills such as conflict resolution, customer service, working collaboratively; and communication

Separating Work from Self

As previously discussed, frequently STPs can be so immersed in their work that it is difficult to determine where performance ends and self-worth begins. Criticism of your work may be interpreted as highly personal comments attacking integrity, intellect, or value. Sandra made the statement, "I wish I could talk to Ken about his work and not have him react as if we are talking about him." It is a rare and valuable skill to be able to separate your work from yourself.

Following are some guidelines for improving your ability to process criticism:

Give Others Permission to Disagree with You. Allowing others to have a viewpoint different from yours raises your tolerance and increases your ability to listen and process their input. Accomplishing this begins with the simple step of acknowledging that no matter whether the critical input of others is right or wrong, valid or invalid, they have a right to their perceptions and opinions. This does not necessarily mean you agree with their viewpoint; it merely means that you are willing to listen to their input and give it fair consideration. It is your obligation not to "shoot the messenger" or dismiss this input. Points of disagreement can be viewed as starting points from which to begin negotiation—they are not a declaration of war. Just because others have critical comments about certain aspects of your work or portions of your assumptions and conclusions does not mean they totally reject everything that you have done. Agreement or approval of your work is not an all-or-nothing proposition. Apparently, Ken interprets criticism of any part of his work to be a total rejection of everything he has done and of him personally as well. It seems as if Sandra is not allowed to disagree with him!

SPEC

Repeatedly say to yourself, "Not everyone thinks as I do, and others have a right to see things their way."

Accept Critical Comment with a Commitment to Learn.   When others offer critical comment, seize it as an opportunity to learn something. If you are open to it, their input can help you to. . .

- . . . consider alternatives or options
- . . . better understand their thought process
- . . . form a clearer view of the bigger picture
- . . . identify more efficient ways of dealing with the task
- . . . develop an assessment of where your vulnerabilities may lie
- . . . see how others' priorities may differ from yours

Lower the Stakes.   Every discussion is not a battle that must be won. The price of disagreement in a discussion does not have to be monumental. Ken appears to be escalating the stakes. It sounds as though he has raised Sandra's criticism to a level of importance that demands that he leave his job. You do not have to quit, take yourself off the project, request a transfer, or refuse to support someone else's efforts just because things do not go your way. Do not perceive every incident of critical comment as a call to arms; most things are just not that important. Some battles are worth fighting, some are not. Do not allow the stakes to become so high in every disagreement that the other party must be defeated, and if not, that somehow equals a defeat for you. There are times when you must stand your ground

SPEC

Repeatedly say to yourself, "Whether or not I agree, I can still learn something from these comments."

This will help to defeat your initial negative response to what they are saying.

and be willing to do whatever is necessary to carry the day. However, those circumstances are few and far between. Threatening to take an adverse action every time someone offers criticism or there is a disagreement is an unpleasant behavior in children and an immature, self-defeating behavior in adults.

Depersonalize the Issue.   In the earlier discussion on giving critical comment to others, we emphasized the importance of depersonalizing the issue—focusing on *what* the issue is and not *who* is involved. The same principle holds true when you are receiving critical comment. Take the *who* out of it, and in this case, the *who* is you. Ken obviously needs to raise his awareness on this issue. Do not allow yourself to see critical comment that is directed toward your work or productivity as a personal confrontation, or an attack on your competency, integrity, or intellect. You as a person are separate and distinct from your work. Allow others to be critical of what you do without perceiving their observations to be personal.

SPEC

Do not interpret statements of disagreement, contention, or critical comments as personal attacks.

One effective technique is to reassure yourself, "This is not about me. This is about a thing [the work, the conclusion] and not about me personally." Just as you recognize your ability to criticize the work of others without attacking them personally, allow others to do the same with you.

Seek Solutions.   When others offer critical comment, assume they are also offering themselves as a consultant or a resource to help you in correcting the problem. If they just offer criticism without identifying options for correction, probe their intellect for solutions.

Use assertive probing questions to begin to identify alternatives:

"Help me understand how I could have done this differently."
"What are some options for verifying [correcting, overcoming] this?"
"May I hear your thoughts on a better way of dealing with this?"

Instead of perceiving critics as adversaries, invite them to be your allies and to collaborate on mutually acceptable outcomes. Do not make them the problem; invite them to become a part of the solution. If you are willing to listen, they probably have some worthwhile insights to share.

Listen for Accuracy, not Emotion.   In later chapters, we will be discussing effective listening techniques. At this point, be aware that everyone has a tendency to listen from a position of preconceived perceptions. The truth is, most people determine ahead of time what they are going to hear, and then they listen to reinforce that expectation. You hear what you want or expect to hear. This is often referred to as selective listening, and everyone is susceptible to it, some to a much greater degree than others. No one is immune. Examine critical messages for content and avoid emotional reactions. Ken expects criticism from Sandra (which is actually a part of her job), and when she offers it, he responds emotionally and his ability to learn from or process her information evaporates.

For example, if you think one of your peers (or your boss, supervisor, manager, etc.) is incompetent and incapable of quality performance, you will judge everything the person says and does through the filter of negative judgment. When the person makes a mistake (and everyone does from time to time), you will seize upon that as proof and reinforcement of your accurate perception. When the person does something right, you will discount that and perhaps attribute it to "luck." These negative perceptions, once imbedded in your listening and interpretation process, make accurate reception of messages extremely difficult. Listen carefully for the specific components of the person's critical comments, and do not muddy the emotional waters with selective listening.

Communication Assessment

1. Do I seek honest, accurate feedback from others?
   yes ☐   *no* ☐
2. Do I allow others to disagree with me without judging their perceptions negatively? *yes* ☐   *no* ☐
3. Do I seize the critical comments of others as valuable learning opportunities? *yes* ☐   *no* ☐
4. Do I attempt to de-escalate the stakes in circumstances of disagreement? *yes* ☐   *no* ☐
5. Do I depersonalize critical comments and avoid taking criticisms of my work personally? *yes* ☐   *no* ☐

6. Am I able to separate myself from my work and view criticisms objectively? *yes* ☐ *no* ☐

7. Do I seek the input of those who offer critical comments in the correction process? *yes* ☐ *no* ☐

8. Do I listen unemotionally to critical comments? *yes* ☐ *no* ☐

Any *no*-responses indicate opportunities to improve your communication effectiveness.

An Effective Model for Processing Critical Comments

There are four specific steps you can take to process critical comments constructively.

Clarify
Acknowledge
Identify
Establish criteria

Step 1. Clarify. Ask for specific examples of the performance or behaviors that are being criticized. Critical comment that is general in nature is meaningless and only escalates your negative emotion. You cannot respond positively and fix problems or correct behaviors that are identified in vague general terms. If someone is offering criticisms of your work, it won't help you if the person uses general statements such as the following:

"This doesn't make sense."
"This report is inaccurate."
"Your conclusions are totally wrong."
"This work is not acceptable."

These are not specific comments. They are not clear enough to help you identify the root issues. Everything you have done, reported, or concluded is not wrong. The most effective way to help your critics become more specific in their observations is to ask for more information. It is important to monitor the structure of these questions, as well as your tone of voice and body language. If you are not careful, you run the risk of appearing challenging, condescending, or insubordinate, and none of these messages are in your best interest. Use phrases such as:

"Exactly what happened that may be open to question?"
"Which parts of the report may be in error?"
"Are there specific conclusions we can discuss?"
"Help me understand where the specific problems lie."

The key to successfully maintaining positive inquiry and not allowing the communication to degenerate into contention is implementing *assertive* communication with no trace of any *you*-based aggressive messages.

Step 2. Acknowledge. Let your critics know that you acknowledge the appropriateness of their input and perceptions, welcome it, and are willing to consider and learn from their insight. (This does not necessarily mean you agree.) It is usually appropriate to compliment them on the quality and depth of their thoughts and observations. Doing so reduces any adversarial positioning and invites them to be more helpful rather than critical in their comments. It also sends a very strong message that you have the maturity and confidence to be willing to accept differing points of view and observations.

Helpful statements you can make include:

"Obviously, you have put a lot of thought into this and I appreciate your insight."
"Your opinions are important to me and I appreciate your efforts in helping me improve."
"I have always found your input to be very insightful and I take your comments very seriously."

Step 3. Identify. As with seeking specific clarification of the criticism, it is important to identify the steps that must be taken to remedy the situation and correct mistakes. You cannot respond effectively to generalized suggestions such as these:

"You need to work harder."
"You need to improve the quality of your work."
"You need to broaden your observations."

These statements do not help you understand what the critic wants you to do. He or she obviously has an expectation of changed behavior. You cannot possibly respond appropriately to the criticism if the critic is unable to clearly communicate her expectation.

Use the same types of clarifying questions as you used in Step 1:

"Help me understand *exactly* what it is that I can do differently."
"What is the single *most* important thing I can do to correct this?"
"What is the most effective *specific* action I can take?"

If you fail to clarify the specific correction necessary, it becomes a heavy burden on you. You are expected to read your critic's mind and try to guess what she wants done. Chances are great that this will only lead you down the path to further criticisms. (You can't work harder or do better if you do not know what those phrases mean to the critic.) The key lies in avoiding generalizations.

Step 4. Establish criteria. An extremely important and often over-looked part of the process of successfully receiving and reacting to critical comment is the establishment of criteria to measure the effectiveness of your action as a result of the criticism. You must determine how the critic (and any other key people who may be involved) are actually going to measure your response or correction. A key question to consistently pose is "How will we know this has been successfully dealt with?" If you are going to take the corrective action, it's not enough for you to know that you have done it; others must also be aware of your response. How the method of measurement or notification is determined really doesn't matter. What does matter is that everyone involved agrees as to what it is. Others should not rely merely on taking your word that you have made a correction. You may perceive that you've done it, while they may perceive that you have not. This only prolongs and exacerbates the situation. Clearly identify what the proof points are so that everyone will have a consistent understanding of the measurement criteria.

In concluding this chapter, I offer this thought: "Positive feedback always feels better and affirms your worth. Negative feedback properly received increases your value."[1]

5

Communicating with Your Boss

We all have at least one person we are accountable to for our activities and results. We are responsible for contributing to the achievement of the goals and objectives with which this person, commonly known as "the boss," has been charged. We not only report to but also depend on him or her for approvals, appraisals, and assistance in accomplishing our goals, tasks, and projects. It's an easy, all-encompassing term, and your boss may, in fact, be a director, department head, supervisor, vice president, CEO, senior technical expert, or any other top-level professional.

The word *boss* probably has its roots in slang. It may conjure up images of the leader of a chain gang or sweatshop who displays highly autocratic, perhaps even abusive, behavior, and an "It's my way or the highway" attitude. Though examples of that stereotype do still exist, thankfully their numbers are dwindling. The term *boss* here is used merely for convenience and is not intended no call up negative stereotypical images. Your boss may well be an extremely talented professional manager or executive who demonstrates no stereotypical negative qualities. Everyone has a boss, and in today's workplace, many STPs are lucky enough to have more than one! Like it or not, with the current trend toward reorganizing, downsizing, rightsizing, or whatever the term of the moment may be, matrix management (or having multiple reporting points) is a common circumstance.

Establishing effective communication with your boss is very important for your current performance, future opportunities, and the overall quality of your professional life.

As we begin this topic, let's evaluate the current status of the communication environment between you and your boss.

Communication Assessment

1. Does your boss consistently and predictably refuse your requests or reject your proposals?   *yes* ☐   *no* ☐

2. Do you and your boss differ significantly in the prioritization of tasks and projects?   *yes* ☐   *no* ☐

3. Do you have consistent difficulty meeting deadlines or delivering performance within previously established timelines?
yes ☐   *no* ☐

4. Do you and your boss have frequent disagreements on the importance and relationships of time, budget, and quality?
yes ☐   *no* ☐

5. Does conflict erupt when your boss is unhappy with your efforts or critical of your work?   *yes* ☐   *no* ☐

6. Do resentments or negative emotions continue to exist in the wake of disagreements, disappointments, or missed opportunities?
yes ☐   *no* ☐

7. Is your boss frequently critical of the depth, accuracy, or scope of your reporting?   *yes* ☐   *no* ☐

8. Does your boss often misunderstand or jump to the wrong conclusion regarding your communication?   *yes* ☐   *no* ☐

9. Do you often have a different understanding than your peers of your boss's message?   *yes* ☐   *no* ☐

10. Do you and your boss often appear to be pursuing different goals and objectives or to be working at cross purposes to each other?
yes ☐   *no* ☐

11. Does your boss seem to require more information in writing from you than from others in your immediate work group?
yes ☐   *no* ☐

12. Do you feel that your boss frequently establishes meaningless criteria for measuring the quality and success of your work?
yes ☐   *no* ☐

13. Does your boss tend to isolate you or prohibit you from communicating with others outside your immediate work group?
yes ☐   *no* ☐

14. Are you unsure about how your boss prefers to receive and deliver communication (visually, written, face-to-face interaction)?
yes ☐   *no* ☐

15. Are you often nervous or uncomfortable when communicating with those above you in the organization?   *yes* ☐   *no* ☐

Obviously, any *yes*-responses identify areas of existing or potential communication barriers between you and your boss and demand evaluation, diagnosis, and corrective action. Left unaddressed, these conditions have the potential to have a negative impact on your career, impede your overall effectiveness, and inflict long-term damage on critically important relationships.

Copy this assessment and ask your boss to complete it, evaluating you from his or her perspective. Compare your results and discuss (not challenge) any significant differences and perceptions. This exercise alone may prove to be invaluable in identifying problems, opening up lines of communication, and creating strategies for effective correction.

As we discussed in Chapter 4, seeking feedback is of critical importance, and this assessment provides the opportunity.

CASE STUDY 3

Ryan is an electrical engineer. He has been employed for the past eighteen months by a relatively small company that specializes in the manufacture of electrical motors for utility vehicles. He previously worked for a very large organization.

He answers directly to the CEO and owner of the company. Currently the utility vehicle manufacturers purchase DC motors for their vehicles. The market is very competitive, and with offshore manufacturing, DC motors yield very little profit.

Ryan is developing a technology that would enable the utility vehicle manufacturers to buy less expensive AC motors and power them with DC. Ryan's technology enables DC to be inverted to simulate AC. This way, the customer, who has traditionally been captive to the DC motor, powered by on-board batteries, can now use the lower-cost AC motors and achieve the same power at lower cost. Ryan has successfully used inverters on these vehicles to convert direct current to alternating current and is confident that his new design will enable the vehicle manufacturer to use the smaller, lighter, and more efficient motors. His biggest problem has been measuring the electrical power as the motor consumes it.

Ryan's boss doesn't completely understand the measurement problem and is indicating he may be ready to abandon Ryan's project and reassign him to work in another area. Ryan feels that his boss is losing confidence in him and seems to be watching him very closely. Ryan says, "Every time I turn around he is asking me what I am doing and wants to know why I am not moving faster in completing this project. He also seems to misunderstand my memos and reports, and lately he seems too busy to meet with me. He has even canceled our weekly meetings, saying he will meet with me on an as needed basis. He hasn't canceled anyone else's meetings, just mine."

Whether you are having a critical problem in communicating with your boss, such as Ryan, or you would like to make improvements on what may already be a pretty good communication situation, there are a number of techniques you can utilize.

Preliminary Communication Action Plan
   Let's consider some of Ryan's options.

- What do you see as the most important issue facing Ryan and his boss?

   _____

   _____

   _____

- List three recommendations you would make to Ryan for improving his communications and relationship.

   _____

   _____

   _____

- List three things you would suggest Ryan *not* do in attempting to correct the current communication problems.

   _____

   _____

   _____

Have you ever been in a similar circumstance with your boss at any time throughout your career? There are a number of things you can do to improve the situation.

Aligning Goals and Objectives

The first consideration in establishing effective communication with your boss is to ensure that you are both working toward the same goals and objectives. It is possible that Ryan and his boss do not share a consistent understanding of goals and priorities. There are six key factors to assess in evaluating whether you are dedicating your efforts to achieving the goals and objectives of your boss and the overall organization, as well as effectively communicating your activities, challenges, and successes. Ryan would do well to consider these issues very carefully.

Once you are accomplishing the things that your boss believes to be important, another benefit comes your way. Being assured that you are "on track," she probably has little or no interest in the other things you may be pursuing. Thus, you will create an increased amount of discretionary time to pursue areas of high interest to you if you are communicating and demonstrating your willingness to accomplish the things most important to your boss. Meaningful amounts of freedom can be earned when the boss is confident you are aware, willing, and focused to pursue the right things. What is "right" is usually what is important to the boss!

Understanding Organizational Goals

First, determine whether you have a clear and accurate understanding of the organizational goals.

Does Ryan have a grasp of the overall big picture? Do you? Do you have a clear understanding of what the organization is dedicated to accomplishing? More important, do you comprehend how the organizational goals and objectives trickle down to impact your area of responsibility? Be aware that there is a difference between understanding the organizational goals and agreeing with them. Do not confuse your possibly frustrating lack of agreement with or disdain for portions of the goals and objectives with a lack of understanding. This issue of organizational goals is not about your agreement, it is about your comprehension. You do not have to like the goals, you just need to understand them!

What can Ryan or you do to increase your understanding of the goals of your boss and the organization?

First of all, revisit your most recent performance appraisals. Clearly stated in those documents are the goals and objectives that your boss deems most important. Have you consistently achieved in these areas? In most performance appraisals, there will be two sources of goals and objectives: those established by your boss and those that you recommend. Are you working as diligently at accomplishing your boss's goal as you are your own? If you believe that some of the boss's goals and objectives are outdated or have become lower priority, ask yourself why you think that. Just because the boss has not mentioned them lately, or he does not seem to be monitoring them closely, does not mean they have been abandoned or forgotten. Ongoing communication is the only way to maintain a correct perspective.

If you see the goals and objectives you were being held accountable for diminishing in importance, priorities have changed. Is this change in priority shared by your boss or does it only seem that way from your perspective? Have you stopped pursuing some goals and objectives owing to a lack of interest on your part? Has the boss communicated to you in specific terms that the goals and objectives have actually changed? Are you just assuming the boss agrees with you? You may be nurturing false assumptions that could have a real, detrimental impact on your development and career. You may be assuming a shift in importance when none exists, and the price you pay could be expensive.

SPEC

 *Initiate regular discussions with your boss to review the goals and objectives of your performance appraisal.*

Make your appraisal a living document. Perhaps on a quarterly or bimonthly basis, request a meeting to evaluate the goals and objectives and summarize your activity and accomplishments to date.

Take this opportunity to determine whether the pursuit of these goals and objectives is still relevant. If it turns out they have changed, generate a brief written summary to formally acknowledge the circumstances and identify the emerging, increasingly important goals and objectives that now demand your attention.

This is a communication responsibility that falls squarely on your shoulders simply because you cannot afford to be pursuing the wrong targets. Your rocket may be headed to the wrong planet. Do not wait twelve months until your next appraisal to discover that the goals and objectives you have been pursuing have become obsolete, and the efforts you have initiated for their completion are seen as unproductive. Do not assume that your boss will take the initiative to provide you with current information. Relying on a "nobody told me" defense later on will not save your hide.

Take personal responsibility for initiating these reviews. Recognize the priority shift and adjust early—do not wait until the damage is done and then try to find a place to put the blame.

How Are You Perceived?

Find out whether you are perceived as supporting the goals of the organization and department, or as pursuing your own self-interest.

Be in consistent communication with your boss to determine his perception of your activities. Does he think you are investing your intellect, time, and resources in pursuit of the most important aspects of your job? Perhaps he believes you are majoring in the minors. If you are seen as pursuing only activities focused on self-interest, your boss and peers may have begun to see you in a negative light. Communication barriers may have been erected without your knowing it. Ryan's boss may see him as foolishly pursuing a meaningless activity.

There are two key questions for Ryan to pose, one to his boss and one to himself:

- Does his boss perceive that the successful completion of his current activities will result in achieving the overall organizational goals and objectives?
- Will successfully developing the new technology he is currently working on make Ryan happy and make him experience the warmth of professional accomplishment, yet make no meaningful contribution to the things that his boss sees as most important?

Both you and Ryan must initiate communications to figure out how others perceive your efforts.

Seek managerial and peer review. Seek input from your closest associates, people whose judgments you trust, to find out whether your activities are on track from their perspective. Encourage honesty and objectivity. Avoid guiding people to tell you what you want to hear. The critical point to remember is not to become engaged in discussions about *how* you are doing something.

If your goal is to head due north, use every method possible to determine if you are on course. Whether someone agrees with your mode of transportation (walking, running, automobile, bus, train, airplane, etc.) is less relevant than their affirmation that you are headed in the right direction.

Your Boss's Priorities

Do you have an accurate understanding of your boss's perception of the critical issues of quality, deadlines, and budgets as they apply to your current activities?

What does your boss believe to be most important? Her priorities probably vary with each separate circumstance. What may appear to you to be inconsistencies may be a very appropriate situational evaluation. In one project deadlines may be critical and budgets flexible. In another, quality may be more important than the deadline. Your boss may not make you aware of changing priorities. She probably assumes you automatically make the same determinations she does (a foolish assumption on her part). You must develop a clear comprehension of the variances when they occur. It's your responsibility! Again, your agreement isn't necessary, just your clear understanding. If you are pursuing the best possible quality that you and the organization are capable of producing while your boss is concentrating on producing an adequate outcome in time to meet a deadline, you and your boss are going to be at cross-purposes. Do not expect yourself to be a mind reader. Initiate frequent communication to determine the specific expectations concerning quality, deadlines, and budgets. Never lose sight of the importance of these three critical issues, and never make uninformed assumptions about their relevant value. Ryan may have greatly exceeded his boss's timeframe for tolerance without realizing it.

Do you know the actual budget constraints of the activities you are currently working on? Regardless of what anyone may tell you, dollars are always an issue. The American effort spearheaded by NASA in the 1960s to put a man on the moon and bring him back safely was probably the last scientific and technical endeavor where money was no object. Quality and time were the critical factors, and probably never again will STPs have the luxury of such unlimited funding. Do you have any control over the budget or the dollars involved? Can you take dollars from one activity and invest them in another? All of these are questions that must be addressed and mutually understood by you and your boss. Deal in facts, not emotions, spend your time addressing the reality, and avoid editorializing or becoming judgmental. Consistent or significant miscommunications concerning these three areas can be detrimental to your career.

Communicate Success

Take the initiative to make your boss aware of any and all progress and successes you are experiencing in accomplishing the overall goals and objec-

SPEC

Many STPs provide a weekly update to their bosses to clearly communicate their current successes.

tives. Typically, every goal has incremental components and the systematic achievement of these components results in the accomplishment of the overall goal. Your boss may be focused only on the end result, and he may be unaware of your headway and momentum. As you reach success at each incremental level, make sure your boss is aware of your current results. Doing so accomplishes a number of things: It increases his comfort level and decreases his anxiety. It has the added benefit of helping him realize that intense monitoring of your work is not necessary. It is obvious that Ryan's boss is aware of the problem he is having, yet it is not clear whether or not Ryan has kept his boss accurately informed on his success as well. It appears he is being successful in developing the technology, yet struggling with the measurement aspect of his creation.

One of the best ways to get your boss to back off and give you operating room is to keep him informed. When he is confident that you are aware of the important goals and are steadfastly working toward achieving them, your relationship with your boss will take a positive turn. As always, effective communication is the key.

A weekly update may contain the following:

- A clear and specific statement of your activities and the goals you are pursuing
- A concise summary of the activity during last five working days in pursuit of each goal
- A clear identification of any goals formally achieved (frequently this is printed in a different color to be sure to attract the boss's attention)
- A list of specific items requiring the boss's attention. This list can serve as an agenda for a requested meeting to decrease the time spent in discussion.

This update follows an executive summary format, preferably one page, not exceeding two.

When you succeed, let your boss know. Do not be shy! Due to the pace of today's workplace and the preoccupation your boss may have with other issues, your successes may be under-recognized. They may get buried in the avalanche of competing demands. It can also happen that someone in a leadership role may take the trouble to identify inadequate performance and take any positive accomplishments for granted. If so, successfully communicating your achievements helps to broaden the boss's field of vision. It also provides excellent documentation of your accomplishments for your future performance evaluations.

Communicate Challenges, Barriers, and Additional Resource Requirements

No plan or project ever goes totally as predicted. There are always unforeseen circumstances that must be addressed. The key is to find the flaw and fix it early so you can continue on your quest toward success. Make your boss aware of any significant issue that could impede your performance. Take great care not to lapse into blaming others. Communicate any impediments to performance as factually and unemotionally as possible. If you need help from the boss in stimulating cooperation from your peers or other departments, or if you need her assistance in acquiring additional resources, the earlier you make her aware of your circumstances, the better she will respond. Do not wait until the situation becomes serious to start identifying the problems. The earlier and more accurate the identification, the better.

It is important for your boss to understand that the identification of challenges and barriers or the request for additional resources or assistance is not an attempt to avoid responsibility or accountability. Some STPs attempt to coat themselves in Teflon by shifting responsibility and accountability to others.

Communicate When You Are Overloaded or May Be Unable to Achieve Goals

Do not agree to take on additional tasks or projects that may overload your capabilities and/or hinder your progress on current activities. Saying *no* to the boss is an art, and you may be unsure of how to do it successfully. If you do not refuse more tasks, it often results in your accepting more work than realistically doable. Increases in stress and decreases in performance soon follow.

Putting too much on your plate creates quality or time failures later.

You often find yourself in a catch-22 situation. As your workload increases due to your failure to communicate to your boss that you cannot take on any more responsibilities, you increase your efforts to accomplish the expanded responsibilities rather than risk failure. You work longer, take work home, come in on the weekends, and ultimately achieve success. This positive outcome only encourages the boss. Success in dealing with the increased workload ultimately works to your disadvantage!

This results in an explosion of negativity. You probably find yourself whining and complaining to others (the people who can do nothing about the situation), and not addressing the issue with the boss (who is the only person in a position to be helpful).

SPEC

 *Avoid any unnecessary escalation of negative emotions by effectively implementing the U-S-S communication model on a timely basis.*

The U-S-S Model. The U-S-S model is a very good method to communicate overload or establish realistic timetables for performance. U-S-S stands for *understand; situation;* and *suggest.*

U: "I *understand* this is important and I'm anxious to work on it."
S: "And [not *but*] here's my *situation*. I have these current projects, tasks, and goals that must be completed by . . . "
S: "I would *suggest* that a realistic completion date on this new task would be . . ." Or: "I would *suggest* that Sean or Brittany may be in a better position to accomplish it sooner." Or: "I would like your *suggestion* on how to prioritize my workload so that everything can be accomplished in a timely manner."

These statements communicate your willingness to perform, clarify your current workload, and offer alternative solutions or solicit the boss's advice on how to make it all happen. He will probably reconsider the timeline, assign the task to someone else, or reassess his prioritization of the tasks you are working on. This communication strategy, if implemented properly, has a high rate of success.

STPs are certainly not the only people who struggle with effectively saying *no* to their bosses. They may experience a higher rate of frustration because of their intense desire to achieve. People in all professions in America today often allow their resentment to escalate as unwanted or perhaps unreasonable tasks and demands are added to the pile. These situations may ultimately result in an emotional exchange with the boss that only makes things worse.

Case Study Assessment

Reread the case study concerning Ryan and his communication problems with his boss. Review the recommendations you offered earlier in this chapter. In retrospect, are there any changes you would make in your suggestions as to how Ryan can increase his communication effectiveness with his boss?

Communicating Tactfully with Your Boss

The importance of tact was discussed in the last chapter. In many cases, exercising tact comes down to the way you say things. There are a number of formulations that may come in handy. The following nine sentences will facilitate effective communication with your boss by helping you frame difficult messages in a positive context. They will help you to exercise more control over your workload and time and are appropriate to use with your boss and peers if they are tactfully structured in an assertive communication package and do not incorporate aggressive messages. They contain no elements that could be construed as a challenge to authority, insubordination, or condescension. If you are not comfortable with these exact words and phrases, feel free to substitute language that reflects your personal style. Take care to use assertive *I-* and *we*-based messages, not aggressive *you*-based ones. Note also the absence of the words *but, or, however*, and other provoking phrases.

> "I would if I could, and this is why I won't be able to." (Establishes agreement and proclaims support and explains why you will not be able to respond.)

"Which of these other tasks I am working on should I delay? Help me to prioritize my work." (Communicates your willingness and dilemma and asks the boss to be your consultant in planning your activities.)

"Considering my workload, I will be able to complete this by . . . " (Creates a realistic timeline.)

"Let me determine what a realistic timeline would be and I'll get back to you on that if you haven't found another solution in the meantime." (Buys you some time and encourages the boss to take an alternative action.)

"I would be very happy to do this as soon as I accomplish these other things. I would also say that Jonathan and Tracy are very capable in this area and could probably do it as well and even quicker." (Suggests alternatives without appearing resistant.)

"I would not be able to give this the time or quality that it really deserves. I would suggest . . . " (Gently explains your reason for declining and offers alternatives. It implies it is in her best interest to go elsewhere.)

"I would feel very uncomfortable with this." (Says no assertively and leaves little room for opposition or expectation that you will reconsider.)

"I'll be very happy to assist on this if you would be willing to take the principal responsibility." (Communicates your willingness while establishing conditions and shared responsibility.)

"I'm sorry, I will not be able to do that." (Gentle, yet firm. Avoid using this statement very often, especially with your boss. It should be so unusual that others will be hesitant to challenge you.)

SPEC

It is important to communicate tact-fully with everyone, and it is especially critical in dealing with your boss.

Communication Operating Plans

A Communication Operating Plan (COP) is a predetermined and agreed-upon plan for dealing with predictable communication problems that you negotiate with your boss. You have been trained to apply an analytical process to predict, correct, or prepare for potential problems, weaknesses, or failures in the scientific and technical aspects of your work, and you can apply the same process to the communication aspect of your work environment. If you take the time to assess the communication problems you have experienced with your current or past bosses, you will quickly begin to identify patterns. It is not difficult to predict where the potential disconnects are most likely to occur. COPs are not methods of avoiding problems, they are planned responses for dealing with problems when they occur as expected.

An effective strategy for negotiating COPs is to discuss with your boss incidents where she has experienced past communication problems, either with you or other STPs. Seek her opinion on where she believes future communication disconnects could occur. This is nothing more than anticipating potential breakdowns and identifying contingency plans before they happen. COPs encourage you to "dig your foxhole before the shooting starts."

Do not wait until you are dealing with a full-blown problem to begin the discussion. It is far better to anticipate and be prepared—it pays off.

There are at least seven areas that call for a COP to be negotiated between you and your boss.

COP 1: Information

It's been said that 80 percent of what you need to know is contained in 20 percent of the information available to you. Eighty percent of the information you receive is relatively unimportant. It is imperative that you and your boss identify and agree upon the 20 percent of information that is truly critical to your performance, how you will ensure access to it, and what you will do with it once you have it.

Discussion Starters.
- What information is currently being generated and channeled to you that is not urgent or critical to your success or the overall success of the department, team, group, etc.?

- What information is contributing unnecessarily to your information overload?
- What information are you currently not receiving on a consistent basis that is urgent and critical to your success (what are the areas where you are repeatedly left out of the loop)?

COP 2: Reporting

Evaluating the practice of submitting reports can yield significant dividends. In many organizations, traditional methods of reporting have become obsolete, yet reports continue to be required because no one has bothered to evaluate their actual relevance. In some cases, reporting has degenerated to a level of "Give me a report to prove to me you have been busy." (If STPs were clearly communicating outcomes and productivity, such reporting would be totally unnecessary.) You may be in the frustrating position shared by many STPs of having to submit reports that you know nobody is reading. In discussions with your boss, it is very important to stress that you are not dismissing the importance of reporting; you are striving to make the reporting more meaningful and efficient for everyone concerned.

Discussion Starters.
- Is all of your reporting necessary?
- Are you reporting information that may be obsolete or traditional and is no longer critical to your boss?
- Are there reporting demands on you that you believe can be streamlined?
- Is there data that could be critical to performance, monitoring, assessment, or early detection of problems that isn't being captured?
- Can the current reporting mechanisms be altered to increase efficiency?

COP 3: Feedback

What agreements can be implemented for the effective communication of timely feedback? Feedback can take many forms, from positive reactions to critical comments. It may include such items as approvals, opinions, criticisms, positive recognition, emerging patterns, answers to inquiries, etc.

Feedback flows in both directions. A mechanism must be in place for you to provide feedback to your boss and vice versa. Is there feedback you are not receiving on a timely basis that is urgent and critical to your performance? (This feedback may include such items as approvals, opinions, criticisms, positive recognition, emerging patterns, answers to inquiries, etc.)

Discussion Starters.
- What early-intervention feedback system is in place for your boss to communicate to you his approval, criticism, general observations, concerns, or disappointments?
- How do you communicate negative feedback upward?
- What can be done to reduce the turnaround time when timely responses are necessary?

COP 4: Crisis or Emergency

Communicating effectively in times of crisis or emergency can prevent small incidents from becoming huge problems. It is important that plans already be in place when a crisis occurs or an emergency situation looms on the horizon, so that your boss and others who may be impacted by the outcome can be alerted in a timely fashion.

Discussion Starters.
- What style of delivery (verbal, written, face-to-face) is required in times of crisis or emergency?
- What are the policies for releasing critical communication to other departments, groups, teams, or organization leaders?
- Have clear guidelines for authority and responsibility during crisis situations been identified and communicated?

Responding to correct a crisis and managing the flow of information are two very distinct and separate issues. Exercise great caution to be sure that everyone involved understands their roles.

COP 5: Conflict

Conflict is inevitable. Resentment and negative outcomes are optional. Predetermined methods for dealing with conflicts must be established. Resolve conflict when it occurs between you and your boss before it breaches your relationship, lowers productivity, or has a negative impact on others in your work group.

Discussion Starters.
- Are there guidelines in place for you and your boss to seek appropriate mediation from others when attempts to resolve your conflict appear to be stalled or impossible?
- Are there policies for determining when your boss should be asked to mediate conflicts between you and your peers under her direct responsibility?
- How are conflict issues to be resolved between you and other individuals outside your department or work group?
- How is intradepartmental or intrateam conflict to be handled?

COP 6: Priorities

As previously discussed, consistent communication and agreement on priorities is critical. It is also a fact of life that priorities change. The quicker any changes are identified, the more productivity and efficiency increase and stress, frustration, and wasted effort decrease.

Discussion Starters.
- What process is in place for you and your boss to consistently evaluate the relative priorities of current tasks, projects, or assignments?
- How are shifts in the importance of quality, time, and cost to be communicated between you and your boss?
- How is the balance between increasingly important projects and those of lessening priority to be maintained?
- When priorities change, how are you relieved of responsibilities for assignments whose priority has gone down and whose value has thus been decreased?

COP 7: Formal Communication

Effective communication is extremely difficult in the absence of a formal structure for scheduled meetings. Though you never want to meet "just to meet," if meetings are not regularly scheduled, they rarely occur, so it is important to establish a structure for formal communication.

Have you and your boss identified dedicated times to meet on a daily, weekly, or monthly basis?

Discussion Starters.
- Do your meetings have a structure for the consistent presentation of information?
- How do either of you establish the need for an urgent, unplanned meeting?
- Where are the best places for you to meet to engage in important communication without experiencing interruptions, lack of focus, or disruptions to the listening process?
- Who is responsible for rescheduling canceled or disrupted meetings?

SPEC

Use these seven COPs as a basis for a formal discussion with your boss.

These Communication Operating Plans may be incorporated into your performance appraisal or into a formal meeting between you and your boss to review your progress, performance, etc. They also can be utilized to negotiate group or departmental communication structure. You can broaden the reach of your communications by negotiating COPs with all of your critical communication points.

Other Communication Challenges

There are two additional communication challenges that relate to communicating with your boss:

Seeking additional clarification of tasks, goals and objectives.
The presentation of negative information or communication failures, delays, or bad news of any kind.

Both of these communication challenges contain elements of high risk. Mishandling these situations can result in intense negative reactions by your boss, and these can cause long-term problems. Relationships can be damaged, career growth disrupted, and your value to the organization diminished if you do not deal with these situations effectively.

Seek Additional Clarification of Tasks, Goals, and Objectives

If not handled properly, a request for further clarification can be perceived by your boss as a challenge to his authority, insubordinate behavior, or a demonstration of resistance.

SPEC

The most effective technique in seeking clarification is to front-end-load your message.

Front-end-loading means prefacing your inquiry with a statement of support. "I'm anxious to begin work on this and agree that it can be very successful. I need some further information to help me get started. May I ask you a few clarifying questions?"

This avoids implying the damaging question "Why are we doing this?" or a questioning of his goals. When you clearly state upfront that you are in agreement and very supportive of him and what he wants to accomplish, your boss will not perceive your inquiry to be insubordination or a challenge to his authority. The boss sees you as an ally, just needing more information to do a better job, as opposed to an antagonist. When you front-end-load the message with positives, you take away any perception of disagreement.

Others often misunderstand the insatiable pursuit of additional data and information that typically drives STPs. What is a logical request for information on your part can elicit a negative response in others, especially those in authority. The front-end-load technique eliminates miscommunication and is one of the most effective communication behaviors you can develop.

This technique is also effective when you must communicate potentially negative information or foresee problems. "I think this project can be successful, and I'm anxious to do everything that I can to support it. Here's a potential problem, and we need to be sure we prevent it from happening."

This replaces an antagonistic statement such as "That won't work and here's why."

Please note: The word bridge between the front-end-load and the bad news is *and*. It is not *but, however*, or any other provocative word. Use of *and* is what ensures the effectiveness of this technique.

Once again you are clearly stating your initial support and then identifying potentially negative issues for discussion. Instead of being seen as a resister, you are now viewed as a visionary who is planning ahead!

Six Steps for Presenting Bad News.   When it is necessary to deliver potentially negative information or communicate failures, delays, or bad news of any kind to your boss that she probably will not enjoy hearing, use this six-step model to avoid or neutralize any negative consequences. Packaging this communication effectively ensures the accurate transfer of information, and lessens the predictable knee-jerk reaction to "shoot the messenger."

Step 1. Clearly State the Tone of the Message.
  "I have some news that you're probably not going to like."
  "A problem has occurred that you need to know about."
  "I am not going to be able to meet this deadline and I don't want you
    to get a surprise."

The point of this step is to set the tone for the conversation and *lower* the boss's expectations. If your initial statement sounds particularly ominous and then you follow with information that is perceived as not so bad after all, your boss may actually have a positive emotional response:

  "Gee, that really wasn't as bad as I expected" or "That really wasn't as bad as it first sounded."

Step 2. State the Specifics of the Problem. Using a clear, concise delivery, present the information, emphasizing facts and data with as little emotion as possible. Do not intentionally omit any relevant information. No matter how problematic it might be, it is far better to get everything out in the open at once. Information left for later discovery only compounds the magnitude of any problem. Be as accurate and complete as possible, and neither overstate problems nor attempt to sugarcoat or lessen the impact of your message.

Step 3. Take Responsibility for the Problem. Clearly state that you accept responsibility for what has taken place. As previously discussed, do not try to involve or blame others. Even if others are at fault, attempting to broaden the scope of culpability is usually seen as weakness and a blatant attempt to avoid accountability. Blaming has become such an overly used strategy in today's workplace that those who refrain from using it elevate their stature. You make yourself conspicuous in a very positive way by refusing to take this path of least resistance. Squaring your broad shoulders, acknowledging that the buck stops with you, and facing the issue head-on reflects great dignity and maturity and increases the respect your boss and others will have for you. Attempts to deflect responsibility work against you.

Step 4. Offer Corrections and Solutions. Once again, we stress pairing a statement of the problem and a recommendation for a solution. Never present a problem without offering a reasonable strategy for solving it. Even if the boss rejects your suggestion (and he may well do so), you still present yourself as a problem solver, not just a problem identifier. Presenting multiple possible solutions and emphasizing the one you see as best gives your boss additional alternatives to consider and underscores the depth and breadth of your solution-oriented thought process. When you offer problems only with no resolutions, you present yourself as inadequate, or perhaps weak under pressure. Avoid offering any unrealistic solutions. They are counterproductive and you make yourself look foolish!

Step 5. Identify the Silver Lining. This is huge. Clearly identify the opportunity for learning that has taken place, for both you and others. How can this experience contribute to the prevention of similar situations? Did you learn to be less aggressive in your predictions? More diligent in your monitoring? More thorough in your research or investigation? What can others in the organization learn from this event? What would you do differently in the future to ensure that certain mistakes are not repeated? Does a policy or procedure need to be altered? Do additional information or resources need to be made accessible earlier or on a more timely basis?

A negative outcome can be turned into a positive experience if the lesson learned is valuable enough. Making mistakes and correcting problems can

SPEC

Today's mistakes can create tomorrow's successes . . . if processed effectively.

be an effective, albeit expensive, education. Let your boss know that the tuition you paid in blood, sweat, and tears is yielding positive results.

Step 6. Strategize the Impact on Your Boss. Does this circumstance create additional problems for your boss? Are there political issues that must be addressed? Are there short-term resource allocation issues to be considered? Are production schedules or reporting procedures temporarily disrupted? Discover your boss's issues of the moment and investigate what you can do to mitigate the negative fallout. Be especially sensitive to any possibility that your boss is going to look bad because of the problem. It is critically important to demonstrate your awareness of her situation and willingness to do whatever it takes to lessen the impact. Without exception, making your boss look good and never making your boss look bad is a sound strategy. Always ask what you can do to be helpful.

Communication Action Plan

1. Identify three areas of communication strength between you and your boss.

   _____

   _____

   _____

2. How can you become even better in these areas? (Sometimes the most effective changes you can make are in areas of current strength.)

Can you transfer these skills to areas of relative communication weakness?

3. Identify three areas of weakness in your communications with your boss.

   _____

   _____

   _____

4. For each area of weakness, list a communication strategy discussed in this chapter that you are not using that may improve the quality of communication.

Would negotiating an effective COP (Communication Operating Plan) be helpful in improving performance in any of these three areas?

6

Communicating Technical Information to Nontechnical People

Communicating with people who do not have training, experience, or orientation in your technical arena is another significant career challenge that you face every day. The importance and necessity of sharing technical information with nontechnical people and helping them to clearly understand it is increasing at an almost incomprehensible rate. Frustrations run high for both the person trying to deliver the message and the nontechnical people receiving it who are trying to make sense out of information they do not understand.

Barriers to effective communication exist even before the transfer of information begins. Negative projections are rampant on both sides. Nontechnical people may be intimidated by the complexity of the information and predisposed to assume they will not be able to understand it. The assumption that they can't understand technical information may have led them to develop a resistance to processing your message. They may shrug their shoulders, lamely proclaim "I never was good at math," and excuse themselves from even trying!

You may also have preconceptions. You may have a negative perception of nontechnical people as incapable of absorbing important information. You may resent having to spoon-feed your information to others and may even be reluctant to extend yourself to implement effective communication techniques. One of the technical professionals we interviewed said,

"There's becoming more of a need to basically lower yourself to communicate with nontechnical people. So many of them just do not try. I have never seen people who cannot understand such simple information. I am amazed they can function at all."

Negative predispositions on both sides can lead to an "us-against-them" mentality, which is alive and well in both camps. One nontechnical professional summed up his feelings like this:

> People with a technical background seem to need more stroking. Basically they have this tremendous need to be right, and many of them arrogantly think they are right in everything they do. They are coming from a world where there are definite right and wrong answers and very little of anything gray. The software will either work or it won't. This knowledge about how to do the technological piece is highly valued and they do not see the important contributions of other people and other types of jobs in the workplace. You have to overcome the ego and power tripping which lends itself to that attitude of superiority.
>
> Knowledge is power, and, boy, do they feel powerful! My experience has been that if I stroke technical people and their egos, I can easily get what I'm after much more quickly than when they sense I dread the interaction. So going to them because my computer is not working or asking them a question goes much better if I'm willing to pump up their ego. They need to feel superior. It would help if they would view themselves as sages or someone having the power to assist the rest of us in the business world so that we can get our job done. That may be a real challenge. It would mean taking a step down off that pinnacle of feeling more powerful or somehow having more worth because they have a particular expertise in a certain area. They need to acknowledge the value of others. This same technical person may have to make a presentation perhaps, or to solve a problem in an area of emotional distress, or one requiring strong interactive skills, and the truth is, they would feel as equally lost in that area as I do in the technical realm. It would sure help if they would be more collaborative.

Wow! Are these the views of isolated individuals or a reasonably clear description of the schisms that exist? Regardless, you have to break down these very real communication barriers if you are going to successfully communicate with the myriad of nontechnical people in your workplace. If you are to be an effective communicator, you cannot allow either their limitations or your internal bias to interfere.

CASE STUDY 4

Shawn is a technical support engineer for a networking company. His role is to provide customer service by answering support calls when the end-users he is responsible for have a problem with their PCs not working properly. Most of his work is done via the telephone or e-mail and the overwhelming majority of the people he communicates with are nontechnical. Every day he must troubleshoot the problems the customer is experiencing by translating their nontechnical descriptions and statements into meaningful technical concepts. On the basis of what they tell him and their responses to his questions, he must diagnose the problem and determine the most effective solution. He must then communicate the solution back to the end-user for them to fix the problem.

Shawn adamantly believes the biggest problem he faces is the lack of technical knowledge and understanding of the people he is required to support. He says, "The problems usually are not with the computer . . . it's the people!"

What can Shawn do to become a more effective communicator?

This chapter gives you some specific tools to assist you in meeting this challenge.

Use Analogies and Examples

It is very beneficial to help nontechnical people grasp complex information by incorporating into your explanation simple analogies or examples that they will understand because they come from their own frame of reference.

Real-World Commentary

Michael Ostack, an IT consultant and Microsoft Certified Systems Engineer, owns NetX Solutions in Charleston, South Carolina. He offered these suggestions.

It is really important to use everyday examples or references when presenting important technical information to nontechnical people. Some of the software programs that I use contain different protocols, and many times when explaining this to nontechnical people, I stress the various types of protocols that the software and hardware utilizes are similar to languages. The protocols are equivalent to English, German, or Japanese. The Gateway device acts as a translator for protocols. I use the example of the United Nations. A highly skilled simultaneous translator will hear a statement in one language and instantly translate and deliver it to someone else in his or her own language. This is a reference that nontechnical people readily understand. When explaining how a router device works, I use the example of a traffic cop. The router directs data signals around the Internet and from your PC to the Internet and back. Many computer terms are intended to relate to everyday references to help everyone who uses one to understand it more quickly and easily. The term "e-mail address" is quickly grasped because people have a regular mail address. The PC "desktop" from which you do all of your work equates to your normal desktop where you do all of your work. These common references help people to grasp the information quicker.

These are good ideas for using examples, analogies, and references that a nontechnical person may quickly be able to understand and apply to complex technical discussions. Shawn should follow Mike's advice and use appropriate nontechnical images and comparisons whenever possible to help his customers understand his information.

When President Ronald Reagan was proposing the SDI program for space-based national defense in the 1980s, he nicknamed it after the movie *Star Wars*, which was at the height of its popularity. This helped many people grasp the general idea of his recommendations and made it unnecessary to bog the American people down in complex discussions that would only have confused the issue.

Limit Your Message to "Need-to-Know" Information

It is important to remember your ultimate goal when communicating with nontechnical people. In general, you want to achieve an accurate transfer of a *limited* amount of information. They do not need to know it all. You are not trying to elevate them to your level of knowledge or expertise.

Your nontechnical peers are not expected to have Ph.D.-level knowledge of your information or data. Their need is primarily for an overview, or for some specifics in a particular decision-making situation. Their need for knowledge and understanding is limited to the bottom line required for them to perform a specific function or grasp a general concept. *You* are the

SPEC

Stay focused on a generalized goal. Nontechnical colleagues only need to know what they need to know, when they need to know it!

one expected to have the intricate knowledge. They need to know what something does and how to make it happen, not necessarily how or why it does it. If they wanted to learn intricate, in-depth knowledge, they would have pursued a scientific and technical education and would have selected a career similar to yours. They didn't!

Determine how much your nontechnical peers want or need to know, and avoid the temptation of trying to make them understand the entire picture. If you are giving too much information, it's not going to do anyone any good. We all know the people who, when you ask what time it is, tell you how to build a watch. If someone asks who won the game, he does not necessarily need all of the detailed information in the box score including the attendance and relative humidity at game time! When STPs do provide too much information, it is usually due to their desire to educate and help nontechnical people broaden their horizons. Nevertheless these good intentions can lead to counterproductive overexplanation.

SPEC

One of the best ways to discover what the nontechnical person really wants to know is to say, "Help me understand what you will do with this information."

Real-World Commentary

Carol Price, the president of Unlimited Dimensions and Training, Inc., is one of the premier communication training professionals in the United States today. She is the author of the book *Assertive Communication Skills for*

Professionals (CareerTrack Publications, 1994) and has also designed and marketed her own training program, "Communication in the Workplace." Carol observed:

> Many people feel that when they ask a technical person a question, they end up getting an entire manual back from them. If they want to know how to send e-mail, they don't have to understand how the Internet works. If the marketing department needs to know specific information on the market they are targeting, they do not need to understand how the information linkage occurs, or all of the sources that were used to gather the data. To provide more information than necessary just reinforces the perception that technical people believe they are smarter than anyone else. Don't provide any more information than they need to know. If nontechnical people want more information, they will ask you, and you can either provide it or help them understand where they can go to get it.

How much is too much? Remember the old story of the five-year-old child who looks at her mother and says, "Mom, where did I come from?" The young mother is obviously distressed because she thinks she has to go through the whole story of conception and birth, and she's not really sure that she's ready to do that with this child. With sweaty palms, she pulls out her old college health text book, finds the pictures and diagrams, and goes through a description of the process, hopefully selecting words that her precious five-year-old will comprehend. As the mother's uncomfortable discussion mercifully draws to an end, the child looks up and says, "That's really interesting, Mom, but Billy said he came from Baltimore. Where did I come from?" Providing more information than is necessary is usually counterproductive for all concerned.

In Shawn's case, the people he communicates with require only very limited, specific information to solve their current problem and prevent its recurrence.

STPs are tempted to provide too much detailed information when nontechnical people ask them a question. They may want a very simple yes or no answer to a complex issue. They may come to you and ask, "Will this product do this?" or "Will our system do that?" You realize the answer is more complex than a simple yes or no because there may be numerous variables that could be factors. Your typical response might be: "Well, I can't give you a simple yes or no answer because . . . " (a dissertation now follows).

Perhaps it would be more effective to make a general response followed by a brief explanation. For example: "I would probably say yes, but there are some issues to consider. Would you like me to go into some detail right now? If not, that's fine, just be sure to delay making any major decisions on the basis of that 'yes' until we have had time to look at all of the relevant factors." This provides the concise preliminary general response your questioner is looking for and clearly makes her aware of additional important information to consider before she make any decisions or takes action. It is probably a prudent move to then follow up with a memo or e-mail (retain a copy), restating in positive terms the importance of looking at more detailed information in future discussions.

This response meets everyone's needs: it gives people the information they want, avoids overloading them with inappropriate minute detail, and qualifies your response so they do not take actions based upon incomplete information without giving you the opportunity to expand the discussion.

SPEC

Involve others in determining the level of detail they require by asking them—before you start your response to their original question.

Offer three options:

I would like to find out how much information you need at this time.

I can give you a detailed technical explanation, which will take considerable time.

"I can supply a foundation or background of information and identify resources for you to follow up with to increase your knowledge or understanding. I'll tell you where you can go to get further information.

I can give you a brief, concise overview, kind of the Cliff Notes version, and then I'll be happy to respond to your questions, or fill in the blanks where necessary.

When you use this strategy with your peers, they will be interested in, not intimidated by your information, and will probably want more detailed information. When you're communicating with people who are nontechnical, who have been educated in a different discipline, or who perform an entirely different function within the organization, they will choose the bare minimum. This results in their not being overwhelmed with information and your not investing unnecessary time in inappropriate in-depth discussions. This strategy provides multiple options and ensures that everyone's immediate communication needs are met.

There are probably many times when you are required to make a group presentation to an audience of both nontechnical people and other STPs. When you are, consider this strategy:

SPEC

 Target presentations to the nontechnical portion of your audience. Offer to provide additional, in-depth material to STPs or others who may benefit from it.

You can provide this additional material in several ways:

- Be available after the presentation for an additional extended session covering more complex, detailed information.
- Provide written technical information for postmeeting review.

Most of the STPs will welcome your additional material or stay for more detail, yet you will not be forcing your more knowledgeable peers to sit through an extended presentation of material they already know. The nontechnical people will grasp the information in the simpler form as presented without being subjected to complex information they neither need nor understand.

This strategy meets the needs of your diverse audience. Rarely do you have the luxury of presenting information to groups where everyone is equal in education, experience, knowledge, or training.

Display Your Thinking Visually

The transfer of information to nontechnical people is enhanced tremendously by the use of visuals. Models, graphs, or any hands-on material will contribute to better understanding. When possible, Shawn should take advantage of every opportunity to provide visual as well as auditory information to his customers. Diagrams, computer keyboard overlays, or simplified troubleshooting guides, provided prior to the problems' occurring or e-mailed or faxed during live discussions, help others to put a picture to your words.

Visual support tools are valuable whether you are addressing groups or individuals. Here are some suggestions for maximizing their use:

Enhancing Visual Aids

Any visual support material should be created to help focus the receivers on your information and put data in a simple, easily absorbed format. Visuals are intended to reinforce your verbal message (to show them as you tell them) and stimulate their interest. Never use visual material merely to impress receivers with your depth of knowledge or intellect. Overwhelmed receivers shut down to your message and no accurate comprehension takes place. Visual aids are intended to help simplify the communication process, not complicate it.

Visuals are very helpful for displaying percentages, comparisons or ranks, time sequences or deadlines, frequencies of occurrence, and correlation between variables. The same guidelines for the creation of visual support materials apply, whether you are making a presentation in front of a large group or helping individuals understand your complex technical information:

- Present one idea per visual. Do not blend ideas or topics.
- Keep it simple. Avoid excessive words, numbers, designs, etc. Use a maximum of six lines per visual and do not exceed thirty-six words. Use more visuals with fewer words, rather than fewer visuals and more words. Don't clutter your information. Visual aids are intended to simplify and clarify, not confuse.
- Good graphic quality is important. Copy must be neat and legible. Use different colors to differentiate. Use large readable fonts. Always proofread carefully before you print.
- The visual is an *aid* to understanding. Do not expect the visual to make your point without supporting explanation. Show them and tell them. What may be very clear and obvious to you may be confusing to others.

Real-World Commentary

Carol Price of Unlimited Dimensions and Training, Inc., encourages STPs to use visuals:

> Graphs are excellent. However, there should only be two points on the graph. As soon as a graph has more than two points, you're dead, you lose a lot of people. Create the graph in front of others, if possible, so they can literally see how the information flows together. When you put things in writing, such as diagrams, actually develop the diagram right there in front of them. This way movement and changes are seen as they happen. Don't give them finished visual product or they lose the development process, which can affect their understanding of the result.

It can be very helpful to the communication process if you encourage nontechnical people to participate by creating their own visuals. Encourage them to fill in and complete the graph as you provide information. This also enhances the kinesthetic aspect of the communication process.

SPEC

How valuable are simple visuals? Consider the success of the newspaper USA Today.

One of the most appealing aspects of *USA Today* is its extensive use of graphics and color. Simple graphs appear throughout the paper and are featured in the lower left corner of the first page of each section. Visuals help the reader grasp the primary message quickly (within nine to fifteen seconds), proving the old adage that a picture is worth a thousand words.

Involve the Listener

Realizing the potential exists for miscommunication with nontechnical people, you can head this off if you anticipate potential trouble spots and take action to avoid their occurrence.

Involving communication recipients reduces negative emotion or an implied superiority by making them partners. One way of involving your listeners is to take the time to establish ground rules and COPs (Communication Operating Plans) with your listeners. (This is an excellent example of the usefulness of COPs in different situations.) Involving your listeners positions you to be the collaborative teacher and not the condescending expert. Become the imparter of knowledge as opposed to the intimidator overwhelming the nontechnical person with complex information. Empower the receiver to be an active partner in the communication and not just a passive "dart board" being struck with information. Create an allied, not adversarial relationship.

Real-World Commentary

Carol Price suggested, "In communicating with nontechnical people, I recommend that you set the ground rules and literally call it that. You would say, 'Here are the ground rules. I am going to give you information and I need you to stop me at any point and tell me if I am not communicating well. If I am appearing condescending, or if I'm too high or too low in communicating the information, please let me know.'"

Carol also recommends that you use a variation of a front-end-loaded message to help decrease any negative reaction and increase the communication collaboration: "This is an important project, to both you and me, and I know it's very important for you to understand this information. I also know this is not something that you are very familiar with, so you tell me how you'd like me to package the information. Do you want me to tell you so you hear it? Put it in a visual form so you can see it? Or actually walk you through the process in a hands-on way?"

Manage the Intimidation

Another important factor in reducing potential intimidation when communicating with nontechnical people is to be aware of your physical presence. Do not stand if they are seated; you may appear to be towering over them. Sit or stand side by side in an informal manner as opposed to positioning yourself formally across a desk or a table. These may seem to be meaningless subtleties; however, they have a big impact.

Your information is probably in itself intimidating enough to the nontechnical person. Do not compound the listener's sense of being dominated with an overbearing posture or menacing stance.

Structure Your Message: Preview—Present—Review

The three-step model called "preview—present—review" is very effective for presenting information to any audience or individual, regardless of the circumstances or their knowledge base. Shawn should use this structure when instructing his customers on how to correct their PC problems. Though particularly valuable when dealing with nontechnical people, it is valuable in all communications, and you should not hesitate to incorporate it into all of your important communications. This is an excellent technique for presentations to any group, at any level of knowledge.

This simple and effective communication model reduces any negative intimidation factors in your communication, increases clarity, and reduces frustration on the part of the receiver. It also uses the critical component of repetition to ensure that your message gets across accurately.

SPEC

Preview, present, and review: Tell your audience briefly what you plan to say, deliver the message effectively, and summarize what you said, for accurate retention of your message.

Preview

Prepare the listeners to accept your message by telling them briefly what you are going to communicate. The preview should mention both content and emotional impact, and help to establish the receiver's expectation for the communication. Properly implemented, it tells listeners what you want to discuss, helps them to focus on your message, and suggests a possible response.

Some examples:

"I want to discuss the results of our testing, and I think you will be very pleased." (Tells them what you want to discuss and implies a positive message.)

"There may be some problems with the results of our latest testing. I'd like to review the figures and identify some possible options." (Tells them what you want to discuss, prepares them to hear about potential problems, and establishes your commitment to help solve any problems that may occur.)

"I have three specific things to share with you and then I want to answer any questions to be sure I have done a good job of communicating." (Tells them how much information to expect and establishes your willingness to clarify unclear points. It also lessens the pressure on the receiver and allows you to take responsibility for the transfer of information.)

An effective preview for Shawn would be: "Get ready to take some notes. I am going to give you two possible options for fixing this problem."

Present

The "present" stage of your communication is the content, the true meat of the communication. You must present information at the appropriate level, in terms of the receivers' needs and their ability to absorb and process the message. The structure of your presentation will vary depending on the background of your communication partners. Use the "tell them, show them, involve them" model to offer information a number of ways. You can further enhance the effectiveness of the delivery of your message by paying attention to your selection of words, your tone of voice, your body language, and the use of supporting visual or hands-on material.

You may want to review the information on the essentials of presenting effectively in Chapter 2.

Review

To conclude the communication, quickly summarize the critical points, themes, conclusions, or recommendations that were discussed. If possible, limit the review to three key points. "I'd like to quickly review the three key things we discussed. First we discussed the data, the results of the recent testing, most important being. . . . Second key point was the conclusions, both positive and negative, that could be drawn, most important being. . . . And the third point was our response, the steps we will take as a result of knowing this information. What we agreed to do was . . . "

Correctly structured review gives you the opportunity to repeat the most important parts of your message again in a very clear, concise manner. It is extremely valuable in imbedding and reinforcing your information. It also helps the receiver understand the connection of all your information, further emphasizing how it all ties together. This is especially critical with nontechnical people. The review, or summary, allows you to nail down the most compelling parts of your information again, allowing the receiver to hear it a third time. Once again, repetition, as an important feature of effective communication, comes into play.

Preview, present, and review is an excellent model for written as well as verbal communication. It is a recommended method for structuring professional papers, findings, and opinions, and ensures that your information will be presented in a format highly conducive to the receiver's comprehension.

Avoid Thinking Out Loud

Sometimes in conversations between scientific and technical peers, there are episodes of thinking out loud. The tendency to think out loud is particularly strong for all STPs and is rooted in high intellect and creativity. Whether limited to you as an individual or in a group brainstorming session, it undoubtedly has resulted in the generation of significant ideas and discoveries. The challenge or idea is presented, one thought leads to another, and creativity escalates, resulting in ideas, solutions, or perhaps a more focused analysis.

When you are communicating with nonscientific and nontechnical people, this same thinking out loud has a major downside. Their challenge of absorbing your information is difficult enough without being further confused by random thoughts, speculations, or disjointed comments. What is stimulating under one circumstance can be overwhelming in another. Plan your communication to avoid thinking out loud.

When you will be presenting technical or complex information to nontechnical people, prepare yourself in advance to deliver the exact message and quantity of information that is appropriate. Lack of planning, which can lead to ad-libbing or rambling, will only end in a higher rate of confusion for your communication partner. Determining ahead of time the scope of your communication will help you to control the volume of data and avoid the tendency to think out loud. Shawn should not confuse his customers by trying to think through the problem with them on the telephone. If he starts a discussion with, "Well, it could be this . . . or it could be that," the customer won't know when his thinking ends and his correction begins. He should gather the data, and if necessary, call them back after he has conducted his diagnosis.

Once again, keep in mind when you are communicating with nontechnical people that it is not how much you know that counts, only how much the receiver absorbs and understands. Planning in advance will avoid wandering discussions.

Avoid Projecting Opinion as Fact

The nontechnical people you communicate with must be able to differentiate between your opinions and factual data. Other STPs most likely know when your information is fact- or opinion-based, yet that is undoubtedly not the case with nontechnicals. While you may perceive there is a clear distinction, it may not be readily identifiable to them. Because of your assumed expertise, knowledge, and command of your areas of specialty, your opinions are given great weight. Others may take as cast in stone information that you have presented as opinion only. You may not realize your level of influence; many STPs do not. Unsubstantiated opinion can get you into trouble, especially if others send it through the internal information chain with the full weight and credibility of your name behind it. The best way to ensure that there is no confusion is to clearly identify when you are stating an opinion.

An effective way to separate opinion from fact is to use qualifying phrases such as these:

> "The information I'm going to share with you is my opinion and is not based on hard data. Obviously, I believe in it strongly or I wouldn't be offering it, and I want to make it clear that it is my opinion."
>
> "Some of what I'm going to say is opinion; some of it is rooted in factual data. I'm going to be sure to differentiate which information is in which category. If you are unsure as to which it is, please do not hesitate to ask."
>
> "First I'm going to share with you the factual data, and then I will be presenting my professional opinion concerning the conclusions we can draw from the data. I will clearly identify when I shift from fact to opinion."

Flawed organizational decisions have been made and action plans implemented because opinion was taken as factual. Your opinions are extremely valuable, and in many cases it is your job to offer them, and it is of critical importance that others know whether you are stating your opinion or scientific and technical fact. Do not assume that nontechnical people have the same ability to discern the difference as your scientific and technical peers.

Helping Nontechnical People Make Sound Technical Decisions

It is very important for Shawn to maintain this focus in his role as a technical support engineer. Many STPs experience frustration with nontechnical people in the area of decision making. Nontechnical people may make inappropriate decisions or hesitate to take action in circumstances that appear very simple and obvious to you. This lack of action can be due to their limited technical understanding. They find it easier, safer, and less risky to wait for you to make a decision or to advise them before they take action themselves. Many of the demands on your time can be reduced and the abilities and performance of nontechnical people can be increased if you are able to communicate more effectively and prepare others to make good, sound decisions.

Obviously, you want the nontechnical people around you to make good decisions and to exercise common sense. In reality, the definition of making good decisions and exercising common sense really lies in the eyes of the beholder, and it is doing things the way you want them to do it! Their common sense is rooted in seeing and reacting to things the same way you do. If you want nontechnical people to make good decisions, you must communicate the specific criteria for good decision making. Before you make a decision or take an action, you as an STP consider the available information and subject it to formal or informal analysis. You then arrive at an appropriate decision or action. You must ensure that nontechnical people understand the process of analysis that brings you to a certain conclusion. What may seem obvious to you and all the STPs of this world is extremely unclear to many nontechnical people. It is of paramount importance that you recall that at one time you "did not understand this stuff either." Do not expect people to be able to reason through problems they have not been prepared to understand. The key to preparing others to make sound technical decisions is to be very specific and methodical in your communication.

Troubleshooting problems is a great example. To prepare people to solve problems, give them very clear steps to take.

"If your computer does not start, check the electrical plug in the socket."
"When you receive this prompt on your screen, take this action."
"When you receive this message on your monitor, go to . . . "
"If the test results are in the range of . . . , do . . . "

It is a common response for nontechnical people to become over-whelmed or intimidated in the face of technical problems or questions. Take the fear out of their situation by providing step-by-step, simple information for making appropriate decisions or solving common problems. It is important to help them understand what to do. They do not have to know why they are doing it or how the results are materializing. It is not necessary to know how an automobile's electrical system functions to insert the key and start the engine.

The Importance of Positive Feedback in the Communication Process

Regardless of their technical orientation, people absorb information more readily in nonthreatening, positive environments. When you present information to nontechnical people, and they begin to have even a glimmer of understanding of your analogies and examples, be sure to give them appropriate positive feedback. No "Ah-ha" or "light bulb" moments should go unnoticed. Clearly acknowledge any progress they make in grasping the information. You have to crawl before you can walk, so as soon as your non-technical people do the equivalent of starting to crawl, give them positive reinforcement. That which gets rewarded gets repeated and if you reward their breakthroughs, you are encouraging them to seek even more. Encouragement increases the willingness to absorb information. Use statements such as these:

"Great! I can see you are starting to really understand this."
"You are doing a good job of understanding some pretty complex data."
"You seem to be getting this information pretty easily. Good for you."

Positive reinforcement encourages nontechnical people to concentrate even harder on processing the information you are presenting.

The Need for Training

One reason for communication difficulties between STPs and nontechnical people may be that the organization is failing to provide basic knowledge or training. Nontechnical people may be dealing with a level of technical or scientific information that they have not been trained to understand. The less training and development they receive, the more dependent they are upon you for basic knowledge and problem solving. The high levels of frustration and the low levels of tolerance you are experiencing in communicating with nontechnical people may be directly related to their lack of training.

Training Assessment
    Here are some key questions to consider:

1. Is your organization failing to offer training programs that provide nontechnical people with the necessary knowledge to understand the technical aspects of their jobs?   *yes* ☐   *no* ☐
2. Are there consistent predictable communication breakdowns that could be eliminated by offering additional training?
    yes ☐   *no* ☐
3. Is it assumed that nontechnical people in the organization have a basic knowledge of certain procedures and technical information that in reality they may not possess?   *yes* ☐   *no* ☐
4. Is the organization doing an inadequate job of keeping nontechnical people informed on technological advancements and information that affects their ability to perform?
    yes ☐   *no* ☐
5. Are nontechnical people being held accountable for performing technically related functions for which they haven't received adequate training?   *yes* ☐   *no* ☐

Yes-responses indicate opportunities to make recommendations to those at appropriate levels of authority to reassess the organization's current training offerings. This may be an area where you have no influence. However, it never hurts to try. Some of your consistent communication problems could be eliminated or reduced by the uniform presentation of information by the training department.

This training issue also relates to the people you serve outside of your organization. Shawn would do well to consider various ways he can influence the training of the external people he supports.

Communication Assessment
1. Am I aware that an "us-against-them" mentality may exist between the technical and nontechnical people in our organization?
   yes ☐   *no* ☐
2. Am I aware of any negative bias I may personally have against nontechnical people in my communications with them? (Be especially wary of a self-serving *no*-response here.)
   yes ☐   *no* ☐
3. Do I adjust the information I present to nontechnical people to be appropriate to the level of information that they need to know?
   yes ☐   *no* ☐
4. Do I realize that it is not how much I know that counts in my communication with nontechnical people, but rather how much understanding I am able to help them develop?   *yes* ☐   *no* ☐
5. Do I effectively use visually displayed information (models, graphs, hands-on tools, etc.) in my communication with nontechnical people?   *yes* ☐   *no* ☐
6. Do I realize that my primary goal in communicating with nontechnical people is to provide general concepts rather than specific in-depth information?   *yes* ☐   *no* ☐
7. Do I identify the method by which nontechnical people would prefer to receive my information?   *yes* ☐   *no* ☐
8. Do I follow the preview-present-review model in communicating information to others?   *yes* ☐   *no* ☐
9. Do I always differentiate between facts and opinion when communicating with nontechnical people?   *yes* ☐   *no* ☐
10. Do I make use of effective analogies and examples when communicating with nontechnical people?   *yes* ☐   *no* ☐
11. Do I dismiss or ignore the importance of providing nontechnical people with specific criteria for making technically related decisions?   *yes* ☐   *no* ☐
12. Am I aware of any potential training opportunities that would decrease personal and organizational communication problems?
    yes ☐   *no* ☐

Yes-responses to questions 1, 2, 11, and 12 and *no*-responses to all others (3, 4, 5, 6, 7, 8, 9, 10) indicate opportunities for increasing your communication effectiveness.

In Chapters 7 and 8 we will discuss the specific challenges that STPs face with the difficult process of listening and accurately comprehending the messages of others.

7

The Challenges of Effective Listening

In this chapter, we address the root causes of poor listening skills, the impediments to effective listening. You will find no SPECs or suggestions for correction; they follow in Chapter 8, where the strategies for improvement are offered.

The challenge of effective listening is universal. It is the least *practiced* skill in America today; poor listening skills influence our professional lives and also play a major role in our personal relationships. The stark reality is that as a people we are not good listeners. Most of us do not really listen, we just wait to talk! In many cases, we are so focused on our internal thoughts, priorities, and agendas that we do not actually listen to what others are saying. We are so preoccupied or our minds so full of thought that there just is not room for the input of others. It has been estimated that Americans on average retain at best about 50 percent of what they hear immediately after they heard it, and that retention rate erodes to 25 percent after the passage of twenty-four hours.[1]

Listening is a consensual activity. No one can be forced to listen. It is a skill over which every individual has complete control and it is driven totally by internal motivation. Listening as a skill tends to be untaught and untrained. Our schools teach reading, writing, mathematics, the sciences, computer technologies, history, art, and the humanities, yet no curriculum focuses on listening. Nor is listening generally a part of the training offerings of today's organizations. People are expected to listen effectively, yet they are not being prepared with the necessary skills.

Among the myriad reasons for our poor listening tendencies is that speaking has much more value than listening. There are professional orators, public speakers, and many people who talk for a living. Have you ever heard of a professional listener? We do far more listening than talking, yet we rarely put much energy and focus into the reception of others' messages. In general, we are unaware of the price we pay for being poor listeners. When communication problems occur, we usually blame everyone else and do not consider that our listening quality may be involved.

We all have a tendency to rate our own listening skills very high. Others would probably rate our skills significantly lower (just ask your spouse or other significant people in your life). We rarely see ourselves as the problem. Everyone else has communication and listening difficulties, but not us!

We are intentional nonlisteners. Our listening becomes retaliatory. "We don't listen to them because they don't listen to us." We punish others by not listening to them. Without a doubt, one of the most demeaning things we can do to another human being is tune him or her out. Listening to other people is a valuable gift that we extend to them and it conveys respect, esteem, and a strong sense of their dignity. Failure to listen sends a negative message of placing a low value on the other person. Listening is not only a skill of communication, it is a skill of relationship building.

Everyone deals with listening challenges. Some of the listening impediments you confront are unique to your scientific and technical orientation, while others are common in all professions. Regardless, all contribute to miscommunication. You are not any less skilled at listening than anyone else. In fact, STPs such as you can be extremely effective listeners. Obviously, you did not develop the wealth of knowledge you possess or gain the depth of expertise you have by not listening. The challenge for you is to develop the ability to listen and effectively absorb all levels of communication as well as you do data and technical communication.

Many STPs view listening as a "touchy-feely" subject and dismiss its value. Things such as small talk, subjective perceptions, and abstract ideas may hold little or no interest. If it isn't technical, it isn't worth listening.

You experience many listening challenges. You are influenced by your physical environment, internal issues, stress, and negative emotional reactions. Others disrupt your listening effectiveness when you allow them to push your emotional buttons. Listening skills include avoiding the traps and maintaining objectivity and personal control. You give others tremendous influence and control over you by reacting to their provocations.

Listening Assessment

For each question, place a check in the column that best describes you.

Do you. . .

	Always	Frequently	Occasionally	Rarely
1. . . . consistently learn about important events or activities later than your peers?				
2. . . . find yourself to be crisis driven; reactively putting out fires?				
3. . . . think that your manager consistently delegates the most critical and complicated tasks to you?				
4. . . . believe that your manager and coworkers often find it necessary to repeat information to you?				
5. . . . find that other people choose to communicate in writing and reconfirm verbal communication in a documentable form?				
6. . . . tend to have the same basic understanding of organizational and managerial communication as your peers?				
7. . . . experience higher rates of criticism or miscommunication than your peers on orally transmitted tasks or requests?				
8. . . . repeatedly feel left out of the loop or not included in important communication?				
9. . . . experience clients voicing their frustrations with lack of follow-up or unmet expectations?				

	Always	*Frequently*	*Occasionally*	*Rarely*
10. . . . concentrate on what is being said, even if you have low interest in the message?				
11. . . . listen to the other person's point of view even if it is in disagreement with yours?				
12. . . . listen to comprehend the entire message, not just specific points or facts?				
13. . . . form a response in your head while the deliverer is still transferring his message?				
14. . . . focus your entire attention on the person who is speaking?				
15. . . . allow the speaker to express criticism or negative feelings toward you without becoming defensive?				
16. . . . project the appearance of listening even when you are not totally focused on the communication?				
17. . . . make a specific effort to increase your effective listening skills?				
18. . . . take notes to increase your listening efficiency?				
19. . . . find your concentration being broken by external distractions?				
20. . . . restate the deliverer's message to ensure your accurate comprehension?				
21. . . . tend to do most of the talking in conversations?				
22. . . . find it difficult to wait until someone else finishes speaking before you begin to speak?				

	Always	Frequently	Occasionally	Rarely
23. . . . find yourself rejecting the messages of others before they begin to speak?				
24. . . . cease other activity and focus on the individual who is speaking?				
25. . . . offer verbal and nonverbal encouragement and affirmation to the speaker?				
26. . . . give equal weight to points of disagreement as to points of agreement?				
27. . . . refrain from seeking clarification on unclear points?				
28. . . . believe that people who disagree with you are wrong or uninformed?				
29. . . . maintain control of your concentration and attention, not allowing them to wander during conversations?				
30. . . . receive feedback from others that you are not an effective listener?				

Now, figure out your score according to the table below. You will have noticed that some questions rate positive traits, and some rate negative traits. For each question, note where your check is, and give yourself the number of points shown for that box.

Question	Always	Frequently	Occasionally	Rarely
1	1	2	3	4
2	1	2	3	4
3	4	3	2	1
4	1	2	3	4
5	1	2	3	4
6	4	3	2	1

Question	Always	Frequently	Occasionally	Rarely
7	1	2	3	4
8	1	2	3	4
9	1	2	3	4
10	4	3	2	1
11	4	3	2	1
12	4	3	2	1
13	1	2	3	4
14	4	3	2	1
15	4	3	2	1
16	1	2	3	4
17	4	3	2	1
18	4	3	2	1
19	1	2	3	4
20	4	3	2	1
21	1	2	3	4
22	1	2	3	4
23	1	2	3	4
24	4	3	2	1
25	4	3	2	1
26	4	3	2	1
27	1	2	3	4
28	1	2	3	4
29	4	3	2	1
30	1	2	3	4

If you scored 105–120: Get a second opinion. Although a score this high is possible, it is highly unlikely. A self-assessment in this range probably reflects a distorted view of your personal listening skills. Seek input from others—show them your test results—and give thoughtful consideration to their feedback. Their insights will help you realistically assess your listening effectiveness.

If you scored 95–104: You have excellent listening skills.

If you scored 85–94: You have above-average listening skills.

If you scored 75–84: You have average listening skills.

If you scored 83 and below: Indicates high honesty and low listening skills. Great potential for improvement.

Ask yourself the following questions:

1. Do you see any trends in your responses? Is there a common thread linking the questions you identified as listening weaknesses?
2. Do you find any inconsistencies (perhaps you are a more effective listener in some circumstances, a poor listener in others)? What would cause these inconsistencies?
3. What are your areas of greatest and least listening effectiveness? What does this suggest to you?

By the time you have finished this chapter, you will have the tools to plan targeted improvement in your listening skills.

Listening Styles

There are at least five listening styles; one is effective, four of them are not. The ineffective four styles are counterproductive or can be dysfunctional.

Four Ineffective Listening Styles

> The "missing-in-action" listener
> The "distracted" listener
> The "selective" listener
> The "contentious" listener

The "Missing-in-Action" Listener.   This is typically a passive or detached listening style. These listeners, although physically present, are clearly mentally or intellectually absent. They may be preoccupied with personal issues and at times even appear to be in a trance. Although there may be a smile on their face, their eyes are blank and distant, and it's obvious they are disengaged from whatever is being said. It is not a question of misunderstanding the communication; they do not even hear it. It is a total lack of reception, not a lack of comprehension.

You could become a "missing-in-action" listener if you have little interest in what is being said or you give little or no legitimacy to the communicator. A person might go missing in action if they feel unable to understand a complex message (this is usually *not* the case with STPs). If people are intimidated by the deliverer or the content of the message, they may choose to zone out of the listening process. Regardless of the cause, being "missing in action" means being missing from the communication and vulnerable to the myriad of problems that can occur from totally missed messages.

The "Distracted" Listener.   This is an active dysfunctional style. These people are obviously distracted from listening by more immediate concerns. Typically they are consumed by "urgent" internal issues of the moment. They may be doing two or more things at one time. They try to appear to be listening while reading, writing, or pursuing some other activity. They may be concerned about time pressures, perhaps they repeatedly glance at their watch, and their behavior usually indicates impatience. They clearly convey a message of wanting to get the conversation over with so they can get back to the things that are really important to them.

This listener appears to be engaged by consistently nodding in agreement or using appropriate verbal cues, yet they realize they are not doing an effective job of absorbing the message. To a degree, they are "listening con artists." They know the importance of listening and are aware of the negative message not doing so sends so they attempt to create the illusion of listening. This is dishonest inasmuch as it is an intentional distortion. Their only goal is to try to bring the communication to a quick conclusion. They have little or no interest in the information. People who experience the distracted listener often feel as though they have been "handled" as opposed to being heard. Trying to get the distracted listener to process information is the equivalent of attempting to jump onto a moving train. It is moving too fast to permit you to board.

You can become a distracted listener when you are under pressure to meet deadlines or are wrapped up in your own thoughts or emotions. When you are unwilling or unable to slow down your thought process enough to allow the introduction of additional information, you are the distracted listener!

The "Selective" Listener.   This listening style involves listening to be right or to confirm previously determined opinions and positions. These listeners sift through the message to glean information to support what they already think, hearing only what they want to hear. They are not listening to the total message, they are only selectively listening to validate their own beliefs. They screen out or ignore information that does not fit their preconceptions. Selective listeners can be either positively or negatively inclined. You have probably had the experience of paying someone a series of compliments while offering one small point of criticism, and all they heard was your criticism. Perhaps you have been in a circumstance where someone has accused you of never saying anything good about their work, and you are frustrated because you could easily cite many examples of recent positive comments you have made. This person may well be a selective listener who chooses to hear only the negative. Conversely, you may have offered someone several points of appropriate criticism only to realize they did not even hear your comments because they were focused on the fact that you complimented their tie or their new hairstyle! They chose to hear only the positive!

You become a selective listener if you do not discipline yourself to listen to someone's total message. It is an arrogant listening style and should be avoided because a selective listener dismisses the messages of others and confirms her own self-righteous positions. If you decide before the communication even begins what you want to hear, and interpret statements to support your previously formed belief, you have succumbed to the trap of selective listening.

Many STPs, such as you, struggle with this listening style when categorizing or judging whoever is delivering the message. If you think someone is an idiot, they prove it to you by what they say. Everything they say goes through your internal selective listening filter of idiocy. If they convey a message that does not support idiocy, you tend to disregard it and wait for them to say something that does. Selective listeners only hear what they want to hear.

Teenagers are a prime examples of selective listeners. They expect to be unhappy with what their parents are going to say . . . and they are! Mom and Dad say "Hello" and somehow that is seized upon as a negative comment!

The "Contentious" Listener. A contentious listener is one who uses a combative or negatively aggressive listening style. It has been described as "listening with a chip on your shoulder." Similar to selective listeners, contentious listeners listen only to find points of disagreement. They listen only to reject, not to actually process the entire message. They are determined to disagree. You may offer twenty-four points of mutual agreement, and one point of contention; they will focus on the one point of contention! Disregarding any areas of agreement, they only wish to focus on areas of disagreement.

You can become the contentious listener when listening with your emotions. Fear, anger, jealousy, resentment, and similar emotions often result in combative listening patterns. This is subjective, reactionary listening. If you feel in any way threatened by someone's message, contentious listening is a common response.

The Effective Listener

Effective listeners are both mentally and physically committed to the listening process. They exercise conscious control over their listening activities. Being focused on the entire message that is being delivered, they are very attentive to the speaker's total delivery. They maintain keen awareness of the alignment of words, tone of voice, and nonverbal communication. Effective listeners practice open-minded objectivity, withholding judgments and interpretations (agreements, disagreements, and emotional responses, etc.) until they have processed the entire message. Effective listeners send powerful messages to their communication partners of holding them in high esteem and finding their thoughts and opinions to be of great interest. Those who truly listen effectively demonstrate great respect for others, and in turn are held in high regard by others.

The Twelve Characteristics of Effective Listening

STPs who are effective listeners. . .

1. . . . have a strong commitment to the listening process.
2. . . . realize that listening skills are neither instinctive nor eternal.
3. . . . are motivated to learn, practice, and reinforce their active listening skills.
4. . . . display high self-confidence and self-assurance by listening effectively.
5. . . . are highly efficient in completing their assignments and fulfilling their responsibilities.
6. . . . demonstrate greater flexibility in resolving disagreements and conflicts.
7. . . . participate more intelligently and effectively in conversations.
8. . . . are as focused on their communication partner's message as they are on their own.
9. . . . make more decisions based on a solid foundation of facts and data and avoid reactionary, shoot-from-the-hip conclusions.
10. . . . experience greater upward career mobility.

11. . . . suffer less embarrassment resulting from foolish mistakes or incompetent decisions.
12. . . . successfully control the listening barriers that affect their reception of messages.

In Chapter 8 you will earn the critical skills that are necessary to increase your overall listening effectiveness, along with specific strategies for implementing these skills. The remaining information in this chapter is designed to raise your awareness of barriers to effective listening and allow you to assess their impact on you.

How Good a Listener Are You?

The following assessment tool invites you to thoughtfully evaluate your listening effectiveness. If you dedicate enough time and attention to this exercise, you will clearly identify your individual listening strengths and weaknesses. As with most things in life, the value of this assessment will be in direct proportion to what you put into it.

The Impediments to Effective Listening

Why is effective active listening such a complex challenge? There are many causes of poor listening patterns. Whether you are willing to admit it or not, you are certainly affected by these factors when you receive communication from others. It is also important for you to realize these same factors work against you when you are communicating with others, because they have the same kinds of impediments to effectively listening to you. Increasing your awareness will not only enable you to become a better listener, it will also allow you to observe the telltale signs of poor listening in others.

The most significant listening impediments facing you and other STPs in today's communication environment are discussed below. While these are not the only barriers, they are by far the most significant. Are STPs the only ones facing these impediments? You and your scientific and technical peers are certainly not the only ones facing these challenges. The fact remains that due to your education, training, and disciplined thought processes, you may have a significantly greater difficulty in dealing with them than others.

Impatiently Waiting to Talk.   Everyone tends to value their own thoughts and issues more highly than those of others. It is natural. What we have to say is always more important than what someone else has to say. We are always anxious to talk. We want to demonstrate our knowledge base, correct the errors and misperceptions of others, and at times, establish or maintain control or primacy. Because you are in such command of knowledge and have such a passion for your area of expertise, it is common to want to actively participate in or perhaps dominate discussions. You are extremely focused on contributing to the communication, especially if you are in some disagreement with what is being said. This desire to contribute often occurs at the expense to others. Instead of listening to them, you are planning what you are going to say!

How many times do you find yourself saying things like the following?

"I don't mean to interrupt, but . . . "
"Before you go any further, let me just say . . . "
"Wait a minute, stop right there. Here's what really happened . . . "
"I know what you are going to say and it's not accurate."

This is a circumstance where being highly knowledgeable and in command of expertise actually works against STPs.

1_____ ____ ____ ____ ____ ____ ____ ____ ____ ____10

Rate on a scale of 1 to 10 (1 being very low; 10 being very high) your tendency to allow this impediment to influence your listening.

Information Overload.   You are deluged with so much information that it is humanly impossible to process it all. The volume of information available to you is increasing day by day, minute by minute. It is very difficult to determine whether information is really valuable or just more of the overall background noise that fills your professional life. Much of the information you are exposed to appears to be important and somewhat urgent, and you have to determine its actual relevance. It is easy for you to become desensitized and assume the information could not possibly be as meaningful as the deliverer believes it to be, or as important as the information you already possess. You can tune out and become a missing-in-action or distracted listener. Someone could be offering to sell you twenty-dollar bills for five dollars, and you may not hear their offer because it is lost in the immense volume of information to which you are already exposed.

When you are in information overload, it is as if your brain is full and there is just no more room for any additional information, regardless of its interest, importance, or urgency.

1___ ___ ___ ___ ___ ___ ___ ___ ___ ___10

Rate on a scale of 1 to 10 (1 being very low; 10 being very high) your tendency to allow this impediment to influence your listening.

Being Preoccupied.   It is difficult to listen effectively when you may have other compelling issues on your mind. If you are under time pressure to complete a project or perhaps submit an important report, you may be too preoccupied to really process what someone else is saying. You may be preoccupied with personal concerns such as marital issues or health problems in addition to professional pressures.

STPs can easily become preoccupied when they are working on a challenging task or are focused on solving a particularly intriguing problem. STPs' intense focus and concentration become an enemy of listening. The active intellect and intense concentration of STPs in general causes preoccupation to be a potentially serious impediment to effective listening.

1___ ___ ___ ___ ___ ___ ___ ___ ___ ___10

Rate on a scale of 1 to 10 (1 being very low; 10 being very high) your tendency to allow this impediment to influence your listening.

Perceived Value of Message.   While people may be delivering messages that are obviously important to them, these messages may be much less important to you. On a scale of one to ten, they may perceive the information to be an eleven, and to you it may be a minus eight! Their priority may have little impact, interest, or importance to you. You may even experience a negative reaction, thinking, "Why are they taking up my time with this?" or "Why would they think that I even care about this or have any interest at all in this information?"

It is difficult to listen effectively if you believe the message is of low importance, and is a waste of your time. Though your lack of interest may at times be justified, if you often find yourself feeling bored and dismissive toward what others have to say, it is a serious impediment to listening and indicates a very selfish listening style.

1____ ____ ____ ____ ____ ____ ____ ____ ____ ____10

Rate on a scale of 1 to 10 (1 being very low; 10 being very high) your tendency to allow this impediment to influence your listening.

The Challenges of Concentration.   This problem occurs when highly intelligent people with very active minds are asked to focus on messages that are not mentally challenging. The result is boredom and a wandering mind filled with other thoughts. This is a big problem for STPs; the issue is not your *inability* to concentrate, it is about the fact that most communication does not challenge you sufficiently to encourage concentration. It has been estimated that the average person speaks between 120 and 180 words per minute.[2] Your brain is actually capable of processing information at a much greater rate (approximately six times higher, 700 to 1,000 words per minute). What this means is that in a typical communication the deliverer is not giving you enough information to tax or engage your intellect. Your underchallenged brain wanders and becomes involved in additional activity. You begin thinking about your next task, what you are going to do when you get off work, or perhaps you even start considering what you are going to order on your pizza for lunch! You may have five or six different thoughts competing for your attention at one time.

To listen and concentrate effectively, you do not have to gear yourself up, you literally have to gear your intellect down. Your brain is very much like a Thoroughbred racehorse that wants to run. When you are listening effectively, you are pulling on the reins and asking this bundle of energy to move at a slow pace while your Thoroughbred brain keeps straining to take you elsewhere. This is certainly not a case of low intelligence; it is the reality of having too much mental capacity to be engaged by weak stimuli. You really must discipline yourself to listen effectively. Left unchecked, your creativity and thought processes will take you to destinations unknown.

This is another example of how STPs' exceptionally high abilities can work against them in the communication process.

1____ ____ ____ ____ ____ ____ ____ ____ ____ ____10

Rate on a scale of 1 to 10 (1 being very low; 10 being very high) your tendency to allow this impediment to influence your listening.

Jumping to Conclusions.   A hallmark of the contentious listener, this impediment manifests itself when you listen to only a portion of someone's message and assume you already know the rest of what they are going to say. You may begin to defend yourself or correct their statements before you give them the opportunity to even complete their message. You have undoubtedly had the experience of making a statement or asking a question and someone began responding before you had even finished your thought. You know how obvious it is when others jump to conclusions? Well, guess what? You are probably guilty of the same listening misbehavior.

This barrier is especially troublesome when you jump to the conclusion that someone is being critical or disagreeing with your positions. This is a hair trigger or knee-jerk listening response. It results in premature judgment based on fragmentary data. They may be attempting to be complimentary or voicing their support, yet you never hear it because you do not give them the chance to complete their communication.

1_____ _____ _____ _____ _____ _____ _____ _____ _____ _____10

Rate on a scale of 1 to 10 (1 being very low; 10 being very high) your tendency to allow this impediment to influence your listening.

Preconceived Assumptions.   This is different from jumping to conclusions. When you jump to conclusions, you don't let the person finish before formulating your response. With preconceived assumptions you make assumptions about what the communication is going to be about before it even begins. You assume you already know what the other person is going to say before he even opens his mouth. You may begin to formulate an emotional or verbal response without actually hearing the message. This impediment is particularly significant when someone is perceived to deliver consistently negative messages. You shut down your listening because you already know what they are going to say and you have already determined you do not want to hear it! Perhaps you have someone in your intimate work group who only seems to communicate when they have a complaint, criticism, or something to whine about. As soon as you see them draw a breath and prepare to speak, you probably say to yourself, "Here we go again" and when that assumption is in place, your listening is impeded.

You may have the same reaction to the Pollyannas around you, people who tell you "Everything is going to be okay" and start pontificating that no matter what happens, "There is a silver lining in every cloud." You could easily assume they are shallow thinkers and lack a realistic view of the problem. Your assumptions contribute to your dismissing what they say and not processing their message, although it may contain some valuable and meaningful information.

Consider the mass preconceived assumptions that would probably occur if your boss issued a general e-mail message stating, "There will be a mandatory meeting at 9:00 A.M. tomorrow to discuss some very important matters concerning our future." How many people would assume the meeting would be about layoffs, or a merger, or some other ominously negative event? In fact, it could be about a change in your IRA investment options!

1___ ___ ___ ___ ___ ___ ___ ___ ___ ___10

Rate on a scale of 1 to 10 (1 being very low; 10 being very high) your tendency to allow this impediment to influence your listening.

Prejudice.   While preconceived assumptions address content of the message, prejudicial listening addresses the worth or value of the messenger. This is a personal rejection of the deliverer. This barrier exists when you predetermine the value of the *person* who is delivering a message. This is not a predetermined prejudice against *what* they are saying, it is a prejudice against *who* is saying it. In its most vile form, this impediment contributes to hatreds such as racism or the rejection of diversity in any form. It results in the ridicule or dismissal of the messages of others because *they are different*. You would be guilty of this if you devalue someone because of their ethnicity, culture, religious beliefs, gender, age, etc., and determine they are not worth listening to before they even begin to speak. While, unfortunately, incidents of such disdainful prejudicial judgments do exist, most of you do not experience such petty hatreds. For the vast majority of STPs, incidents of this barrier are rooted in a form of professional prejudice. It is devaluing someone because of what they *do*. You may not hold in high esteem people whose training, education, or functions are not scientific and technical in nature. How often have you heard (or yourself given voice to) statements such as these:

"You know how those marketing people are, they are all hype."
"All the people on the second shift are lazy and don't do anything we ask them to do."
"Management is only interested in the bottom line, and I really don't listen to anything they have to say."
"Those financial people are clueless."

Prejudicial listening impediments take the form of absolute value judgments based upon the predetermined low worth of the message deliverer. The healthcare industry experiences circumstances where some doctors do not value the input of nurses or other professionals, and specialized RNs may not value LPNs, etc. In the scientific and technical community, degrees, certifications, publications, and honors frequently place people in a communication value hierarchy. While it is easy to see the danger of this impediment intellectually, it is easy to fall prey to it unintentionally.

This impediment can also work in reverse. If you hold someone in very high esteem, you may accept his messages as gospel without appropriate thought or questioning. You may assume they are divinely inspired and everything they say is the absolute truth. This would be a listening pattern of prejudicially high acceptance and could have as many negative consequences as refusing to listen to somebody because of a judgment of lesser value.

The challenge for you is to consistently and objectively separate the message from the messenger.

1___ ___ ___ ___ ___ ___ ___ ___ ___ ___10

Rate on a scale of 1–10 (1 being very low; 10 being very high) your tendency to allow this impediment to influence your listening.

Selective Listening. This is both an impediment and a flawed style unto itself. Selective listening is the culling through the communication to selectively separate the information you will choose to embrace from the information you will dismiss. It is the dubious art of only hearing selected portions of the message. You may choose to embrace only that with which you agree, or only that with which you disagree. Either way, it results in a distorted perception of the information.

An example of selective listening is the interpretation or spin of the political discourse that takes place, especially during elections. No one is surprised when Republicans and Democrats interpret statements of their own party's candidates or office holders as positive and selectively interpret statements made by the other side as false, misleading, or negative. The response of politicians can be easily predicted by whether they have an *R* or a *D* in front of their name. It has little to do with the actual content of the message.

When listening selectively, you readily embrace messages that support your previously held positions and beliefs without listening to the information objectively.

1____ ____ ____ ____ ____ ____ ____ ____ ____ ____10

Rate on a scale of 1 to 10 (1 being very low; 10 being very high) your tendency to allow this impediment to influence your listening.

Embracing the Minutia.   This is another listening impediment that has a particularly significant impact for you. Similar to selective listening, it is the focusing on and magnifying fragmentary parts of the message, disregarding the greater body of information. When this barrier is in evidence, issues of commonality or agreement are dismissed and obscure bits of information become the focal point, not the intended message.

This impediment is especially challenging for STPs such as yourself because your education, experience, and thought process is geared toward identifying the minutia. You are taught to seek, investigate, and analyze. You are conditioned to search for the obscure opportunity. You are trained to pursue the minute point, and are often rewarded for doing so successfully. In fact, great achievements have resulted from this willingness to painstakingly investigate and pursue. In communication, these same skills can actually be counterproductive. As you listen to identify the minutia or areas of disagreement and inconsistency, it is important for the points of agreement to be identified as well. For you to be an effective listener, you must develop a reasonable balance.

1____ ____ ____ ____ ____ ____ ____ ____ ____ ____10

Rate on a scale of 1–10 (1 being very low; 10 being very high) your tendency to allow this impediment to influence your listening.

Lack of Empathy.   It is extremely difficult to be an effective listener when you really do not care about the message that is being delivered. If you have no connection, involvement, or relevant frame of reference, there is very little motivation to listen intently. This is a common complaint voiced by many of you and your peers concerning team, departmental, or organization-wide meetings. "There is so much information that just does not pertain to me or my area of responsibility, yet I have to sit there and listen to others drone on about things that just don't matter. I could be doing my work if I didn't have to sit through this meaningless stuff."

Once lost, it is difficult to regain an effective listening focus due to lack of empathy. It is nearly impossible to drift in and out of effective listening. Once you abandon it, you lose it all. Creating and maintaining empathy can be difficult. It requires you to see things from your communication partner's point of view and subordinate your own.

1___ ___ ___ ___ ___ ___ ___ ___ ___ ___10

Rate on a scale of 1 to 10 (1 being very low; 10 being very high) your tendency to allow this impediment to influence your listening.

Emotions (Fear, Anger, Grief, etc.).   When emotions run high, listening is impeded. The emotion of the moment takes priority and it is common to become so engrossed or consumed that it is difficult for information to penetrate through this barrier of emotional intensity. In circumstances of high emotions, physical reactions frequently dominate: breathing becomes rapid, dry throat, sweaty palms, etc. Emotional outbursts may occur. You may be driven almost compulsively to vocalize what you are feeling, clearly demonstrating little or no interest in what others may have to say. Emotional balance is a huge factor in the listening process. It is not only negative emotions that impact message reception. If you are excited or happy, listening becomes equally distorted as well.

Emotions can be a factor before the communication ever begins, or they may be triggered during the listening process. Regardless of when the emotional interference occurs, listening is severely impacted from that point.

1___ ___ ___ ___ ___ ___ ___ ___ ___ ___10

Rate on a scale of 1 to 10 (1 being very low; 10 being very high) your tendency to allow this impediment to influence your listening.

Physical Distractions.   The physical environment always has a significant influence on anyone's ability to process information. Interruptions, lighting, the bustle of activity, and background noise are just a few of the factors that disrupt the listening process. When lighting is poor, people frequently perceive that they cannot hear. Incoming phone calls are very distracting and it is difficult to come in and out of the listening process in between telephone interruptions. Competing activities, or disruptions within your field of vision, even at a distance, have a negative impact on your listening effectiveness. If you have a view from your window that is pleasant or interesting, you may find yourself focusing on the visual stimulation rather than listening to the message someone may be delivering. Some physical distractions can be corrected, and in Chapter 8 you will learn some very specific actions you can take to minimize their impact. Other physical distractions cannot be easily addressed, such as noise levels in manufacturing areas, paging systems, or even external traffic sounds, trains, etc. You can learn to tune out some of these distractions, while others will continue to disrupt your listening efforts.

1___ ___ ___ ___ ___ ___ ___ ___ ___ ___10

Rate on a scale of 1 to 10 (1 being very low; 10 being very high) your tendency to allow this impediment to influence your listening.

Poor Delivery of the Message.   When the person delivering the message does so in a monotone, whining, or otherwise distracting style, it is very difficult to stay focused on their message. There is little you, as the receiver, can do about their style of delivery. These circumstances challenge you to increase your commitment to the listening process and re-emphasize your listening attentiveness. As frustrating as it may seem, you cannot afford to allow the poor communication style of others to reduce your ability to comprehend their message.

1___ ___ ___ ___ ___ ___ ___ ___ ___ ___10

Rate on a scale of 1–10 (1 being very low; 10 being very high) your tendency to allow this impediment to influence your listening.

Replaying the Positive.   Your listening is also disturbed when you may receive positive comments and replay them over and over in your mind, continuing to enjoy them. Someone may compliment your work and you may become so engrossed in that portion of the message that you tune out or ignore anything else that is said. Wanting the glow of positive recognition to last as long as possible is certainly understandable. While basking in the rush of high compliment, it is easy to tune out the messages, both positive and negative, that follow.

1___ ___ ___ ___ ___ ___ ___ ___ ___ ___10

Rate on a scale of 1–10 (1 being very low; 10 being very high) your tendency to allow this impediment to influence your listening.

Communication Action Plan

Review your assessment of each of the listening impediments. Any rating of 6 or above indicates an area of potential listening weakness. The higher the rating, the more significant the challenge. Assessing listening impediments is a very personal, individualized exercise, and may result in conclusions that do not make you happy or proud. Realize they are invitations for growth and development.

For the most part, these barriers are internal, and you are in a position to initiate correction and exert some level of control. You are responsible for your own listening effectiveness. The buck stops in the mirror!

Many of the barriers become intertwined or contributory to each other. Jumping to conclusions typically leads to negative emotional reactions. Lack of empathy and disparity of prioritization are very similar, perhaps even varying degrees of a common issue. Some of the barriers are more easily corrected than others.

Strongly consider supplying a copy of this assessment to your direct manager, and at least one other person who is a critical communication point in your professional life. It would also be helpful to include at least one significant person in your personal life as well. Ask them to rate your listening skill level from their perspective. Assessing a composite of all their ratings and comparing them with your own will give you valuable insight into your current level of listening effectiveness.

In Chapter 8 you will find many practical, real-world guidelines for increasing your listening effectiveness.

8

Developing Effective Listening Skills

Your listening efforts are completely under your control. If you are willing to be an effective listener you can become one. The first steps in becoming a better listener are to assess accurately your current level of listening skills (which you did Chapter 7) and to make a commitment to improving those skills in a specific time period. Just as you make a commitment to completing projects and tasks, meeting customers' expectations, and satisfying organizational performance standards, you can also formally commit yourself to increasing your listening effectiveness. Make your commitment known to the people you communicate with on an ongoing basis, especially your boss and other critical communication points—include also the most important people in your personal life. If possible, make improvement in your listening skills a formal part of your performance appraisal. Give others permission to evaluate your progress. Invite their feedback. Commitments not shared with others are secrets. Take a risk by declaring your intent.

Six Communication Realities

1. There is good news! Effective listening skills can be learned.
   Good listeners are made, not born. Some people may have inherently better listening skills than others, yet everyone can learn to become a more effective listener. Because the skills are acquired, the playing field is level for all. No one has a listening advantage.

2. To become an effective listener you must be committed to your personal skill development.

It takes a willing student. The skills are not necessarily easy to learn; if they were, everyone would already have them! You will experience success in direct proportion to the effort you are willing to invest in the learning process. Increasing your listening skills must become a personal goal. Establish incremental goals. Do not expect yourself to become a more effective listener in one giant leap. Monitor and track your success to verify your growth and development. You must consistently strive to increase your skill. Listening is a journey of constant improvement. It is not an end to be achieved. You will never be a perfect listener. Continue to strive to become a more effective listener.

3. Active listening skills must be practiced.

Increases in your skill levels will erode if not reinforced. Repetition is the key. Effective listening becomes second nature when the skills are embedded, and the only way this can be achieved is for you to practice, practice, practice. The active listening skills and SPECs designed to increase your abilities outlined in this chapter will not become second nature unless you are willing to use them repeatedly. The first time you try them you will probably experience only limited success. The truth is, some of you will give up if not instantaneously successful. A limited number will keep at it until increased levels of effectiveness are achieved. Surgeons practice their techniques, pilots spend countless hours in flight simulators, and professional golfers make regular visits to the driving range. You must be willing to invest the same effort if you are going to increase your listening prowess.

4. Time is an important tool.

If emotions are high, buy yourself some time and allow your intensity to ebb before you ask yourself to be an effective listener. Earlier we discussed peak energy times. Give strong consideration to scheduling important listening opportunities during those times when you are at your highest levels of energy and productivity. Many of your listening opportunities are subject to your control and many are impromptu where planning is not possible. Exercise your influence when you can. Make time work in your best interest.

5. How well you listen to others depends in great measure on what you say to yourself when the listening process begins.

Your listening skills evolve around your ability to manage your own internal communication. The internal dialogue, listening instructions you give yourself, have tremendous influence over your abilities to accurately absorb the messages of others. To be a good listener, you must have the self-discipline to identify and overcome the listening impediments discussed in Chapter 7. Do you prepare yourself to be an ally or an adversary? Do you focus on absorbing information or rejecting it? Your self-talk plays a huge role in preparing you to accept information. The internal tone you set for yourself when you encounter a listening opportunity determines whether you will listen objectively or prejudicially.

6. Some effective listening techniques are more difficult to implement than others.

The unique nature of individual listening strengths and weaknesses places varying degrees of importance and challenge on active listening skills for different people. You must decide which techniques are most productive for you. Your assessment activity from Chapter 7 will help you determine where your greatest problems lie and this in turn points you in the direction of the techniques that will have the greatest impact for you. Also consider that the greater the degree of difficulty you experience in implementing a specific technique, the greater its importance or necessity. If it is easy, you are not challenging yourself.

In Chapter 3 we discussed how you can present your message so that others can absorb it with accurate comprehension. In this chapter we look at some of those techniques from the opposite perspective . . . that of you as the receiver of information, the listener. You will understand how to use these techniques when the person delivering the message may not be skilled in effective communication.

The five-step model offers many recommendations for developing and honing the skills of effective listening.

Five Steps to Effective Listening

This five-step model will help you to develop a *listening ritual*. Rituals are an important part of many of your repetitive behaviors. You have a routine for going to bed (changing into sleep attire, brushing your teeth, laying out clothes for the morning, a cup of warm milk, etc.). You have also developed rituals for eating (washing your hands, perhaps reciting a blessing, placing the napkin in your lap, etc.). You probably have evolved a certain ritual that you do when you arrive at work to begin your day. It is also important to develop a *listening ritual*. When you do, your transition into a listening mode will become second nature. You will engage effective listening without having to think about it. Ritualized behavior is ingrained, habitual behavior.

Following these five steps as you enter into a listening opportunity will help you become a much more effective listener.

Step 1. State your intention to listen.
Step 2. Manage the physical environment.
Step 3. Make an internal commitment to listen.
Step 4. Assume a listening posture.
Step 5. Participate actively in the listening process.

Following is a list of strategies and techniques to help you achieve success in each step of developing your listening ritual.

Step 1. State Your Intention to Listen.

Making an audible statement of your willingness and commitment to listen accomplishes two things.

It creates an environment of respect and dignity, and helps your communication partners realize their message is welcomed. The risk of approaching you is automatically lowered and they are encouraged to be very open in their communication. This simple statement on your part helps to reduce any anxiety they may be experiencing by sending a very clear message that you are interested in what they have to say. This is a compelling indication that you place a very high value on them and their ideas. You might use one of the following sentences:

"I am anxious to hear what you have to say."
"I'm sure this will be very interesting, and I am looking forward to hearing about it."

Your statement of your intention to listen also prepares you internally to shift from your current thoughts and activities into an active listening role. You are giving yourself an internal command, literally instructing your ears, mind, and body to focus on the incoming message. It helps you to transition from whatever you may have been involved in to the process of receiving information. It is the very first step in becoming a committed listener. You prepare yourself to listen and send a signal to your communication partners that you welcome their message.

Step 2. Manage the Physical Environment.

Managing the physical environment means clearing the decks of any and all distractions that you can. Can you eliminate every listening distraction? Of course not. But eliminate the ones you have influence over, and increase your awareness that remaining physical distractions have the potential to interfere with your listening effectiveness. Awareness is the key. Just as you turn the lights out to sleep more soundly, you manage distracting influences to listen well.

Eliminate as many distractions as possible, such as the following:

- Hold telephone calls.
- Reduce as much background noise as possible.
- Put down whatever you are currently working on and focus on the speaker.
- Clear your desk or put papers, letters, etc., into a closed file folder.
- Position yourself to remove potentially distracting activity from your line of sight.
- Turn off your computer or reposition the screen away from your immediate line of vision.

SPEC

Your effectiveness is enhanced when you and the speaker move to a more conducive listening environment.

Changing your location to one that is more conducive to listening sends a very powerful positive message to your communication partner. It tells him that you are interested in what he has to say and want to do everything possible to give him the quality listening and dedication of your attention that is deserved.

Explain your intention by saying something like this:

"I may not do an effective job of listening here in my office. There are too many distractions. I want to give you the quality of concentration you deserve. Let's take a walk, go to a conference room, or go to the lunchroom for a cup of coffee, whichever you prefer."

Step 3. Make an Internal Commitment to Listen.

This is by far the most critical step in being an effective listener.

Here are five specific recommendations to help you manage your internal self-talk, eliminate or reduce listening impediments, and prepare yourself to effectively absorb information.

SPEC

Before you begin to listen, say to yourself, "I realize she may have a different view of this than I do and it is important that I discover her perspective."

Remove Internal Barriers.   This technique primarily addresses the impediments of preconceived assumptions and prejudicial listening patterns. Exert control over your internal belief system and allow yourself to give appropriate value to the communications of others. This is best accomplished by eliminating the internal labeling or negative judgment of people who may be different from you in background, function, or discipline, etc. This helps you to separate the messenger from the message.

Correct your internal perceptions by giving others the right to disagree. Others are permitted to have different priorities, goals, and conclusions than you.

Rather than starting to listen with a predetermined opinion of the speaker's message, commit yourself to a process of communication discovery. This does not mean giving other people's views precedence over yours; it merely acknowledges that to communicate effectively, you must understand their point of view.

When you acknowledge the rights of others to have differing perceptions and you refrain from judging them negatively because their training, education, and organizational function are different from yours, internal barriers begin to disintegrate. When you reach the point of truthfully being able to say to yourself, "Even though I may not like this person or think her job is as important as mine, I realize there is value in what she has to say," you will immediately become a more efficient and mature listener. Preconceived assumptions and prejudicial listening patterns exist in your head; use this technique to break them down.

Avoid the Assumption of Negative Motives.   It is fairly common to make assumptions about the negative motives of your communication partners, especially if you do not like or value their contributions. This occurs most frequently if you have reason to believe they may disagree with your own thought processes and activities. If someone disagrees, you may assume he is stupid, he is an idiot, or just out for himself. You are quick to think he is pursuing his own personal negative agenda and is only motivated by selfishness or greed. It is interesting to observe that when you are in an adversarial position with someone else, you view your own motivations as rooted in fairness and see yourself as only trying to do what is right. Everyone does. At the same time, you assign very negative, and perhaps vile, intentions to your communication partner. You rationalize your reactions by blaming him for being a bad person!

To avoid assumptions of negative intent, say to yourself:

"Even if we disagree, he is doing what he thinks is right."
"Even if she is wrong, she is motivated by the same things I am, which
 is to solve this problem, do what's best for the customer, or
 maintain our budget constraints (etc.)."
"Their intentions are as valid as mine, even though we disagree."

There are times when communication becomes contentious or disagreement escalates because you do not want your communication partners' intentions to be validated. You do not want them to *win*. You may fall into the trap of disagreeing on principle to make sure that greed, unethical behavior, or selfishness do not win the day. You lose sight of your actual message and focus only on them as negative individuals. You allow the communication to become personal, not driven by content. Making this internal commitment to avoid assumptions of negative intent lessens that tendency. Once again, it allows you to validate the messenger and fairly process his message.

Challenge Yourself to Remember What Has Been Said.   Prepare yourself to listen as if you were a spy!

As you enter into a listening opportunity, challenge yourself to listen so intently that you could accurately write a detailed summary of the conversation as much as two hours after its completion. Commit yourself to receiving and recalling the communication accurately.

SPEC

Say to yourself: "I am going to listen so carefully I could write a word-for-word account of this conversation at the end of the day."

As a follow-up to significant communications, it is always a valuable exercise to put your perceptions and recollections in writing while they are still fresh. Doing so helps further embed the communication in your mind. Remember the importance of telling, showing, and involving in communication—you can do that with yourself also. It also gives you a written summary of your perceptions of the communication, which may be helpful in preparing for future discussions or taking subsequent action and making decisions.

SPEC

Give others the benefit of the doubt and acknowledge that your lesser prioritization does not diminish the importance of the communication.

Prioritize and Process the Communication from the Messenger's Vantage Point.   Often the message being delivered is much more important to your communication partner than it is to you. You can neutralize the normal reaction of dismissing the importance of others' communications by attempting to understand the priority of the message from their point of view. This is the listening equivalent of the Golden Rule, "Listen to others as you would want them to listen to you."

Prepare yourself by saying:

"She obviously places a greater value on this than I do. If I were in her shoes, this would have much greater importance and I would certainly want others to listen to me with great intensity. I'm going to listen to her as I would want someone to listen to me."

This is an example of empathetic or partnered listening. You actively shift your focus to validating the perspective of the messenger. While the message itself may be of low importance or priority to you, you realize your responsibility in supporting the deliverer of the message. This technique develops a greater connection between you and your communication partners. If you limit yourself to judging the importance of communications by your own criteria, not only do you dismiss the information, you deny others the value of your input, which they are obviously seeking. Be wary of becoming the antithesis of the empathetic listener, i.e., rooted in selfishness and only willing to listen when self-interest is high.

Manage Your Emotions.   To be an effective listener, you must learn to distance yourself from impulsive, negative emotional responses. STPs who are effective listeners develop the ability to choose their preferred reaction and do not allow themselves to be provoked by either intentional or unintentional messages from their communication partners. If others are intentionally trying to provoke you and you respond with a negative emotional reaction, you allow them to be victorious. Your quick negative reaction may be your communication partners' most effective weapon. The best way to exercise your internal control is once again to manage your internal dialogue.

Manage your emotions by saying to yourself:

"I'm not going to allow him to control me."
"I'm not going to give in to her by allowing my emotions to show."
"I'm not going to react negatively; that's probably what he wants me
   to do."
"Her *you*-messages are not going to get the best of me."

This is especially helpful if your communication partner is using aggressive *you*-based messages, which as we learned increase negative reaction and reduce listening efforts. Whether they use these aggressive messages intentionally or not does not matter—the impact is always the same. You are as vulnerable to the aggressive messages of others as they are to yours.

Always keep in mind, there is no statute of limitations on negative reactions. Once you have heard the message and have taken the time to process it thoughtfully, you can always react later if a negative response is appropriate. You have the option of going back and saying:

> "I thought about the discussion we had this morning and I really don't agree with the conclusions. Here's why . . . "
> "I've thought about the discussion we had last Thursday and I find I'm not handling it very well. I'd like to talk further."

SPEC

When you feel yourself starting to react negatively, assert internal control and do not allow yourself to be victimized by their provocation.

You can address negative emotions anytime you choose. Taking the time to process a communication and choosing your reaction ensures that you maintain control and stay focused on the content of the message and avoid becoming embroiled in the sideshow of emotion.

If you find that certain people push your emotional communication buttons regularly, you have taught them how. By consistently reacting to aggressive or provocative messages, they have learned exactly what to say or do to create a negative reaction within you. Provocation can be a very effective weapon in the communication process, especially when a person is uncomfortable with a communication or finds that your thoughts, ideas, and conclusions are preferred by supervisors and peers over theirs. Rather than acknowledging your points, they choose to alter the course of the conversation by provoking a negative response in you, which conveniently deflects attention from the content. When you respond with negative emotion, they blame you for any miscommunication or communication breakdown. You may be their unwitting accomplice allowing them to push your button, by failing to manage your emotions and responses internally.

Managing your internal emotion is also very important when receiving information in meetings, even though you may be having a very strong negative response. A public display of your negative emotional response is generally unwise. Try to delay your response and then let go in private, alone or with a trusted friend, not a coworker. This will usually be more beneficial in the long run.

SPEC

Other people will actually take your re-action more seriously when they realize you have taken the time to thoughtfully process their message.

A Note on Written Communication.   Messages received in writing—memos, e-mails, formal documents—can also be provocative. This may or may not be the intent of the deliverer. It is an effective strategy to delay any response until your negative emotions subside and you have the opportunity to seek further clarification. There are many reasons why communications do not always mean what they appear to mean at first reading. Firing off inflammatory responses without managing your internal emotions not only compounds communication problems, it can do long-term damage to your career! Memo or e-mail wars can escalate to unnecessary levels of intensity, and can result in the high cost of breached relationships and disrupted productivity. When you are responding to e-mails in which you have some level of emotional involvement in the communication, your best friend is the "Send Later" option.

Step 4. Assume a Listening Posture.

In addition to managing the physical environment, you must also manage and communicate your own physical readiness to listen. The visual demonstration of your readiness to listen—or the lack of it—has a significant influence on your communication partner. The nonverbal messages you send can encourage, inhibit, or perhaps even intimidate them. Body language is just as important a factor in receiving messages as it is in effectively delivering communication. You can alter a person's message and create incomplete, abandoned, or distorted communication by means of your nonverbal reception.

Body language that conveys readiness to listen includes the following:

- Establish and maintain appropriate eye contact. Effective listeners maintain eye contact with their communication partner 90 to 95 percent of the time.
- Avoid staring at fixed objects or off into space.

- Limit your field of vision. Avoid letting your eyes dart around or looking beyond your communication partner.
- Keep your eyes alert and interested, not projecting a dazed or confused state.
- Lean slightly toward your communication partner, when you are both standing and sitting.
- Maintain an open posture. Avoid crossing your arms and legs, slumping your shoulders, or assuming the "flamingo position"— perched precariously on one leg
- Don't fidget or present the speaker with other distractions.

SPEC

Avoid making yourself too comfortable in communication circumstances. Increased comfort can give the appearance of decreased listening.

Slouching, propping your elbows on the table, resting your head in your hand, letting your chin drop to your chest, etc., all decrease your listening effectiveness. Listening takes self-discipline, and maintaining an alert physical posture is a part of it.

Show that You Are Listening by Giving Verbal Affirmations. Affirmations may take the form of utterances and include appropriate "Ah-ha's" for important points, as well as affirming statements such as, "That's interesting," "I see," "Oh," "Uh-huh," "Yeah," "Good," etc. These affirmations are tangible proof to your communication partners that you are listening and are engaged in what they have to say. They are verbal demonstrations that you are connected to the message.

Your verbal and nonverbal listening responses can either increase or decrease the self-esteem and confidence of your communication partners. They encourage or discourage them to communicate with you more honestly and completely. Any tangible signs of intimidation, disinterest, or negative judgment on your part inhibit both the effectiveness of their delivery as well as the volume and quality of the information they present. You may never know the importance of what they did not say. By the time you discover any incomplete or withheld information, complications may have begun to occur.

If you find yourself being left out of the loop or always being the last to know, it may be because people are hesitant or uncomfortable in providing you with information. Shooting the messenger can be a nonverbal action! It is in your best interest to avoid miscommunications and future problems by encouraging others to communicate as effectively as possible. You do not want to do anything that causes them to hesitate or fail to share all of their relevant information with you.

Step 5. Participate Actively in Listening.

The six actions listed below are perhaps the most powerful strategies of all for making you a more effective listener.

Take notes.
Ask appropriate questions.
Prevent yourself from talking.
Summarize internally.
Seek and acknowledge areas of agreement.
Summarize and restate.

Take Notes.   Actively take notes when others are delivering a message. Always ask their permission and tell them why you want to write down the key points of their message.

Begin the note taking process by saying:

"This is important information and I want to be sure that I am
   listening effectively. Do you mind if I take some notes?"
or
"I am really interested in what you have to say and I would like to
   take some notes to be sure I get it right. Is that okay with you?"

If someone objects to your taking notes, obviously honor their wishes.

When you take appropriate notes, you will not only encourage yourself to pay closer attention, you will also have a written summary of the communication, which could have great value for you. Rarely will others object to your taking notes on what they have said, and if they do, it is generally a sign they are not confident about what they are saying.

These are your notes to yourself and you can write them as an outline and use any codes, abbreviations, or shorthand notations you please. They should not be a laborious task. They are for your use only, and no one else will see them. Note taking augments the communication; it does not dominate or detract from it.

As long as your communication partners understand why you are taking notes and what you are trying to accomplish, they are going to be both appreciative and supportive of your efforts. Your dedication clearly communicates the high value you place on them and their message.

SPEC

Taking notes helps you to stay focused on the conversation and should not detract from the communication process.

Be wary of the pitfalls of taking notes:

Do not assume the role of a court stenographer, writing down word for word everything that is said.

If you pay too much attention to writing notes, you will not maintain eye contact and will disconnect from your communication partner. Do not let your focus become the accurate recording of the words instead of the accurate comprehension of the message.

Avoid the temptation to begin doodling or absent-mindedly fidgeting with your pen or pencil.

Doodling or fidgeting indicates your apparent distraction, boredom, and lack of concentration on what is being said.

Some STPs find that keeping their hands busy by doodling or absent-mindedly making marks on a piece of paper actually *increases* their ability to concentrate and contributes to their accurate reception of communication. If this is true for you, be absolutely sure you explain this to your communication partner. For example: "I'm going to be taking some notes and you might see me drawing shapes or doodling on the pad. Please don't be distracted by that. I find that I actually pay better attention if I give my hands something to do."

Taking notes during telephone calls is also a very powerful listening technique. You may become easily distracted or bored when talking on the telephone and may try to do several other things at the same time. Perhaps you simultaneously work on the computer, continue writing, or review documents or data while trying to maintain telephone conversations. This can almost always be discerned and sends a very obvious negative message to the person on the other end of the phone. They realize you are lagging behind in the conversation and assume you are uninterested. This is disrespectful and conveys a message of very low value or importance. If your communication partner says things like "Hello . . . are you still there?," you have clearly communicated your lack of focus on their message.

When your telephone rings, consider the strategy of picking up a pen and paper before you answer the phone. When you do pick it up, let the person on the phone know you are taking notes: "I want to be sure that I capture all of the information that you are telling me. I'm going to be taking some notes to be sure I get it right. If I'm a second or two behind you in the conversation, I just want you to know why."

Callers quickly realize that you value what they are saying and interpret any conversation delay on your part positively because they know you are taking the time to write down what they say. You will find that in their quest to be helpful, callers will talk slower and louder. They want to help you get it right! People like it when you think what they are saying is important enough to write down.

Ask Appropriate Questions.   Questioning can be a very effective listening technique. It helps you keep your communication partners focused on their topic if they should begin to wander and it helps clarify your perceptions of their message. If you are unclear on something that has been said, seek immediate clarification to avoid compounding any misunderstandings. Exercise extreme caution to make sure that your questions are perceived as positive inquiry and are not misunderstood as challenges to the speaker's competence or authority.

Increase your listening and decrease miscommunication by prefacing your questions with a phrase or statement that communicates your desire for clarification, not argument.

"Let me be sure I understand this correctly. Did you say . . . or . . . ?"
"As a point of clarification, did you say . . . ?"
"I'm not sure I understood. Was your point . . . or . . . ?"

Asking appropriate questions can also help your communication partner overcome her poor delivery skills by breaking up her monotone or redirecting her ineffective delivery style. Your focused questions can help them deliver a more concise, effective communication.

There are four types of good-listening questions:

Closed-ended questions
Open-ended questions
Duplicate questions
Hypothetical questions

Closed-Ended Questions.   Closed-ended questions are intended to evoke a one- or two-word response, usually "Yes" or "No," or a specific point of information. Here are some examples:

"Did you say you agree or disagree with the conclusion?"
"Were the results seven or twenty-seven parts per million?"
"Do you see this as a positive or a negative development?"

Open-Ended Questions.   Open-ended questions are asked to elicit a less structured, more discursive response, or a detailed narrative. Open-ended questions are very effective in helping people expand their communication. They also provide more complete information on specific points. Typical open questions ask for opinions, recommendations, or explanations, or can be invitations to provide more information.

"How would/did you handle . . . ?"
"Tell me more about that."
"How would you deal with . . . ?"
"Please cite some examples of . . . "
"If you could, what would you do differently?"

Duplicate Questions.   Duplicate questions ask for the same information two or more times in different ways. They are usually most effective when asked sometime after the first complete delivery of the information. This type of active listening questioning can be especially effective in verifying facts and bringing out inconsistencies.

"Earlier you outlined the actions you took. What steps or thought process did you go through to make that choice?"

"Tell me again the sequence of events."
"How can you be absolutely sure of your accuracy?"

Hypothetical Questions. Hypothetical questions ask what would happen in some hypothetical scenario. They usually begin with "What if . . . ?" or "Just suppose . . ." They are used to weigh different possible outcomes:

"What if everything goes exactly as scheduled? What will the positive outcome be?"
"What if all of the conclusions are accurate? How soon can we verify them and begin the next step?"
"Just suppose we cannot get the support from management that we need. What would we do in that circumstance?"
"Just suppose time wasn't an issue here. Could we meet the customer's quality expectations?"

To be an effective listening technique, questions must be posed clearly and concisely, and then you must *stop talking*. Allow your communication partner to respond to your question.

SPEC

Avoid the deadly questioning trap of answering or responding to your own questions.

Unfortunately, many scientific and technical professionals misuse this active listening technique by posing a question and then answering it themselves. This results in their taking over the conversation and shutting their communication partner down. It's just another way of not listening and continuing to talk. For example: "Let me be sure I understood. Did you say the results were seven hundred parts per million or seven thousand parts per million? If the results were seven hundred, I don't think that's accurate. I would be happy to support a finding of seven thousand, yet if the results said seven hundred, I think we need to go back and retest. If we took action on a faulty test reading . . . *blah, blah, blah* . . . that happened a few years ago . . . *blah, blah, blah* . . . I can't tell you all the problems it caused . . . *blah, blah, blah,* . . . did I ever tell you what happened where I used to work? . . . *blah, blah, blah* . . . which reading was it, I forgot what you said?"

Prevent Yourself from Talking.   Since the tendency is to want to control communications by doing most of the talking, it can be very helpful to do something specific to inhibit your ability to begin talking or blurt out a premature response. Here is an excellent technique that can be one of the most powerful listening tools ever conceived by mankind.

SPEC

Point your index finger in the air, bend it downward at the second knuckle, and stick it in your mouth!

When it is appropriate for you to listen rather than to talk, this technique makes it more difficult for you to impulsively blunder into the conversation. Before you can talk, you have to hesitate at least long enough to take your finger out of your mouth, and perhaps at that point, you will regain momentary control. You may feel self-conscious about looking silly with your finger in your mouth, but in fact, your communication partners *don't care* if you look silly as long as you are truly listening to them. Although you may walk away from conversations with tooth marks in your knuckle or blood dripping from your finger, you will be able to take satisfaction in the fact that you truly listened and allowed the other person to share his information without interruption.

Some people choose to put a pen in their mouth or the ear frame of their glasses. It really doesn't matter. The whole point is to make it a little more difficult to impulsively begin talking when listening is appropriate.

Summarize Internally.   You can form a diagram in your mind just as if you were drawing a schematic on paper of the most important issues and all the supporting related points. You can begin to identify the end of one train of thought and the beginning of the next by analyzing and categorizing the information your communication partner is presenting.

When you are engaged in an important listening opportunity, continually ask yourself the following questions:

What are the three most important points she has made?
Are there several issues that should be discussed separately?
What data or measurement could we develop to clarify some of these issues?
What are the strongest and weakest points in his presentation?

This internal summarizing process helps you stay engaged in the message without making any verbal interruptions. You are actively summarizing, cataloging, and analyzing their message, and this active participation in the message controls or defeats any tendency to lose your concentration.

Seek and Acknowledge Areas of Agreement.   It is important to identify and acknowledge all areas of commonality, consistency, and agreement be-

SPEC

As you are listening, silently summarize in your mind the salient points of the communication.

tween you and your communication partner. Give him positive credit. Keep score mentally by identifying his valid points, areas where you share a common viewpoint, along with the areas of disagreement. Allow yourself to take in the total message and not zero in on areas of disagreement. Do not interrupt your partner by fastening on each individual point as it surfaces. There will be more points of agreement than points of contention.

After you have listened to your communication partner's message and you are beginning your response, use the following kind of language: "It's obvious that we agree on a number of things, especially X, Y, and Z [list three specific points of agreement as concisely as possible], *and* [not *but* or *however*] there are a couple of points that I think we need to discuss further. They are . . . "

SPEC

Hear the entire message and acknowl-edge the points of agreement.

This strategy allows you to gain momentum by acknowledging the areas of agreement and then positions you to discuss points of contention in a positive, nonthreatening manner. When you commit yourself to identifying and focusing on the points of agreement with the same intensity as you do the points of contention, you will become a more balanced listener. Your balanced response will also work against having negative emotions to overcome.

Do not rely on your communication partner's invitation to summarize and restate. She may not possess the communication skills necessary to seek your input and you cannot allow her lack of skill to cause any miscommunication.

SPEC

Proactively offer your summarization and restatement.

Summarize and Restate.   Just as it is vitally important for you to seek a summary of your message from the people with whom you are communicating, it is equally important for you to summarize when you are on the receiving end of someone else's message.

Summarizing and restating your perception of the communication accomplishes three things:

1. You offer concrete proof of your listening efforts.
2. You prove your willingness and motivation to understand the message.
3. You verify the accuracy of your comprehension.

If you summarize and restate accurately, your communication partners will give you a simple affirmative response, such as "Yes, that's what I said" or "Yes, that's an accurate summary of my points."

If you summarize and restate inaccurately, it gives them the opportunity to correct any misunderstandings.

SPEC

 *This is not about how much you already know, it is about how much you accurately comprehend of what they said.*

Your summarization and restatement should be reformulated in your words, not theirs. The aim is to verify your comprehension, not your ability to repeat words and phrases. Your word selection should be appropriate both to communicate your understanding and to match their level of knowledge. Do not lapse into jargon, acronyms, or complex terms just to demonstrate your depth of knowledge of the subject.

It is of critical importance to summarize and restate assertively, not aggressively. This is the appropriate kind of statement:

"Let me be sure *I* understand accurately. This is what *I* heard . . . "
or
"Let me be sure that *I'm* listening effectively. Here's *my* summarization of the points that were made . . . "

Do not include the word *you* in your summary and restatement. Using the phrase "Here's what I heard *you* say" or "Here's what *you* said" implies that the responsibility for accurate communication is somehow shifted back to the deliverer of the message. It indicates that if there is a misunderstanding, it is rooted in what your communication partner said, not your listening or reception. If there is any point of inaccuracy in your summarization, the deliverer is going to have a very defensive response. The communication will then degenerate into "yes, you said it," "no, I didn't," "yes, you did," "no, I didn't." If there is one comma or inflection out of place, or a statement interpreted improperly, the summary becomes an argument rather than a good-faith attempt at clarification and correction.

After you have made an effective summary and restatement you can begin the next phase of your communication, confident that both parties have an understanding of the issues involved. Keep in mind once again: accurate comprehension does not equal agreement. You are not affirming that you agree with the other person's positions; you are stating that you understand their message correctly.

Summarizing and restating has another valuable benefit. If others are delivering an emotional message containing anxiety, anger, resentment, or some other form of negativity, you will help reduce their emotion by summarizing and restating their message. The key is to listen, summarize, and restate the basic content of the message without mirroring back to them their emotion. When they deliver their message, they do so with passion. When you feed it back, they hear their message without the accompanying emotional content, and they themselves can focus more clearly on the content instead of giving way to their emotion. It is important to control your body language and tone of voice. Any sarcasm, condescension, or hint of negative judgment will only escalate their emotion. An effective restatement, devoid of any emotion on your part, will help your communication partner hear their message from a more balanced perspective.

Communication Assessment
  1. Can you identify three of the active listening techniques discussed above that you are currently using effectively?
  2. Can you identify three of the active listening techniques that you are currently not using? Do you believe they could be beneficial in increasing your listening effectiveness?
  3. Can you identify specific circumstances where your listening efforts are most challenged?
  4. Are there certain individuals with whom you maintain regular communication who represent more of a challenge to your listening ability than others? Why?

5. After considering the information in this chapter on impediments to effective listening and effective active listening techniques, would you respond differently to some of the questions in the listening assessment in Chapter 7? Try the test again and see whether your score is the same as your earlier score. Which questions do you answer differently now? Do you see any pattern in the different answers?

In subsequent chapters, we will discuss how you can apply your increased communication skills to communicating with customers, clients, and funding sources, as well as communicating in environments of change.

9

Dealing with Customers and Funding Sources

The triple challenges of dealing with internal and external customers and those who fund your programs and projects are treated collectively in this chapter. Why are they in the same chapter? Because the communication challenges are very similar. People in all three of these categories have expectations and standards that must ultimately be met by your performance. Their satisfaction, or lack thereof, determines both your current success and future opportunities. Communicating effectively with these three vital constituencies is becoming more important for STPs with each passing day.

People in all professions and functions are required to communicate with customers to some degree. In today's competitive marketplace, deficiencies in this area can spell economic disaster. Your technical superiority won't give you a competitive advantage unless it can be translated into value for the people who need it. This challenge is compounded for many people in the scientific and technical community because you are often dependent on other sources for the funding and resources for your work. These sources must be treated as customers and their needs and expectations met or their support and cooperation could be put at risk.

Internal customers are defined as any individuals, groups, departments, or teams within your organization that directly benefit from your efforts. They are those you serve within the organizational structure and those who support you in your service to others. They may be the next link or the preceding link in the process chain. It is important to maintain partnered relationships with all those who form your supplier/customer connections.

External customers are those outside your organization who directly receive the end results of your collective efforts. They may be customers, clients, patients, student members, constituents, taxpayer, etc., and they are the individuals or groups who benefit from what you do. They will either accept or reject the ultimate product or service you provide. With external customers, there is usually a monetary exchange. You provide a product or service for which they pay money.

Although not all scientific and technical professionals deal directly with external customers, your organization has some form of external customer whose needs must be satisfied. Every organization has some form of customer whose needs must be fulfilled for the organization to thrive. This is true whether the organization is in the private sector and provides products or services to end users or the public sector and serves taxpayers. In the healthcare industry the customers are patients; those in the education sector meet the needs and expectations of students and their families.

It is extremely important for you to stay focused on the significance and value of the external customer. The undeniable fact is that professionally you serve both the internal and external customers in your environment. If they did not need the products, services, and the results of your efforts, your position would not exist. If you do not consistently meet their needs individually and organizationally, your function becomes obsolete or inconsequential and you are ultimately replaced.

Funding sources are the individuals or groups that provide the resources for you to do your work. These sources may be internal or external to the organization and could include individuals, agencies, or foundations, as well as the internal financial gatekeepers who make budget decisions. These are the folks who provide funding for specific research or contractual projects and decide what portion of the operating budget will be dedicated to funding your work.

Without internal and external customers to serve, and without appropriate resources to fund activities, the important work of scientific and technical professionals grinds to a halt. No matter how important your work may be, if it does not provide value to someone else, and if no one is willing to fund it, it cannot continue unless you have access to significant personal resources. The bottom line is that we all have people we must keep happy. Effective communication is an important aspect of driving customer and funding-source satisfaction. For many in the scientific and technical community, their level of success and professional achievement will be determined by their ability to support their technical expertise with positive customer and funding-source relationships.

In your dealings with your internal and external customers and funding sources, it is important to remember that you are not only satisfying current needs; you must also always be focused on the next task, project, or contract.

CASE STUDY 5

Mack is a network consultant for an IT company specializing in systems for large law firms. His role is to analyze the existing systems and needs of current and prospective clients and make recommendations concerning the design and implementation of network configurations that will support the client's goals. It is imperative that Mack clearly understand not only the technical aspects of the system but also the total needs and expectations of his clients. Once he has the big picture, he is in a position to recommend the appropriate technical solutions to meet their objectives.

His recommendations must be structured to communicate effectively with everyone involved, from the network administrator to the office manager, and in some cases, even the law clerks. One of his biggest challenges is helping his clients communicate exactly what they want their network system to do and explain how their needs might change in the future. He says:

> Once I know what they want, I can design a network system that will work. The problem is that many clients are not always clear about what they want. Sometimes they aren't sure themselves, and even if they are, they don't always explain it very carefully. Everybody wants the system to have a DMJ (do my job) button and yet they aren't really good at telling me what that job or function actually involves. I have to ask a lot of questions, and if I can't get people to open up to me, it can be a real problem. If I start guessing, I might make recommendations that aren't right for that particular client.
>
> When I have gathered all of their information, I make my recommendations, and then I have to make sure the client has a realistic expectation of what the network system can do. Everyone wants the perfect system but they don't always want to pay for it, and

many times I have to tell them that the DMJ button doesn't really exist. If they don't clearly understand the system's true capabilities, we can have major problems later. Some clients are easier to work with than others.

Once the system is designed and is being installed, Mack must maintain ongoing communication with the clients to ensure that their needs are being met and must continually update them on the current progress. He says: "When we start the design and installation phases, all of a sudden everybody wants it done yesterday! And then halfway through the project, the client decides they want to make a major change and they don't see why it should impact either the time or cost."

He must also communicate effectively with his company's internal engineers, who understand the systems, and be certain they are meeting the agreements with the client. Mack's responsibilities aren't just technical; he must also excel at customer service if he and his company are to be successful.

Four Realities of Dealing with Customers and Funding Sources

Understanding these four realities will serve as the solid foundation upon which to build your communication efforts. They may challenge your current thinking and increase your awareness of previously unconsidered issues, or they may serve as reinforcement for your current activities. Regardless, these are realities you must deal with regularly.

1. Effective communication with customers and funding sources addresses the needs of today and becomes the foundation for continued activity in the future.

The ultimate goal for all STPs as it is for Mack is to consistently meet the standards and expectations of their customers and funding sources. If you do, you get to keep your job and continue your professional pursuits. Problems occur when there is a difference between your customers' expectations and you or your organization's actual performance. Though the client will often have predetermined standards and expectations, it is your role to make sure that you and the client have the same understanding of exactly what those expectations are, temper them with reality, and make sure they are unequivocally satisfied.

2. It is dangerous to assume that you already know what the customer wants or that the deliverables you provided in previous transactions will meet their current demands. Such assumptions can easily lead to dissatisfaction.

Customers' needs and expectations change. What was acceptable in an earlier transaction may not be acceptable now. Perhaps some of your competitors have increased their capabilities and the customers expect you to meet or exceed that new standard. It is also possible the customers' knowledge and awareness has increased and they have greater expectations of you now than in the past. Mack would be unwise to assume activities and levels of service that previously achieved customer satisfaction will continue to do so today. What made them happy yesterday won't necessarily make them happy today and tomorrow.

Exceptional listening skills are required to determine the customer's or funding source's expectations. In addition, you need the ability to communicate the level of product or service that can actually be provided. Unrealistic expectations must be corrected in the early stages of the project. The time to tell customers that something cannot be done is not at the midway or end point of the process. Your role is to find out what they want, assess your ability to provide it, and communicate what you can do to provide the level of products or services they expect.

3. Standards and expectations can vary dramatically from customer to customer and among various funding sources.

There is no guarantee that what makes one customer happy will meet everyone's expectations. Mack appears to understand the importance of discovering exactly what individual clients want their networking system to accomplish. What works for one law office may be ineffective for another.

4. You do not determine the success of the project—customers and funding sources do.

Always keep in mind that it is ultimately the customers' or funding sources' perceptions that determine whether or not their standards and expectations have been met. The funding sources' and customers' point of view drives the process. What you think doesn't matter; it is their opinion that matters.

This requires you not only to assess what you and your organization are capable of providing, it also calls upon you to communicate these expectations, standards, and commitments to others who may be supporting you in your efforts to provide satisfaction. Overpromising and not following through destroys critical customer and funding-source relationships. Promising them the moon and delivering a pizza erodes credibility, creates perceptions of dishonesty, and results in customers' and funding sources' pursuing other avenues.

Five Causes of Customer and Funding-Source Dissatisfaction

As we consider your challenges in communicating with customers and funding sources, let's first take a look at the typical causes of their dissatisfaction.

For STPs there are at least five communication-related factors that contribute to problems.

Unmet expectations
Perceived dishonesty
Resentment
Indifference
Internal problems caused by your actions

Usually these circumstances evolve unintentionally and go undetected until major problems occur. Communication breakdowns contribute significantly to these negative outcomes.

1. Unmet Expectations

This is probably the most common cause of dissatisfaction. The customer or funding source was expecting something—a specific product or service, expected information flow, or a level of personal treatment—that in their view was not provided.

Three crucial communication skills are necessary to avoid the problem of unmet expectations:

- Effective listening
- Restatement for accuracy
- Ongoing updates and summaries to the customer or funding source

You must ask the appropriate questions, listen effectively to their responses, restate their communications, and communicate clearly your capabilities. Restatement on both sides is necessary to ensure mutual understanding and agreement.

To avoid unmet expectations, Mack must gather in-depth information from his clients, including:

- The number of different functions the network will be expected to perform
- The type of electrical wiring in place and potential upgrade capability
- The current software being used and any anticipated future changes
- The client's accounting procedures
- The specific needs for e-mail, faxing, printing, and Internet usage
- The security demands
- The experience of the people using the system
- The vulnerability to computer viruses
- The use of floppy disks or network backup

These are just a few of the issues that must be identified and addressed to ensure that the client's expectations will be met.

Along with establishing specific expectations, the universal expectations shared by all customers never vary. You must always:

- Listen
- Pay attention to the details
- Take responsibility
- Remember it is their time and money
- Keep your agreements
- Treat them with courtesy and respect at all times

2. Perceived Dishonesty

This is an escalation of unmet expectations. If customers feel their expectations were not met unintentionally, they perceive you to be disorganized or incompetent. If they believe that you intentionally did not keep an agreement, they quickly begin to question the honesty of you or your organization. When customers and funding sources believe you conned them when you promised the moon while all along intending to deliver that pizza, they perceive you to be dishonest. They begin to feel victimized, convinced that you intentionally took advantage of them. If Mack's clients believe that he understood their expectations and promised they would be met when he really had no intention of following through, they assume he was dishonest. Relationships that have been breached owing to perceptions of dishonesty are extremely difficult to repair. Once a perception of dishonesty rears its ugly head, it is very difficult to overcome. Customers and funding sources frequently quote the old adage "Get me once, shame on you; get me twice, shame on me." They are forever vigilant and reluctant to be vulnerable in the future. Mistakes are forgiven; dishonesty is not.

It can become an ominous problem if your customers and funding sources have the opportunity to share their perceptions with others. Allegations can spread like wildfire, especially through a customer base, with potentially dire consequences.

SPEC

It does not matter whether you were intentionally dishonest or not. It is the perception that determines the customer's reality.

3. Resentment

Resentment is created when customers or funding sources perceive that:

They have been treated rudely or unfairly
You are not being responsive to their priorities
You are not being responsive to their issues of time, cost, and quality

Resentment is an emotional response that surfaces when customers and funding sources feel you are not treating them with the importance and respect they are due. If they feel you are more focused on yourself or other issues than on them, or you value other tasks or responsibilities more highly, you create resentment.

If you are not taking the time to listen or keep them informed, resentment escalates. When you tell customers how busy you are and describe the burden of all the work you have to do, they become resentful because they believe they have become a lower priority. Mack placed specific emphasis on the importance of communicating regularly with clients to assure them of his ongoing responsiveness to their needs and keep them updated on all current progress.

4. Indifference

Problems occur when customers and funding sources perceive they are being ignored or treated as if they do not matter. If they think they are just a number as opposed to someone who has great importance to you, they quickly become dissatisfied. Unreturned phone calls, being unresponsive to e-mails, memos, or faxes, and procrastinating on their requests of any kind contribute to this perception. Customers want to be treated as if they matter. They want personal attention. They want to be treated as if they were "custom-made in an off-the-rack world."

Customers experience your indifference when they are handed off from sales and marketing to technical support. When their business was being pursued, they received lots of attention. If there is any perception of diminished importance or lack of follow-up, they probably feel they are being treated with indifference.

Any communication or behavior of yours that contributes to making them feel as though they are just part of the herd results in a very negative perception. If you have ever waited to be seated in a half-empty restaurant while the employees stood around chatting, you have experienced a minor dose of being ignored or treated with indifference.

If customers believe your overall attitude is "It really doesn't matter if you do business with us or not; somebody else will," they are going to seek other options where they will be treated with greater value. If funding sources perceive that you already have what you want from them (their dollars), and your responsiveness and attentiveness to them have declined, they will find other places to apply their resources.

5. Your Actions or Inactions Cause Customers or Funding Sources to Experience Internal Problems

If those who depend upon you experience problems within their organization or department due to your inadequate performance, they perceive you to be more of a hindrance or liability than an asset. If they are embarrassed or are themselves held accountable because of something you have or have not done, they quickly determine that they do not really need you after all. If you do not deliver on time, fail to meet quality objectives, or unexpectedly and inappropriately raise costs, they are probably put in the position of having to defend these results internally. This creates a hassle for them and they may be held negatively accountable for your failure.

If those who have made a decision to do business with you or to provide resources or funding for your activities are made to look as though they made a bad decision, you are in serious trouble. If you want to create instant dissatisfaction, get someone in trouble with their boss.

SPEC

Always make customers or funding sources look good and never make them look bad.

Communication Assessment

1. When you or your organization experience dissatisfaction among your customers or funding sources, which of the five communication factors are most frequently involved?

   Unmet expectations? *yes* ☐   *no* ☐
   Perceived dishonesty? *yes* ☐   *no* ☐
   Resentment? *yes* ☐   *no* ☐
   Ignored/indifference? *yes* ☐   *no* ☐
   Creation of a hostile internal environment? *yes* ☐   *no* ☐

2. Which of these do you consider to be the most significant challenges for you and your organization?
3. Can you identify behaviors, policies, or internal procedures that may create these dissatisfactions with your customers or funding sources?
4. List three actions you are willing to take that will help you communicate more effectively and avoid creating or contributing to dissatisfaction.

   _____
   _____
   _____

The Critical Communication Areas

In addition to establishing mutually agreed upon expectations, there are four critical communication areas for STPs:

Information flow
Problem solving
Managing customer- or funding-driven change
Follow-up

Each area provides an opportunity to solidify relationships and reemphasize your value and responsiveness. These four areas also constitute the primary traps or potential weaknesses in transactions with customers or funding sources. Failing to communicate effectively in these circumstances leaves you vulnerable to criticism and the perception of unacceptable performance.

I. Information Flow

It is important for you to provide ongoing, timely updates, progress reports, and summaries. Transactions with customers and funding sources have numerous midcourse communication points in addition to the heavy communication demands at their beginnings and endings. Effective relationships are not built in a communication vacuum. Information must be provided on progress, achievements, and the review and reinforcement of expectations. To overcome customers' perceptions of being ignored or treated with indifference, it is important to create a consistent communication stream:

Tell them what you have already accomplished.
Summarize your current activities.
Advise them of what your next steps will be.
As you accomplish specific goals and meet and exceed their interim
    expectations, always make them aware of your progress.

Never assume that customers and funding sources have a clear picture of all of your efforts or that they are aware of your ongoing accomplishments.

SPEC

*"The expectation we agreed upon was
. . . That expectation has been met,
and here is the result . . . "*

They may not know when their expectations have been met. Even if they are, seize every opportunity to reinforce their understanding of your efforts on their behalf. In many instances, the only way Mack's customers will develop knowledge and awareness of his activities is if he takes the initiative to tell them. Repetition is a key to communicating this critical information. Assuming awareness can be a foolish and an unnecessary mistake. Providing consistent updates is always productive. Err on the side of providing too much information. If they feel you are overwhelming them, they will let you know.

SPEC

The most effective way to establish a communication stream is to negotiate initial customer and funding-source COPs (Communication Operating Procedures).

There are three crucial questions to ask customers and funding sources to establish effective COPs:

1. How often would you like me/us to provide updates and progress reports?
2. In what form would you like these updates and progress reports to be provided (in writing, verbally, face-to-face)?
3. How will you let me/us know if we're providing too much or too little information? (This is extremely important. It establishes an early warning system for potential problems.)

Mack would be well advised to address these three areas with every one of his clients. While it is becoming more common for STPs such as Mack to be involved in the initial establishment of expectations with customers and funding sources, the actual provision of critical updates and ongoing information is often assigned or delegated to others. You may find yourself not having direct involvement in the ongoing communication process, yet you will be responsible for keeping agreements that have been established. Increasingly you are being held accountable for the activity of others. If there is a breakdown or disruption, the customer or funding source considers it your responsibility and they expect you to react and initiate corrective action.

When you are in this situation, it is important to maintain constant awareness of ongoing progress as well as the quality of information that is being provided. This will undoubtedly require establishing internal COPs to ensure that you remain in the communication loop. If Mack is going to keep his clients properly informed, he must take responsibility for managing his own internal communication flow. Do not allow yourself to be put in a position of receiving a negative surprise concerning the transaction or information that was provided, or perhaps withheld, without your knowledge. Regardless of who is at fault, you will ultimately be held responsible for any damage control. Many times the root causes of poor information flow with customers and funding sources lies with internal communication problems within your own organization.

II. Problem Solving

Frequently, the responsibility for dealing with customer-service problems or providing damage control with funding sources is falling to you. More often, people are demanding to go directly to the source they feel can best solve their problem or address their issue. You are frequently that "go to" source because of your extensive knowledge base and expertise. The use of effective communication skills in providing customer service is rapidly becoming part of the job description for today's STPs. Tasks mishandled by others are brought to you so you can resolve the situation. Customer-service firefighting is becoming a common occurrence for STPs. In many cases, others have made promises that you are expected to keep! You are counted on to have a magic wand that will instantaneously make things right. Today's scientific and technical professionals are expected to be miracle workers in problem situations.

Guidelines for Dealing with Customer and Funding-Source Problems. While every problem is unique, there are a number of common actions and responses that will help in dealing with these circumstances.

The Relationship Is Primary. Always think in terms of the total value of the customer or funding source and the importance of maintaining positive relationships with them.

Do not just view them in terms of the current transaction. They have much greater value than just the circumstance of the moment. Failing to solve a current problem puts all future interactions at risk.

In reality, customers or funding sources are not always right. Even so, that does not change your responsibility to be responsive, address their needs, and create positive outcomes whenever humanly possible. Remember, right or wrong, they are still the critically important customer or funding source that is the basis for what you do professionally!

SPEC

Customers are not always right. Just remember they are always the customer!

Be Responsive. When problems occur, people want you to listen and hear what they have to say. If they are unhappy, they want you to know it and to acknowledge their perception. In many cases, listening intently and allowing them to vent or get their issues off their chest may be all that is necessary. It is not uncommon for customers to tell you that their only intention is to be sure that neither they nor anyone else *ever* has to experience this again. Though that may sound very high-minded and positively motivated, what they really want to do is vent their frustrations. Allow them to do so and give them great leeway in their communication. Do not interrupt and do not start offering responses and solutions until they have finished talking and are ready to listen and problem-solve.

Take Responsibility. When there is a problem, avoid blaming others or distancing yourself from responsibility. Customers and funding sources do not care whose fault it is; they only want the problem resolved. Statements such as "This really wasn't my fault" or "Our team didn't create this problem, it was really the fault of those people in another area" are self-serving and only inflame whoever is experiencing the problem. The customer is holding you accountable for fixing the problem and has no interest in your making yourself, your team, or your department look innocent or blameless. While you may have great interest and concern about who is at fault, the customer couldn't care less. Customers want responsiveness. Once problems have been resolved, it may be appropriate to accurately identify any trail of adverse responsibility. Think seriously about whether there is really anything to be gained by informing the customer or funding source of your internal problems.

Why the problem occurred is your issue. How it is resolved is your customer's issue!

SPEC

Problems are opportunities to create positive outcomes. They are not invitations to run for cover.

Do Not Trivialize the Problem. Your assessment of the importance of the customers' or funding sources' problems may be vastly different from theirs, yet do not show this. It is important to them; therefore it must be important to you. If you act as though you don't find their problems very important, you risk generating great resentment or at least perceptions of indifference. Customers may refuse to do business with you in the future, formal complaints may be lodged criticizing your personal performance, and future funding could be denied because of a perceived lack of understanding or responsiveness on your part.

SPEC

Few things escalate negative perception more intensely than giving customers or funding sources the impression that you are not taking them or their problems seriously.

Use assertive affirming statements in dealing with customer and funding-source problems.

"I understand there is a problem and I am anxious to solve it."
"I know how important this issue is and I will do everything I can to make sure it is quickly resolved."
"We know how important your business is to us and I will take responsibility for seeing that this is corrected."

These statements identify both your awareness of the issue or problem and your willingness to take responsibility for the customer's satisfaction.

SPEC

Always structure your communication to positively affirm what can be done on their behalf, and avoid any discussion of what cannot be done.

Avoid Negative Communication. When dealing with customers and funding sources, exercise great caution to avoid any implication that their requests, issues, or problems are in any way unreasonable. A negative message is often communicated unintentionally by STPs when they emphasize what *cannot* be done to address the problem.

Place great emphasis on what you *will* do. Avoid any statement of what you can or will *not* do.

"This is what I *can* do to solve the problem." *Not* "I/we *can't* do that."
"Our procedures *would allow* us to do this . . . " *Not* "Our policy will *not allow* us to do that."
"Our system *could* provide this information." *Not* "Our system *can't* provide that information."
"I think the *best way* to handle this is . . . " *Not* "The *only thing* we can do is . . . "

Your communication should not indicate that there are predetermined limitations on what you can or will do to address their problem. Even when such limitations do exist, the customer or funding source must perceive that you are doing everything possible to address their problem or concern. Help them to see that you are making the best possible recommendation, not the only possible recommendation! Focusing on what you cannot or will not do indicates unwillingness on your part to comply with requests they deem to be reasonable and appropriate. Customers perceive that you are capable of doing something, yet you are choosing not to do it. Once that perception is established, it is extremely difficult to change.

Another negative communication to avoid is any indication of unhappiness, loss of patience, or negative emotion on your part. Do not allow their problems to trigger a negative reaction on your part. Even if they are angry or upset, do not match their emotion with a similar response of your own.

Never communicate any personal negativity. The customer or funding source does not really care if you are having a bad day. If you are unhappy with your job, in conflict with your boss, or resentful of how you are being treated by your organization, you should never share that information. Regardless of the quality of your relationship with your customer or funding source, he is not your buddy or confidant and should not be the recipient of either personal or organizational negative "inside" information.

One scientific and technical unprofessional (STUP!) was overheard telling a customer, "You are the fourth person to call about this same problem just this morning. We have really been screwing up. You should have heard the last guy, he was really angry." That would *not* qualify as effective customer communication.

SPEC

You cannot treat every problem or request the same.

Respond Appropriately. Become a situational communicator, making sure that your response is appropriate to both the content and emotion of each individual circumstance. A response that is appropriate in one circumstance may actually be ineffective or contribute to negative emotional escalation in another.

Tailor your response to the emotion expressed by the funding source.

If she is *angry,* communicate *concern.*

If he is overburdened, communicate *empathy* (not sympathy).

If it is an emergency situation, communicate *urgency* and *sensitivity* to quick response.

Communication Models for Problem Solving and Dealing with Anger.
Here is a specific communication model that summarizes many of the previous guidelines.

Customer-Service Problems

1. Acknowledge empathy and responsibility.

"I understand this needs to be addressed and I am anxious to help. I will take responsibility for being sure we deal with this appropriately."

2. Initiate positive inquiry.

"Help me understand what happened" or *"Help me understand how I can help you"* or *"Help me understand what you need."*

3. Restate their response.

"Let me be sure I understand this accurately. The issue/problem is . . . "

4. Seek a partnered solution.

"What would be the best way to handle this?" or *"What would you like us to do?"* or *"How do you think this could best be handled?"*

5. Confirm your commitment.

"This is what I will do . . . " or *"This is what will happen . . . "*

6. Conclusive postproblem follow-up.

"We had agreed that . . . would happen, and I'm following up to make sure that it was done" or *"We took the action that we agreed upon and I wanted to follow-up to make sure it was satisfactory"* or *"I perceive the problem was solved and I want to follow-up to be sure that you are in agreement."*

Postproblem follow-up is extremely important to ensure that the customer or funding source is satisfied with the outcome. Never assume that the action you have taken has been totally successful. Initiate a follow-up contact within forty-eight hours of the problem's resolution to make sure they are satisfied. If they are, it gives them the opportunity to recognize your responsiveness, competence, and willingness to address their issues. If they are not satisfied, your timely follow-up identifies their continuing unhappiness quickly and gives you another opportunity to respond before their situation is exacerbated by perceptions of failure or inactivity. Customers or funding sources left to seethe become much more difficult to satisfy.

Dealing with Angry Customers

When you find yourself dealing with customers who are angry or emotionally upset, implement this effective communication model.

1. Maintain your control. Do not respond in kind. Their anger will only escalate if you feed it with your negative response.

2. Allow customers to vent their emotions. Listen, never interrupt, and do not respond or offer alternatives until all of their story has been told.

3. Diffuse the emotions. Acknowledge the validity of the customers' reactions. (You are not telling them they are right, you are telling them they have a right to feel that way.)

"I understand why you are angry" or *"I realize this has been difficult."*

4. Restate their message factually and accurately without duplicating their emotion.

As previously discussed, restating is an excellent technique for calming emotions. They hear the facts restated without the impact of the emotion and the problem does not sound as important or complex.

5. State your concern and willingness. Build a bridge of empathy with statements such as these: *"I know this is not acceptable and I want to be sure you are happy"* or *"I realize this has caused a problem and I want to correct it as quickly as possible."*

6. Seek agreed-upon solutions. Clearly identify the problem separate from the emotion. *"The problem appears to be . . . "*

Discover their preferred solution. *"What would work best for you?"*

Partner with them to collectively work to solve the problem. You are not the problem; you are their collaborative partner in seeking a solution.

Identify the best response satisfying all concerned. *"This appears to be the best solution for everyone."*

III. Managing Customer or Funding Source–Driven Change

One of the ongoing frustrations for scientific and technical professionals in dealing with customers and funding sources is that changes frequently occur. These changes may include additional requirements for products or services, deadline shifts, design alterations, or variations in reporting. Just when you think the rules have been established, customers or funding sources change the rules and their expectations become different. They are not concerned with the disruption their changes cause and they expect you to demonstrate flexibility in meeting their newly defined needs. Customers and funding sources do not want to hear about your frustration or how their changes cause a hassle to you or your organization. All they care about is seeing their changes implemented.

To communicate effectively in the face of these changes:

Discover what customers need.
Identify tradeoffs.
Offer additional options.

SPEC

Always expect customers and funding sources to change their minds, needs, and expectations.

Discover What Customers Really Need.   Customers often say they want one thing, while they actually need something else, and you must discover what they really need, not go on what they say they want. The key is to help them identify their desired outcomes. There may be many different options, each having varying degrees of impact on time, cost, and quality that could be considered in attempting to achieve a specific outcome. However, if the customer or funding source just tells you what they want you to do without identifying what it is they want to accomplish, they are often limiting the available options. This escalates frustrations and does not result in providing what they actually need.

Mack cannot design the appropriate system for his clients if he does not completely understand what outcomes the customer needs to achieve. Poor communication in these circumstances often results in a distortion of roles. Customers or funding sources turn to you and professionals like Mack because of your expertise and ability to provide products, services, or information they cannot provide for themselves. When their proposed changes limit your available options, the usefulness of your expertise becomes limited or negated. You are unable to do your job and will ultimately be held responsible when they are unhappy with the result.

Communicate effectively and help customers and funding sources discover their actual needs and desired outcomes. When they say, "Here is a change I want to make" or "This is what I want you to do," respond with phrases such as these:

"Tell me what it is you would like to accomplish with this change."
"Help me understand what you want to accomplish and maybe we can find an alternative that will reduce cost/save time/enhance quality."
"If I have a clear understanding of what we want to accomplish, we may identify additional options."

Identify Tradeoffs.   For every change there is an opposite and often unequal reaction. All changes have some degree of impact on either cost, time, or quality. There is always a price to be paid. It is imperative for you to analyze and communicate the price exactly. Will the cost be increased by the change they want, and are they willing to absorb the higher cost? The change may cause time delays. Are they willing to wait? Is it realistic for them to do so? Will resource availability be affected? Does using additional resources to accommodate the change now mean those same resources may be unavailable later? Does adding or subtracting something at this point affect quality in other areas? Is the gain from the requested change worth the price that must be paid?

Some STPs have come to believe that making customers happy means doing everything they want without question. That is a dangerous misperception and results in dissatisfaction when the ultimate price is realized.

When customers and funding sources understand the results of their proposed changes, they can make informed decisions concerning the implementation. It is your responsibility to create this understanding. The more information you effectively communicate, the better their decisions. You will also find yourself having to deal with fewer changes when they have a more complete understanding of how changes impact on the project.

Offer Additional Options.   Once again, customers and funding sources rely on you for recommendations and options. You are the expert. You have the expertise and responsibility to help them understand the range of their options. Given your knowledge and experience, you undoubtedly have the greatest insight into the many alternative ways something can be accomplished. Help them stay focused on what outcomes they want to achieve and offer your input into how they can best be accomplished. If your customers and funding sources already knew the options, they wouldn't need you! Let them know the advantages and disadvantages for each option and guide them through the process of weighing pros and cons and eliminating weaker options to make the best decision.

IV. Follow-up

When you have completed a project, provided a product or service, concluded research, or accomplished any type of task on someone else's behalf, it is important to review the overall outcome from the customer's or funding source's perspective. There is always valuable information to be gathered and lessons to be learned by a thoughtful follow-up and reevaluation of the concluded project.

Post-transaction Conferences.   You can benefit tremendously from initiating post-transaction conferences with customers and funding sources when projects have been concluded. Such conferences demonstrate a high standard of professionalism, offer a significant opportunity to learn from the experience, and positively influence the customer's desire to collaborate with you in the future. If you have provided products or services to customers, communicate with them to evaluate their perceptions of your performance and seek recommendations for increasing future satisfaction. When a specific project or task has been completed in accordance with a funding source's requirements, it is very beneficial to *initiate* inquiry to determine overall satisfaction and find out whether the customer perceives the investment as worthwhile. Make a point of trying to see the outcome from their point of view.

Post-transaction conferences should encompass three specific themes:

1. Things that went well. Identify the areas where customers were satisfied and identify specific needs that were met. Celebrate your successes!
2. Areas of concern or perceived unmet expectations. Find out what customers perceive to be areas of weakness or disappointment. Their perceptions are their reality, and it is critically important that you have an accurate understanding of their perceptions.
3. Recommendations for current or future changes or corrections. What would they recommend that you do differently? This gives you the opportunity to identify key elements that encourage them to maintain your relationship and gives you the benefit of their problem solving and creativity. Their recommendations can

become the basis for future activity. They will probably be willing to tell you what you can do to keep their business if only you take the initiative to ask.

SPEC

Post-transaction conferences are quality communication opportunities to emphasize the value and importance of the customer or funding source to you and your organization.

Post-transaction Conference Communication.   To make sure the three themes are discussed at the post-transaction conference, ask these three questions:

1. What did I (or we) do that met or exceeded your expectations? (Always start out with the positive.)
2. What did I (or we) do that fell short of meeting your expectations?
3. What should I (or we) consider doing differently next time? (Always end on discussions of the future.)

A post-transaction conference also provides a forum for a formal expression of appreciation for the customer's business or funding. Never ignore an opportunity to communicate their value and your gratitude. The customer will be much more open to pursuing future opportunities to collaborate with you.

Communication Assessment
1. On a scale of 1 to 10 (1 being very low; 10 being very high), how would you rate your effectiveness in providing timely updates, progress reports, and summaries to your customers and funding sources?

1____ ____ ____ ____ ____ ____ ____ ____ ____ ____10

2. Identify three specific improvements you are willing to make in providing more effective updates, progress reports, and summaries.

———————————
———————————
———————————

3. On a scale of 1 to 10 (1 being very low; 10 being very high), how would you rate your effectiveness in dealing with your customers and funding sources in problem situations?

1_____ _____ _____ _____ _____ _____ _____ _____ _____ _____10

4. In dealing with problems with your customers and funding sources, do you:

Always remember customers' total value and the importance of maintaining positive relationships? *yes* ☐ *no* ☐
Listen closely to their perceptions and observations? *yes* ☐ *no* ☐
Avoid blaming others or distancing yourself from any problem or responsibility? *yes* ☐ *no* ☐
Refrain from diminishing or dismissing the importance of the customers' problems? *yes* ☐ *no* ☐
Avoid communicating any negative messages? *yes* ☐ *no* ☐
Respond appropriately to their circumstances and emotions? *yes* ☐ *no* ☐
Deal effectively with angry customers? *yes* ☐ *no* ☐

Any *no*-responses indicate opportunities for growth and development.

5. On a scale of 1 to 10 (1 being very low; 10 being very high), how would you rate your effectiveness in dealing with changes generated by your customers and funding sources?

1_____ _____ _____ _____ _____ _____ _____ _____ _____ _____10

6. In dealing with changes requested by customers and funding sources, are you:
Surprised when frequent and significant changes occur?
yes ☐ *no* ☐
Focused on what they say they want versus what they really need?
yes ☐ *no* ☐
Hesitant to identify the costs or tradeoffs involved in changes?
yes ☐ *no* ☐
Guilty of not identifying additional options? *yes* ☐ *no* ☐

Any *yes*-responses offer opportunities for growth and development.

7. On a scale of 1 to 10 (1 being very low; 10 being very high), how would you rate your effectiveness in conducting post-transaction conferences?

1____ ____ ____ ____ ____ ____ ____ ____ ____ ____10

10

Communicating Effectively in Environments of Change

It is not unusual for scientific and technical professionals to serve as the driving force behind organizational change. The quest to expand technological capabilities and to increase knowledge leads to the ongoing recommendation and implementation of new ideas and processes. You are frequently at the forefront of establishing the standards of change and guiding others successfully through the process by your leadership and example.

Invariably, you also find yourself struggling to deal with some of the change initiatives imposed upon you by others. As change-oriented as you and most STPs are, there are times when you experience significant resistance to the change process. Because of this dichotomy of being on both ends of change—both driving and being driven by it—communicating effectively in environments of significant change is a growing challenge for all STPs. It is one filled with the highs and lows of exhilarating achievements and disheartening frustration.

CASE STUDY 6

Shirley is an analyst with an environmental laboratory. She is a specialist in semi-volatile testing. She conducts extensive tests and analysis on soil samples, primarily for consultants whose clients are considering purchasing property for commercial or manufacturing use. Her tests determine the presence of materials such as pesticides, PCB content, herbicides, and polynuclear aromatic hydrocarbons. The results of her work have significant influence on the actual sale of the property, qualification for various required permits and certifications, as well as negotiations concerning who will be responsible for the cost of any necessary environmental cleanup.

Her company has recently experienced tremendous growth. Through several acquisitions and an increase in overall business, Shirley is now required to conduct four times as many tests and analyses as she was eighteen months ago. She faces the following challenges:

The purchase of a new gas chromatograph (GC) is necessary to process the increased demand for sample testing within the company's time and quality requirements. Though her manager is in favor of acquiring the new equipment, he has many pressing needs at the moment and is not sure he can accommodate her request. Shirley must successfully communicate the importance and urgency of obtaining the new GC or she will begin to fall behind in her completing her work.

The project managers who submit most of the samples for testing on behalf of their clients understand her increased workload, yet they all continue to pressure her to complete their samples on a timely basis. Everyone believes that their work is most urgent and important and they all want Shirley to stop whatever she is doing and work on their requests NOW! She must communicate her true workload and establish realistic timelines.

When Shirley requests help from some of her peers, she is frequently frustrated by their lack of support. They are all facing their own increased workloads, and naturally they place much higher priority on their own responsibilities.

Temporary analysts are being hired to assist Shirley, and though they are all qualified, she must help train them on company policies and procedures and monitor the quality of their work.

She is recommending some significant changes to streamline the company's testing procedures and has raised the controversial issue of eliminating a number of the less profitable and time-consuming tests they perform. Her manager supports most of her recommendations. The sales and marketing people disagree and are concerned that altering their test offerings in any way will result in unhappy customers and a loss of business.

How do you, Shirley, and other STPs communicate effectively in an environment of such tremendous change?

In fact, there are really only two types of change:

* Change that is chosen—which we welcome
* Change that is imposed—over which we have little or no control [1]

Shirley is obviously dealing with both types of change, and you face them on a never-ending day-to-day basis.

With elected change:

* You choose to pursue the challenge of finding a new and better way.
* You choose to challenge the assumptions of yesterday and today.
* You choose to expand the knowledge of tomorrow.
* You choose to increase the capability of the science and technology that you influence.

This type of change—chosen change—is very exciting and professionally stimulating and is usually pursued with great enthusiasm and tenacity. When individuals or groups choose change, they feel no resistance. Quite the contrary, they feel resistance toward remaining the same and not changing.

You also deal with imposed change. The issues involving this type of change include:

* Reorganization, downsizing, rightsizing
* Budget cuts, restraints, limitations
* Ownership changes, mergers, acquisitions
* Leadership changes
* Relocations
* Shifts in a business's priorities (replacement of today's hot area of research, growth, and development by tomorrow's new program, product development, or compelling need)
* Explosive growth

To be highly successful in today's workplace, you must learn to communicate effectively in both change environments. The increase in business and the escalating workload are changes that are being imposed upon Shirley. She has not influenced it, did not invite it, and she may have preferred to have her circumstances remain as they were before. Being very competent and taking her professional responsibilities seriously, she is choosing to identify and recommend new strategies, actions, and procedures to meet the reality of her redefined challenges. In doing so, she is attempting to impose additional change on others. Her situation is very familiar to you and to most people in the scientific and technical community: becoming a catalyst for change, having to implement change, even when you may not be in total agreement with it yourself, and dealing with resistance in yourself and others.

There are two significant categories of issues involved with any change circumstance. In any change there are elements of pain. There are issues of remorse: having to give something up or have something taken away. The opposite also exists: perceptions of opportunity and potential great gain: "In any change circumstance, there are always two compelling, inevitable issues: what we are giving up and what we perceive we are gaining. In change there is loss and gain; there is separation and attainment. The degree to which we focus on either of these issues determines the extent of our resistance or acceptance to change. If we perceive what we are giving up is too valuable to us or the pain of separation is too great or the price too high, we resist change. If we believe what we are giving up is actually harmful to us or the expense is minimal, compared to the good to be achieved, we embrace or pursue change. Avoiding pain can be a very motivating reason to accept change.

We will use Shirley's situation as a basis to discuss the role of communication in both the elected-change and imposed-change circumstances.

Communicating Effectively When You Are Driving the Change Process

When change is chosen, the focus is usually on what is to be gained. The positive outcomes are identified, including the payoffs for. . .

. . . individuals
. . . funding sources
. . . the overall organization
. . . society as a whole
. . . customers

Shirley believes the changes she is recommending will have positive results. The purchase of new equipment will allow her to continue to produce accurate test results in a time frame that meets the needs of both her internal and external customers. This increased capability will reduce the need to hire additional analysts, saving the costs inherent with adding people. Streamlining testing procedures will result in greater efficiency and lower costs and will actually increase her overall testing capabilities. Eliminating some tests will also reduce costs and provide more time to focus on the tests that make up the bulk of the work the company does for its customers.

Though she has clearly identified all of the things to be gained by initiating her change recommendations, Shirley is finding that not everyone, including her boss, some peers, and people in other areas, share her enthusiasm or vision.

It is extremely frustrating when others do not share the same drive, dedication, enthusiasm, and motivation to pursue and accomplish change. You are probably surprised to find that some individuals and organizational groups do not share your positive perception of the change initiatives you are pursuing.

SPEC

Do not expect others always to share your positive outlook concerning the pursuit of change.

They will not! Such assumptions will only result in your disappointment and frustration and may trigger anger and resentment in you. This will only compound your problem of pursuing change.

Expect resistance. Do not let it blindside you! The important thing is to learn how to correctly deal with change resistance and not allow it to become a significant impediment.

There are three important communication challenges when you are championing and leading others through the change process, points were effective communication is of paramount importance:

1. The presentation of change
2. Communicating effectively with those resisting change
3. Actual implementation of change

1. The Presentation of Change

How you introduce your recommendations for change is very important. Good beginnings contribute to good endings. There are four critical elements in the effective presentation of change.

Announce the change early and often.
Communicate the vision.
Focus on the Future.
Communicate the consequences of not changing.

Shirley will be successful in accomplishing most of her changes if she addresses the four critical elements of the presentation of change. Each contributes to the likelihood of increased willing participation by others in the change initiatives.

1. Announce the Change Early and Often.   Give others as much notice as possible of impending change. When the change actually arrives, it should never be a surprise. Much of the resistance to change can be addressed in the anticipatory phase and significantly reduced before the change becomes reality.

Your announcement of change can be communicated with firm decisiveness:

"Here is what I am recommending we do beginning next quarter."

Or, you may use a tentative, thoughtful style:

"I am thinking of making these recommendations for our next project."

Either way, it gives others an appropriate notice that change is on the horizon.

Shirley should give her boss an early indication of her equipment purchase request, prior to actually submitting it, which allows him time to plan his expenditures. If her workload increase is cyclical or predictable, she may be able to let her peers know in advance of any potential requests for help. Notifying other departments prior to recommending or implementing changes ensures that new developments will not be a surprise.

2. Communicate the Vision.   If you want people to focus on the things to be gained by embracing and supporting your change efforts, they must clearly understand the gains. For them to focus on where you are going, they must understand your intended destination. Do not assume others will bring the same vision or perception to the change process that you do. You are electing the change, and are focused on the positive outcome. For others, it is imposed change and they are probably focused on what is being taken away from them or the pain involved in change.

A successful vision identifies both *what* you are going to do and *why* you are doing it. Obviously, you must have a clear understanding of your own vision before you can communicate it accurately to others. You cannot lead others through change if you do not understand it yourself.

Through her communication, Shirley must communicate her intent, motivation, and what she hopes to accomplish by implementing the changes she is recommending. To say, "I want to buy a new gas chromatograph" is incomplete. It must be linked to a *why* statement: "because it will increase our testing capabilities and ensure that we continue to provide the excellent turnaround time our customers expect."

Even if the *why* seems crystal clear to you, others may not see it with the same clarity. If you do not effectively communicate *why* you are making or recommending change, others will assume you are acting in your own narrow, perhaps selfish, self-interest.

It is also necessary to link the *why* of change to the self-interest of others. People always act in their own perceived self-interest. If you help them to see that your imposed change will serve and support their interests, they will enthusiastically embrace your initiatives. Do not assume they understand how the change will impact them. You must communicate the benefits no matter how obvious and elementary they seem to you.

Streamlining testing procedures means fewer hassles in the department, perhaps more time to spend on additional projects, and satisfied customers who maintain a business partnership with the company and allow everyone to keep their jobs. Reducing costs means more money available for additional equipment or the funding of new projects or endeavors. Increased profits mean raises in salaries, increased bonus opportunities, and perhaps the hiring of more staff. (Some may see increased profit in a negative light . . . corporate greed, etc.) If costs are reduced and profits are increased, the stock price goes up!

Others must have a clear understanding of *what* it is that is to be accomplished and *why* it is important to them. Your communication of the vision of change should be flexible and vary in order to be appropriate to the background, experience, and motivation of the specific individuals or groups to whom you deliver your message. The vision you communicate to other STPs will be different than your message to people in other organizational functions. Different groups and individuals have different interests. The perceptions of change vary and your vision must be expressed accordingly. If other individuals or groups do not perceive the change you advise will somehow be beneficial to them, their responses will range from varying degrees of indifference to significant resistance.

SPEC

If there is no perceived payoff, there is no motivation to implement the change.

Vision is the initial motivator of change. Vision helps others to understand the ultimate rewards of embracing new ideas and processes. The clarity of your vision has immediate and lasting influence on whether people choose acceptance and implementation or resistance and rejection.

Your responsibility is to communicate to others the vision of change. You are not responsible and you have no actual control over whether they accept your vision. (Influence, yes—control, no.) They are not compelled to accept your vision or "buy in" to the change. All individuals control their own internal acceptance or rejection. You are not responsible for their agreement. You are responsible for their understanding and comprehension, even if they disagree with your explanation of *why*. The explanation must be crystal clear. Many times change is resisted because it appears to be driven by an impulsive, ill-considered reaction. Be sure others realize that your change has been well thought out and very carefully considered. An effective vision communicates that message clearly.

Vision must also be "preached" repeatedly. Change can be painful and frustrating, especially because you are asking people to give up past methods or thought processes with which they are very comfortable. You are requesting that they embrace something new and possibly take some degree of risk. You may be asking them to expose themselves to potential short-term failure as they practice and develop new methods and skills. Obviously they are not going to be as good initially at doing something new as they were at doing things by the tried and true methods of the past. If you want others to break through the restraints of the past and embrace a new direction, they must be repeatedly exposed to your vision.

Shirley cannot present her recommendations one time and expect others, including her boss and peers, to understand and enthusiastically support her ideas. The presentation of change and vision is an ongoing process.

SPEC

There are three keys to successfully communicating your vision: Repetition, Repetition, Repetition.

Attention spans are short in conditions of frustration or resistance. People must be continually reminded of the vision and positive reasons for change.

3. Focus on the Future.   The vision of change must be focused on the future. When communicating your vision of change to others, be sure the change is perceived to be addressing future needs and not past inefficiencies. The change cannot be seen as your criticism of how people have been doing it in the past. No matter what the realities of the past may be, people will resent your criticism. While most will acknowledge there is always room for improvement, all will want to be recognized, not criticized, for their past achievements. Any change initiative must be presented as a necessary response to the future, not an affront to the past. The change is necessary to meet the emerging challenges of today and tomorrow. Statements implying "You have been performing poorly and I want you to do better" will be resented and rejected with intense passion. Statements implying "We all have to do things differently because the challenges we are facing are changing dramatically. The thoughts, processes, and behaviors that have brought us to our current level of competency cannot take us to the next level. The external challenges we are facing are dramatically different" will have a much greater chance of being positively embraced.

Shirley must be sure to emphasize that the changes she is championing are necessary to meet the current and future needs of increased demand. As she and her peers are being asked to do more, it will be necessary to do things differently.

In your communication of change, take enough time to acknowledge and celebrate past achievements. Shirley's communication should include a statement such as this: "We have always done an excellent job of providing the accurate testing and analysis our customers need in the shortest time possible. None of our competitors come close to our performance. Because we have been so good, our reputation has led to huge increases in our business. If we are going to maintain our professional excellence in the face of our ever-increasing workload, we are going to have to do some things differently. Here is what I recommend . . . "

It is important for Shirley, and you, to avoid any statements of past negative judgment.

"I've always thought the way we were doing that procedure was wrong, and now I'm going to fix it."
"I have always been concerned about the accuracy of that test, and this is an opportunity to improve it."

Statements such as these are counterproductive because someone, or some group, has taken pride in how it was done in the past and will rally to defend both themselves and past practices. Even if your statements are accurate, you are picking an unnecessary fight. Stay focused on the future, not the past.

SPEC

Change is about today and tomorrow, it is not about yesterday. A successful presentation of change cannot be perceived to be an indictment or criticism of the past.

4. Communicate the Consequences.   In communicating the necessity of change to others, there must also be a clear understanding of the inherent consequences of failing to successfully implement the change. This does not imply issuing threats or innuendos of punishment or retaliation. This is not about threat; it is about reality. What will happen if we do not successfully embrace this change? You will not successfully implement change that is imposed on others unless you communicate to them that there are negative consequences for resistance or failed implementation. Without consequence, there is no change. You must communicate the potential consequences of resisting change:

SPEC

Consequences drive change implementation.

Will competitors develop processes and technology making yours less competitive?

Will the organization become obsolete, forcing layoffs, closures, or abandonment of specific markets?

Will other people successfully embrace the change, allowing them to overtake and replace those who do not?

Will funding be withheld or rerouted to other entities if we do not adapt to the new realities?

Consequences reduce resistance by identifying the individual or organizational price to be paid for stubbornly clinging to the status quo. What do you perceive the consequences would be if Shirley's recommended changes are not implemented?

2. Communicating Effectively with Those Resisting Change

Resistance to change is very normal, especially when it is inflicted or imposed on individuals or groups. Anticipate it and prepare for it. Realize that other people's focus is not on the future or the good to be gained by the change but rather on the pain involved. Others will dwell on what is being taken away, and how the change may impact them negatively.

The three primary root causes of this resistance to change are perceptions, real or imagined, of loss, fear, and unfairness.

Some typical issues of loss concern the erosion of. . .

... access
... stability
... dominance
... economic status
... expertise
... control

Some typical fears include:

... the unknown
... job elimination
... inability to maintain competence and performance
... pending personal obsolescence

Perceptions of unfairness lead to resentment, which can lead to anger and retaliation. People are resentful of. . .

... criticisms of their past
... increased workload
... failure of compensation to match increased demand
... lack of influence
... not being included in the change decisions or process alterations
... being ignored or treated with indifference

In Shirley's situation, the issues of resistance could include the following:

Her boss may fear escalating costs from the purchase of new equipment.
The boss could also be perceiving a decrease in budgetary dollars, leaving other priorities without funding.
The sales and marketing departments could perceive a loss or reduction in the scope of their test offerings and a fear that

customers will be forced to turn to competitors for their testing requirements.

Can you identify some of the issues of loss, fear, and unfairness that others may be perceiving in your change initiatives?

There are several ways to communicate effectively in the face of these issues of resistance:

Listen.
Acknowledge their issues and share information.
Involve others in deciding how change will take place.

Listen.   When you are leading others through the change process, be willing to listen to their perceived issues of loss, fear, and unfairness. Though you can probably anticipate and understand the general nature of their resistance, it is important that you allow them to voice their specific concerns. Once you have presented your vision explaining *what* and *why*, give them the opportunity to voice their thoughts and concerns. Your active listening skills will come into play. Even though you anticipate their responses, it is important to encourage them to articulate their perceptions. Being anticipatory allows you to preplan and consider how to respond to the issues of your boss, peers, and others in the organization, yet it does not mean that you can eliminate the step of listening to what others say.

The best way to encourage people to identify issues is to pose open-ended questions:

"I've explained what I perceive to be the advantages of the change. Do you see as possible downsides? What are they?"
"I'd like to hear your ideas on both the good and bad aspects of this change."
"How do you think this change will directly affect you?"
"I have given you my information. Tell me what you think."
"I would like to hear your thoughts."

Some people may be initially hesitant to share their thoughts. Be patient. There are always issues of loss, fear, and unfairness. Rest assured, they will be telling each other. You want to be sure they feel comfortable in telling you. You cannot deal with resistance of which you are unaware.

SPEC

There are always issues of loss, fear, and unfairness in the change process.

To Reduce Fear, Affirm Issues and Share Information.   You cannot lead people through significant change and focus them on the issues of the future until you break down the barriers of resistance. Encourage others to raise their issues so you can deal with them and move on. Ignored issues of resistance will only resurface with a vengeance.

Position yourself as an ally, not an adversary. Dismissing, belittling, or ignoring issues only drives entrenched resistance deeper and provides motivation for others to fight back by refusing to implement the change. Passive-aggressive behavior then escalates and your change initiatives can die a slow death. Acknowledging and affirming their issues demonstrates your willingness to see the changes from others' viewpoint as well as your own.

Affirmations include the following:

"I understand your viewpoint."
"I know this may be difficult."
"Your issues are very valid."

Acknowledging and affirming does not mean agreement!

The best way to reduce fear of change is to share as much information as possible. Fear thrives in a communication vacuum. Once again, when people do not understand something or information is withheld, they make it up for themselves. Consistently restating the vision of *what* we are doing and *why* we are doing it makes it less likely people will manufacture their own fear-dominated interpretations of why it is occurring. If the change is being driven by facts and figures or bottom-line financial considerations, share that information openly. Certainly you yourself are not always aware of all the relevant information, share what you can. Helping others to see the long-term advantages of change diminishes their fear.

It would be a good idea for Shirley to develop supporting data for her recommendations, perhaps identifying any erosion of actual turnaround times on testing, or actual costs in time and dollars of conducting obscure or unusual test requests. Any supporting information would be helpful.

Involve Others in Deciding How Change Will Take Place. Whenever possible, involve others in determining the methods of change, or *how* the change will be accomplished. When change is inflicted or imposed, and people have little or no choice in the matter, they feel powerless or victimized by the change. They see change as happening to them and feel helpless to deal with it. They certainly do not feel a part of the initiatives or connected to the process in any way. When you include them in discussions and decisions of *how* the change can best be accomplished, you reduce these perceptions of victimization. People tend to readily support change initiatives when they are part of the process. If you want them to have ownership, give them something to own!

Another advantage in getting input into *how* the change will be implemented is that people are brought into the process at their greatest level of expertise. Being very close to the situation and having ultimate responsibility for the outcome of change, the people involved usually have the most creative ideas of *how* it can be accomplished.

If you tell people *how* they must implement the change, they will be resentful and focus on the unfair aspects, and their resistance will escalate. If you involve them in decisions of how to bring about the change, it becomes partially their idea. They will think their ideas are brilliant! Involvement increases comfort and control.

SPEC

Including others in how-based decisions reduces the potential for negative resentment.

When you tell people how to do it, they actually have a stake in failure. If the change initiative fails, they get to say "I told you so," and they are probably in a position to increase the likelihood of failure. When you involve people in how to do it, they have a stake in success. They also get to say, "I told you so" when it succeeds. Allow them to celebrate their achievement, not their failure.

Shirley will increase her possibility for success if she says to her peers, "I think it is in our best interest to streamline our testing procedures. How do you think we can do that? What changes do your recommend?"

3. The Actual Implementation of Change

When your change initiatives are adopted, it will be important to make sure they are actually carried out properly and on time. There are four basic types of communication that give you a measure of control over the behaviors that are necessary for the change process to occur.

Identify specific new behaviors.
Communicate timelines.
Measure the progress of change.
Train the change.

Your ability to control these behaviors will vary according to your position, organizational culture, and support from management. Influence and control what you can, seek help from others if possible, and realize you cannot control everything. Yours is not a perfect world. But you can get a good start by planning.

Identify Specific New Behaviors.   You cannot give people general direction and expect them to create specific achievement. Suggestions to people that they should try harder, become more professional, or work at things more globally, will not result in successful change.

You must be very specific in communicating what must be done. Communicate your detailed expectations and then use the restatement and summary technique discussed throughout this book to make sure everyone understands what new behaviors are necessary.

SPEC

General directions allow for personal interpretations. Specific directions create specific responses.

Successful change does not occur if expectations are not communicated in a precise and clear manner. When the receiver has an accurate comprehension of the specific actions and behaviors required, success and achievement happened.

Communicate Timelines.   When you are driving change in others, timelines must be set to establish when the change is to begin and to identify specific deadlines for completion. Deadlines drive performance. Others must know when they are expected to perform and achieve. Attempting to drive change without clearly communicated timelines allows those who may be resistant to justify or rationalize their lack of active support. Failure to communicate specific timelines shifts control of the change process to the people who are the least motivated to accomplish the objective.

Shirley must recommend specific dates by which the new equipment need to be purchased or certain tests eliminated. She can recommend detailed timelines to begin any new streamlined procedures and deadlines for achieving benchmark performance. People will take change initiatives more seriously if there is a deadline involved.

Do not fall into the trap of waiting until people are ready to change. If they realize you are waiting for them to be ready, they will choose never to be ready! Your role is to clearly communicate your vision, identify consequences, listen to their issues of resistance, involve them in how to bring about the change successfully, and insist that the change process begin at a certain time. They must realize that success will be measured in large part by meeting deadlines.

Monitor Change Initiatives.   The activities, success, and momentum of change must be measured on an ongoing basis. The measuring tools, or metrics, must be clearly identified so that everyone involved in the process knows how their progress is being measured. Monitoring and measuring add a dimension of importance and urgency and serves as the primary bases for evaluation. The measurement tools must be shared openly, so that everyone has access to the information on trends and results. It is very important that those responsible for implementing imposed change realize their activities are being measured. They are being held accountable for the results, and there are consequences for lack of achievement.

When Shirley and her peers establish new internal procedures for testing, they must also determine how the results of change will be measured. The key question is "How will we know if our changes are actually giving us the results we want?"

Train the Change.   When you are responsible for driving change, the necessity of training. The people who will be held accountable for making the change successful must be trained to perform any new skills associated with the change. Whether you provide the actual training or it comes from another source, change must be supported by skill development or it is doomed to failure. New procedures must be trained. It is not enough to just declare intent. New equipment, software, etc., cannot be effectively utilized until everyone has been trained to use it. If you do not provide appropriate training, you provide a built-in excuse for others to fail!

The enthusiasm that accompanies the learning process can be an excellent momentum builder. The frustration inherent in being required to do something you have never been prepared or trained to do frequently sabotages change initiatives. Do not fall prey to overlooked necessity for training. Use your influence to communicate the importance of preparing people to change successfully.

You may make the mistake of assuming that others have the same abilities and skills as you, and can automatically adapt the new behaviors and skills necessary for accomplishing the change. Never assume . . . train.

SPEC

The most important factors in successfully driving change are communicating vision, providing training, establishing deadlines, and measuring the results of change.

Communication Assessment

1. Do you understand the difference between imposed and elected change? *yes* ☐ *no* ☐
2. Do you experience high frustration when others do not initially support your change initiatives? *yes* ☐ *no* ☐
3. Do you understand the two issues of change: moving away from something (pain) and moving toward something (gain)? *yes* ☐ *no* ☐
4. Have you underestimated the importance of communicating your vision of change? *yes* ☐ *no* ☐
5. Do you focus on the future when you present change recommendations? *yes* ☐ *no* ☐
6. Do you fail to acknowledge past achievements when recommending change? *yes* ☐ *no* ☐

7. Do you clearly communicate the consequences of failing to successfully achieve change?   *yes* ☐   *no* ☐

8. Do you fail to listen to and address others' statements of loss, fear, and unfairness in the process of change?   *yes* ☐   *no* ☐

9. Do you share information to help reduce the fear of change?   *yes* ☐   *no* ☐

10. Do you fail to involve others in determining how change will be accomplished?   *yes* ☐   *no* ☐

11. Do you communicate the specific behaviors and expectations necessary to accomplish change?   *yes* ☐   *no* ☐

12. Are the timelines and deadlines of your change recommendation frequently unclear?   *yes* ☐   *no* ☐

13. Do you clearly communicate how the success of change will be measured?   *yes* ☐   *no* ☐

14. Is the importance of training frequently overlooked in your change recommendations?   *yes* ☐   *no* ☐

15. Of the five change issues of vision, measurement, deadlines, consequences, and training, which one provides your greatest communication challenge?   _____

Any *no*-responses to the odd-numbered questions (1,3,5,7,9,11,13) and any *yes*-responses to the even-numbered questions (2,4,6,8,10,12,14) offer opportunities for growth and development. Question 15 is self-explanatory.

Communicating Effectively When Change Is Imposed

When change is imposed upon you and you have no choice, your resistance is the same as anyone else's. No one likes imposed change. Resistance to change by scientific and technical professionals may even be more intense than others' because of your broad knowledge base and passionate identification with your work. You have intense pride in what you do, and when anything threatens to disturb it, your reaction to defend, preserve, and protect is understandable. You may perceive that you know more about the situation where change is being imposed than the people who are actually imposing it. The reality is, you have to manage your response to change just as you expect others to do. There are no exceptions.

You deal with the same issues of loss, fear, and unfairness as others. Unfortunately, in many circumstances the people imposing the change do not have knowledge to communicate to help you deal with your resistance. Others, especially organizational leaders, do not always understand the importance of listening, acknowledging issues, and communicating effectively in the change process. You are often left on your own to work through the challenges of change resistance. Change-related communication is commonly mishandled and the costs of resistance high. Productivity is disrupted and careers can be damaged if change is not dealt with successfully. Do not let this happen to you.

If you have the unfortunate experience of being commanded to change without having the benefit of effective communication, there are a number of things you can do to enhance your own success. Do not allow the weaknesses of others to make you a victim of change. Take personal charge of change!

Seven-Step Model to Effectively Process Imposed Change

The seven steps to process imposed change are these:

1. Discover the *why* of change.
2. Discover the *what* of change.
3. Discover the *when* of change.
4. Discover the *how* of change.
5. Discover the *consequences* of not changing.
6. Review your *options*.
7. Make a *plan*.

Step 1. Discover the *Why*. Understanding *why* change is taking place is just as important to you as it is to others. If the vision is not clearly communicated, your resistance will escalate. Avoid this by actively seeking explanations. Your goal is to clearly understand why the change is being implemented. As with everyone else, your agreement with the change does not matter. By understanding change, you can participate intellectually in its achievement, even when you have no choice.

Avoid any communication that could be perceived as an argument or challenge when you are seeking to discover the *why*. Front-end-loading your message can be very effective in ensuring that your inquiries will not be misunderstood.

SPEC

When you understand the vision of imposed change, you are a participant. When you do not understand the change, you are relegated to the role of reluctant observer.

"I'm anxious to participate in successful change. I need a better understanding of why we are doing this."

"I will be able to more effectively contribute to the change process if I have a better understanding of why it's being implemented. May I ask a few questions?"

"It's difficult to implement something successfully when you're unclear as to why it is necessary. Can you help me understand the necessity for change?"

The people who are leading the change have a stake in your support and success in carrying out tasks necessary for the change to take place. Make it very comfortable for them to share the information with you that will contribute to everyone's overall success. Never become argumentative. Seeking clarification of *why* is not an opportunity to debate. If you do so, people will quickly become reluctant to share information with you, and that is never in your best interest.

Step 2. Discover the *What.* It is imperative that you discover *what* is actually expected of you in processing the change. Encourage others to be specific in their explanation. Ask questions to get clear information on the following:

What they expect of you
What you will be doing differently
What new actions or behaviors are necessary

You might frame your questions in the following ways:

"I'm anxious to begin implementing the change. Help me understand
what you would like me to do differently."

"I want to be sure that I have a clear understanding of what I'll be
doing in this new process."

"I'm a little unclear on what will be changing and what will remain
the same. Can you help me to better understand?"

Step 3. Discover the *When*.   What are the timelines? *When* will you be
expected to begin implementing the change and how long do you have to
accomplish it? As we discussed earlier, a worst-case scenario in a change
environment is to be uncertain about deadlines. You may ultimately be
held accountable for satisfying deadlines of which you were not even made
aware. Ignorance is not bliss. What are the timelines? Do not allow others'
lack of effective communication or unintentional oversights negatively impact your efforts in supporting any change initiatives.

"Help me understand the timelines."

"I need to know the specific deadlines for completing this."

"When is this required for submission?"

"How soon will these changes begin?"

SPEC

*Whenever possible, make time-
lines moot by accomplishing
change initiatives early. It
never hurts to be ahead of the
pack in responding to change.*

Step 4. Discover the *How*.   Has it been determined *how* the change will
actually be implemented? Can you have any input into that process? If so,
always position yourself to be a contributor of creative ideas and solutions. When you see a problem, do not hesitate to articulate it, and make
recommendations to avoid the problem, if possible, and correct it. Once
again, just communicating potential problems without offering solutions
can be deadly. It positions you as being antagonistic toward the change,
not an active supporter. Always communicate solutions in tandem with

problems. It is the difference between being perceived as Chicken Little, squawking that the sky is falling, or as a thoughtful collaborator who anticipates potential problems and develops contingency plans to meet the challenges.

"It's possible that . . . could happen. If it does, this is how I recommend we deal with it."

"Have we given thought to how we would react if . . . happens? This is what I would suggest."

You will have greater identification with the change if you have a measure of influence over *how* it is to be accomplished.

Step 5. Discover the *Consequences* of Not Changing. Do you understand the consequences of not successfully implementing the change? What are the consequences for you personally as well as the entire organization? Confronting consequences sometimes leads to the weakening of resistance. If you realize that failure to comply with this change could result in reduced performance ratings, a negative impact on job security, or perhaps a drastic reduction of your funding, your personal motivation to support and successfully implement the change will probably increase dramatically.

The greater the consequence of not changing, the greater risk you take in not actively supporting the change.

SPEC

Confronting the worst consequence that would happen if you do not successfully implement the change will help you to determine whether allowing your resistance to inhibit your actions and support is wise.

Step 6. Review Your Options. Do you have any additional options concerning the change? Is it reasonable to continue to do things as you always have? Do you have an option to abandon the activity being impacted by the change and perhaps move in a different direction or focus on other pursuits? Can you switch projects, change functions, move to another job or another area of the organization? What are your alternatives? What options best contribute to your long-term goals as well as those of the organization?

Once you identify and assess your options, you increase your control and you make the choice. Now you have actually shifted your personal focus from inflicted change to chosen change, and if you choose to implement and support the change, it will now be chosen change. Options contribute to making you an active partner in the change process and avoiding change victimization.

Step 7. Make a Plan.   Making a plan of action is probably the most important step of the model. By developing an action plan, you commit yourself to supporting the change. An action plan may be personal or formally submitted to others. It may answer questions such as these:

What are you going to do to bring about the change?
What commitments to action and behavior changes are you willing to make?
How will you demonstrate your positive attitude toward the change?

This is not about words; it is about action. How will you walk the walk? You determine how you will demonstrate your commitment to participating in the successful achievement of change initiatives. How will you measure your own performance? Develop your own specific goals and hold yourself accountable. Communicate your goals to the people driving the change and give them permission to help you measure your success. Be willing to take risks and lay your support and commitment on the line.

Communication Assessment
Use this guideline to assess your willingness and ability to support and implement change successfully.

1. Do you know why the change is taking place? *yes* ☐ *no* ☐
2. Are you able to overcome any possible disagreement and support the change effectively? *yes* ☐ *no* ☐
3. Do you understand exactly what is expected of you in support of this change? *yes* ☐ *no* ☐
4. Do you have a clear understanding of the timelines and deadlines? *yes* ☐ *no* ☐

5. Are you clear on how the change is to be accomplished?
   yes ☐   *no* ☐
6. Do you have any input into how to accomplish it and do you have any positive and creative suggestions to enhance accomplishment?
   yes ☐   *no* ☐
7. Have you clearly identified the consequences of not supporting the change initiative? *yes* ☐   *no* ☐
8. Do you understand the potential upsides and downsides for both you and the overall organization concerning the success or failure of this recommended change? *yes* ☐   *no* ☐
9. Have you clearly identified all of your options in dealing with this change? *yes* ☐   *no* ☐
10. Do you have a specific action plan for implementation?
    yes ☐   *no* ☐

Any *no*-responses offer opportunities for growth and development.

What actions will you take?
When will they be completed?
How will you measure your success?
How will others know of your support and achievement of the change initiative?

•   •   •

Because scientific and technical professionals play such an important role in every organization, your support of change initiatives is extremely critical. You must have the willingness and commitment to visibly support the change, not only in your communication but also in your actions and behaviors. Talking about positive change is not enough. You have to be willing to support positive change. Your actions are an important part of your effective communication; they send powerful messages. Whether you are driving the change in others or implementing change that has been imposed upon you, visibly demonstrate your commitment and willingness by letting others witness your supportive actions. If the change requires new behaviors, be the first to implement those new behaviors. If the change requires refraining from past activities, be the first one to give them up. STPs lead by example, whether the change is chosen or imposed. If you want others to support your change initiatives, be an active partner in supporting theirs.

Change is not a one-way street; you cannot support it only when you want to and reject it when it may be uncomfortable or perceived to be unnecessary. Resistance to change is normal. Help others to work through theirs and be willing to deal with your own. Fewer skills will serve you better in your career than effectively communicating in change environments and becoming a committed innovator, supporter, and implementer of change. Nothing is more certain than the inevitability of change. Use the process to your best advantage.

11

Effective Communication in Meetings

You are being called upon to function more and more in interactive team environments. The hierarchical, top-down departmental alignment of the past has given way to the interactive, collaborative team environment. As organizations reorganize and flatten their internal structure, there are fewer front-line and middle managers. Tasks and responsibilities that were previously the domain of managers and supervisors are becoming the responsibility of those who are in staff support or line positions. In the past, information, goals, assignments, and decisions traditionally flowed from the top down. Today, individuals, departments, teams, and groups are finding authority and responsibility at much deeper functional levels of the organization. You are now more interactive and have accountability, not only for accomplishing your own responsibilities, you are also expected to enhance the performance of others.

Frequently you are asked or are required to participate in various types of teams. You contribute to cross-functional process-improvement teams, which are usually charged with reviewing and analyzing a specific function and then making recommendations for improvements (costs, time, efficiency, and so forth). These teams are given a definite period of time to accomplish their objective and then they disband. You and other STPs are highly valued and sought-after team members, owing primarily to your knowledge, intellect, and creativity. It would not be uncommon for you to be involved in a significant number of process-improvement teams during your career.

Crisis management is an area where you are playing a more visible role, especially in these areas:

- Crisis prevention: Anticipating problems and correcting them before they occur
- Response planning: Developing contingency plans to deal with a crisis
- Critical response: Being actively involved in responding to actual crisis when they occur

At one time, damage control was the sole domain of public relations, yet today's scientific and technical professionals are playing a more active role as advisers and counselors in these sensitive circumstances.

Many scientific and technical departments have evolved into self-directed work teams where the members themselves, not a traditional manager or supervisor, make the day-to-day decisions. In many instances, the role of management has shifted from assigning work and approving decisions prior to implementation to reviewing the work and decisions after they have been completed. Shifting more accountability and responsibility to an empowered workforce has changed many of the functions of management in a growing number of organizations.

You may be called upon to lead various types of teams, as well as serve under the leadership of others. Unfortunately, being on teams and contributing to the accomplishment of team objectives is usually *not* a skill taught to people in the scientific and technological communities. You have probably found yourself in the frustrating position of being expected to function in a team environment without having a complete understanding of either the process or the role you are expected to play.

Inherent in any team environment is participation in meetings. The effectiveness of meetings runs the gamut. They can be productive or a waste of very valuable time. Meetings tend to be either very good or very bad. The more people understand their roles, and the greater the team members' communication skills, the more efficient and productive everyone becomes when working in these collective environments. Sometimes scientific and technical professionals are not the best team players. Many of you would much rather work independently, be assigned your own individual goals, and be judged by the quality of your performance rather than be part of a functioning team. Given a choice, most of you would rather work alone or in close collaboration with a few selected peers who share very similar backgrounds. When you are compelled to work in a team, you can become a very productive contributor when you are given the proper guidance and information to understand your role in the process.

In this chapter we will discuss effective participation in team meetings and give you guidelines for success when you are responsible for conducting them or are playing a lead role.

Aligning Your Communication with the Meeting Objective

There are four general functions of a team meeting:

Presentation of Information
Open Discussion
Team Decision Making
Crisis Response

Some meetings will contain elements of all four phases, some will be specifically focused on one. Your communication challenges vary with each function. The team leader may clearly announce the meeting's function or you may have to analyze the circumstance to determine the meeting's function. The effectiveness of your participation is influenced in great measure by your being aware of the meeting's intended purpose and reacting accordingly.

Presentation of Information

At meetings or during segments of meetings that are designed for the presentation of information to the group, group interaction is minimal, and the information is presented in a lecture style (though various visual aids, etc., may be used). One or more designated presenters do most of the talking. Information-only meetings for the whole team are an excellent way of ensuring that everyone has equal access to information and hears the same thing at the same time. Informational meetings or segments are an opportunity to impart information to a wide audience and also avoid the situation where the favored few of the "in" crowd receive their information directly from leadership, while everyone else is forced to scrounge information from rumors, gossip, and the grapevine. Well-conducted informational meetings give people the opportunity to both hear and see information (if visuals are used) and to ask clarifying questions.

Inconsistencies in information occur when people are not given information all at the same time. For example, if a team leader conducts two separate meetings with separate portions of the team, questions are probably asked during one session that may not be asked during the other. This results in one part of the group hearing information not available to the other, which contributes to misunderstandings and to some people feeling left out of the communication loop. Whenever possible, information-only meetings should include the entire team.

SPEC

Your responsibility as a meeting participant is to absorb the information accurately.

Following are some guidelines for participating in information-only meetings.

Showcase Your Listening Skills.   Commit yourself to listening intently. Process all of the information before jumping to any conclusions. Listen as intently to the information whether you agree or disagree. You are not there to discuss, disagree, or analyze the information. The purpose of this meeting is to transfer information from the presenter to the receiver and ensure that everyone is informed.

Limit Your Questions to Clarification Only.   If the information is not clear, it is very appropriate to ask for specific clarification. Take steps to make sure your inquiries are not perceived as challenges. Once again, the best way to avoid this is to front-end-load your message: "I'm not sure I understood. Is it . . . or . . . ?"

Do Not Disrupt the Information Flow.   It is inappropriate to offer comments or to engage in any type of editorializing at an information-only meeting. The information is not being presented to invite your discussion. It is being presented to enhance your knowledge and understanding. Some people seize the opportunity to attempt to debate the leader or other team members, and this usually results in miscommunications and misunderstandings for all. If this becomes a common occurrence, leadership frequently responds by not conducting meetings, which means everyone goes uninformed.

Disagree in Private.   If you are in disagreement with the information that is shared, do not show this publicly, either verbally or nonverbally. When the meeting has concluded, ask to talk to the leader privately to discuss your thoughts or feelings. Do not attempt to engage her publicly. Doing so will look like an inappropriate challenge to either her information or her authority and it invites others to do the same. You may unintentionally

SPEC

While confronting publicly may impress some of your peers, it will erode any relationship and trust you have developed with the leader.

subject the leader to public embarrassment, which rarely works in your favor. She may not get mad . . . she may get even!

The "I'm mad as hell and I'm not going to take it anymore" reaction is not appropriate during an information-only meeting. Be courteous and respectful and withhold comments for private discussions.

Keep Your Own Counsel.   If you disagree with the information shared, avoid the temptation to join in a postmeeting negative criticism frenzy with your peers. If others engage in criticizing and whining and griping, stay clear of their conversations. Sidebar discussions critical of the information, whether they take place in the lunchroom, parking lot, restroom, or wherever, are inappropriate and counterproductive. If you have a point of contention, take it to the leader. She is probably the only person who can do anything about it. Venting to peers cannot bring about any change or positive resolution. It only makes you a part of the problem!

Typical types of meetings for the presentation of information may include the following:

- Updates by management or new policies or procedures
- Results of any follow-up from previous discussions or commitments for action
- A project team learning about the scope of a new project
- A product development team being informed about the results of field tests or their latest prototype
- A network consultant like Mack (Chapter 9) debriefing his internal support people on the feedback from a post-transaction client meeting

What are some typical presentation-of-information meetings in which you are regularly involved?

Open Discussion

Open-discussion meetings or segments are designed to encourage discussion from the entire team concerning information, incidents, strategies, and so forth. They are intended to stimulate interactive group communication: identify options, formulate recommendations, and share opinions. This may be a specific meeting designated to discuss a predetermined topic or it may be a follow-up segment scheduled after the presentation of information.

Here are some guidelines for participation in open discussions.

Do Not Dominate the Discussion. Every group has its habitual discussion dominators. Do not be one of them. Generally people who dominate group discussions do so for positive reasons. They are interested in the discussion, anxious to add their creativity, and of course, feel their input is extremely valuable. It is usually not their intention to override others or deny anyone the opportunity to participate. Dominators are frequently thinking out loud, and the whole group is subjected to listening in on their thought process! They can also be competitively driven, focused not on their contribution but on not allowing someone else to have the last or better word. If you have ever witnessed a couple of meeting dominators play "Can you top this?" you have seen what a negative impact they can have on group discussions. Just as you resent them and dismiss their input, others will resent you if you fall into dominating behaviors.

To avoid dominating, carefully consider what you are going to say before you begin your delivery. This avoids the trap of thinking out loud, as previously discussed. Also assess the percentage of time you are talking in relation to the other people involved in the discussion. If two people are having a discussion meeting, it is probably appropriate for each to talk for 50 percent of the time. If ten people are involved in the discussion, talking fifty percent of the time is obviously dominating.

SPEC

STPs can inadvertently become dominators by attempting to share too much information or becoming defensive if someone disagrees with them.

If you have a special expertise or you feel exceptionally passionate about a specific subject, unequal participation on your part is understandably necessary. Meeting-dominating behavior is often predictable and habitual. The same people do it over and over. Carefully monitor and manage the level of your input.

Encourage the Nonparticipants.   Encouraging all those present at the meeting to participate in the discussion is technically the leaders' responsibility, yet it is appropriate for all team members to encourage others to talk. Some people do not participate in discussions because of risk: perhaps they fear either saying something stupid or getting a negative reaction from certain individuals or the group. Others may not feel that their opinions are valued. Many may refrain from competing with the dominant ones for the opportunity to talk. Nonparticipation is usually not caused by a person's having nothing to contribute. The person may be uncomfortable with the discussion process. Create a safe environment for your peers. Encourage everyone to participate. It is very helpful to say something like this:

> "John, you look pensive and I'm sure you have something to add to this discussion."
> "Susan, you're sitting there quietly and you look like you might have something to say."
> "Shawn, you have a great background in this area. What are your thoughts?"

Do Not Tolerate Criticism of Others.   Have you ever attended a meeting where certain attendees played the role of "input assassins"—

quick to pounce on somebody's comments and reject contributions with their words or behavior. Have you ever been guilty of such negative discussion behaviors?

Never encourage or tolerate any verbal or nonverbal rejection of someone else's comments. Remarks critical of what someone else has said not only inhibit the person's further participation, it limits the input of others as well. If anyone is rebuked, ridiculed, or embarrassed, others are going to refrain from participating to avoid incurring the same reaction. Silent gestures such as rolling your eyes or wincing when someone speaks are as damaging as verbalized comments. If others involved in the discussion participate in any such negative rejection, make it clear that you do not tolerate such behavior:

> "Let's not get into being critical of each other. Let's stay focused on our discussion."
> "Everyone's ideas are valuable. Let's not criticize anyone for their opinions."
> "Everyone has the right to participate without being embarrassed."

Create Multiple Options.   Discussions are more fruitful when they are focused on developing or expanding options rather than limiting them. As the meeting function shifts from discussion to decision making, options begin to be narrowed. In the discussion process, however, the team is best served by looking at all available alternatives. Freely contribute your ideas and encourage others to think creatively. Significant scientific breakthroughs have resulted from the development of ideas that initially seemed irrelevant. The goal of open discussion is to generate a large quantity of information; evaluating the ideas for their quality is done later.

One of the best ways to enhance discussions is to play the hypotheticals.

> "What if . . . "
> "Just suppose . . . "
> "In a perfect world, what would be the best way to address this?"

Examples of typical open-discussion-type meetings may include the following:

- Ideas for interpreting conflicting test results

- Suggestions for correcting a customer-service problem
- Brainstorming the best options for meeting a customer's expectation
- Alternatives for dealing with temporary workload inequities
- An environmental analyst like Shirley (Chapter 10) presenting her change recommendations to the testing team and gathering input from the entire group

Team Decision Making

Many team meetings or meeting segments are specifically intended to generate a formal collective decision. The decision may be recommendations only, or to take specific actions. The first critical step is for the entire team to understand its decision-making authority. If the limits of its authority are unclear, the team may exceed its authority and make the wrong type of decision, which leaves it open to criticism and reluctance by team members to participate in the future. If in doubt about the level of the meeting's authority, seek immediate clarification.

Reaching team decisions is challenging by the mere fact that it is difficult to get a group of people to agree on anything. Rarely is there 100 percent agreement. Team decision making generally means acheiving a group consensus and not just operating on the basis of majority rules. The definitiion of consensus is 75 percent agreement, 25 percent willing to support. Consensus is not always easy to acheive, and the chances for acheiving it are best in an environment where all the team members are given equal opportunity to participate and have their contributions heard.

Resentment runs high when communication is not effectively managed or input is limited only to the leader and the favored few.

SPEC

 *Involvement is the foundation of consensus.*

Following are some guidelines for team decisions.

Do Not Always Expect to Win.   In a team environment, it is unrealistic to expect always to get your way. As in all aspects of life, it is necessary to pick your battles. If it is a decision you feel passionate about, by all means argue intensely and passionately if necessary. In circumstances where you do not have a direct interest or involvement with the decision, or you will not be adversely affected by the outcome, it is probably best to allow others to influence the decision. Realize that discretion is the better part of valor. It is necessary to let others win also. When you support others in the decisions of high interest to them, they are much more likely to support you in yours.

Make Decisions by Systematically Narrowing Options.   In a discussion meeting or meeting segment, the goal is to offer as many options as possible. In decision making the process of elimination begins. The number of possible options is whittled down while the least appropriate are culled out. When you recommend that a particular option not be pursued, always remember that whoever made the initial suggestion probably has some ownership of the idea you may be eliminating. Avoid criticism or off-the-cuff remarks that could be provocative or embarrassing. Always be aware of the importance of helping others save face. Be complimentary of all recommendations, whether they are implemented or not. If one option is being rejected, do not be critical of its value; emphasize instead why another option may be better.

Avoid Malicious Compliance.   "Malicious compliance" means apparently going along with the decision but undermining its success in various ways. Once the team makes the decision to go ahead, it is imperative that you support their collective efforts, even if the decision is contrary to your opinion. Avoid any communication or behaviors that indicate any lingering reluctance or resistance. Never appear to have an internal desire to see the decision be invalid. You gain nothing by trying to be right in the wake of failure. Positioning yourself to say "I told you so" will do untold long-term damage to relationships and perhaps your career. Let your team members know that though you are not necessarily in total agreement, you will do everything within your ability to help this decision succeed. You can say something like this:

> "As you know, this is not necessarily a decision that I totally agree with, and I want everyone to know that I will do everything possible to help it be successful."

"Although this is not my decision of first choice, I support what the
team is doing and will do my share to ensure success."

Don't forget, there will be many times when you will want others to give
you their total support even in the face of their doubts or reluctance.

Scientific and technical professionals are involved in many decision-
making meetings. Typical of such meetings are these:

- Making a final decision on equipment or material purchases
- Allocating budget dollars
- Selecting components for computer design
- Selecting products for specific field applications
- Determining measurement or testing criteria

Crisis Response

Crisis response meetings are called when there is an emergency requiring
immediate action. Though crises differ, there are general guidelines for
managing them that apply to most situations.

Dedicate Time Immediately.   A crisis demands a quick response. Participating in crisis response must become your number one priority. If you
are unable or unwilling to dedicate your time appropriately, communicate
your circumstances immediately. Do not allow others to linger, waiting for
your input. Any worsening of the crisis could be blamed on you, whether
you deserve it or not.

If you decline to participate in a crisis-response meeting situation, always
recommend other people to serve in your place. Never say no without offering alternatives for support. Use the following four-step communication
model:

State your response: *"No, I will not be able to participate."*
Communicate why: *"This is why I will not be able to help."*
Suggest alternatives: *"I would recommend Brittany as my replacement."*
Explain your alternatives: *"The reason why I recommend her is that . . . "*

Stay Focused on the Problem. Not Assigning Blame.   It is important
to focus on the problem and finding a quick solution, not on assigning
blame. The investigation of causes comes later, after the solution.

Your role is to deal with an acute situation that has occurred. Once the problem has been corrected, then any appropriate finger pointing can begin.

If your software has failed, do not begin ranting, raving, or taking in vain the name of the person who designed it. Fix the immediate problem.

It is also important to avoid playing CYA (cover your anatomy) in crisis situations. Valuable response time can be wasted while team members laboriously defend themselves from being made accountable: "I am anxious to work on solving this problem but first, I want to be sure everyone realizes that what happened is not my fault or the fault my department/team/group. I did everything I could to avoid this . . . " ad nauseum.

And the chorus chimes in:

"Yeah, me too."

"Yeah, me too."

"Yeah, me too."

And the crisis-management team hasn't even begun to solve the problem. Position yourself to be the driving force for staying focused.

"Let's be sure we solve the problem first, then we can address accountability."
"Let's avoid blaming and focus on fixing."

Consider Only the Solutions That Are Immediately Available.　Do not get bogged down in hypothetical discussions in crisis situations. Avoid "If only we had this," or "I wish we could do that." Deal only in reality. You can only respond to the crisis with the resources that are available. Lamentations about limitations does nothing to solve the problem. There will be plenty of postmortem time to concentrate on the hypotheticals.

When the Apollo 13 spacecraft experienced the failure of its electrical system and disaster threatened, the crisis response team could only consider the factors they could control on the ground and the resources, equipment, and supplies the astronauts actually had on board. Lamenting the hypotheticals could have cost the astronauts their lives. The Apollo 13 situation is one of the most visible and successful scientific and technical crisis-response efforts in history.

Guidelines for Communication in All Types of Meetings

There are additional communication issues that apply to all types of meetings. Increasing your effectiveness enhances your influence in collective environments. Some of these guidelines may be more applicable for you than others. You decide which ones are most effective in your circumstances.

Digressions

As we all know, it is very easy for meeting discussions to lose focus as the comments and questions begin to wander in many directions. Some meetings meander slowly into oblivion, while others fall apart very quickly. It is always difficult to stay on the topic, especially when those involved are highly creative and knowledgeable. When meeting participants ask questions, make comments, draw analogies, and use examples, it can sidetrack or dominate the discussion. In some cases, people create digressions intentionally. For most groups and individuals, wandering from the primary topic is unintended, yet unavoidable.

To communicate effectively in meetings: *Do not contribute to topic digression.*

If you have an issue to discuss that is not directly related to the current topic or that has the potential to divert the group from its current discussion stream, refrain from raising it until the time is appropriate, or clearly state, "I would like to discuss . . . as soon as we have brought this topic to conclusion."

SPEC

Never allow yourself to be the cause of a digression. Always stay within the communication stream of current topic.

Help Neutralize the Digressions of Others.   If others digress, avoid contributing with statements of agreement, example, or even disagreement. Digressions will become more significant if the fire is fed. Try to steer the discussion back on track.

To neutralize the diversions of others, implement these strategic phrases:

"Those are very interesting comments. Let's be sure to discuss them
    further when we have concluded our current topic."

or

"This change in our discussion is very interesting, and I think we
    should be sure to discuss it in greater depth during our next
    meeting. Let's be sure that we stay on our current topic."

or

"We have established a time limit for our meeting, and although this is a very interesting discussion, we need to get back to our original topic or we won't be able to keep our time agreements."

You do not have to be the meeting leader to address the problem of digressions. It is in everyone's best interest to deal with them as soon as possible. Digressions gain momentum, take on a life of their own, and completely change the focus of the discussion or perhaps the entire meeting. How many times have you left a meeting, mumbling to yourself, "We called a meeting to discuss one topic, and we end up talking about everything but that and now we have to schedule another meeting!"?

Avoid Reacting Emotionally

Do not allow negative emotions to be triggered by team or group discussions. If you feel a negative reaction, allow yourself some time to process the discussion content before you give voice to your reaction. Do not allow yourself to be egged on by others. Many STPs find themselves in the trap of being encouraged by others to engage in negativity. Be wary of people who display "I'll hold your coat while you fight" behaviors. They want to remain in the background while encouraging you to say the things they are not personally willing to risk. Exercise great caution in not allowing others to exert any such negative control over you. Do not become a mouthpiece for your cowardly peers.

Avoid Sending Consistently Negative Messages

Sometimes you may unintentionally create the perception that you are against everything! If there is a new initiative or policy, do you always seem to be against it? If someone proposes an alternative method or process, are you perceived to be the one who can be counted on to regularly shoot such proposals down? Do you always have reasons why anything new will not work? If this is the case, the outcome of your consistent negativity is that people begin to tune out your messages before they are delivered. You know the people in your meetings who are always against everything. Could you be one of them without realizing it? Repeated negativity lowers the impact of your message.

To avoid this pattern of negativity and give yourself more legitimacy and influence in meetings, emphasize your positive messages. It does not serve you well to speak out only when you disagree and remain silent when you are in agreement with a decisions, recommendations, or changes. Silence does not equal affirmation. Make people aware of your agreement by verbalizing your support. As you are willing to speak out when you are not in agreement, make sure that everyone realizes that you also speak out when you agree!

Practice the Positive/Negative Communication Rule

When you have an appropriate negative or critical comment to make, be sure that you preface it, or front-end-load your message, with something positive. This does not detract from the impact of your comment. It establishes the fact that you have a balanced view and sends the message that you are focused on contributing to achievement and cooperation, not obstruction or failure.

If you were in disagreement with some of Shirley's recommendations for change that were outlined in Chapter 10, you could implement the positive/negative communication rule by saying:

"I understand the importance of maximizing our testing efficiency and reducing as many costs as possible. What concerns me is that if we eliminate even some of our more obscure test offerings, we are inviting our clients to seek out our competitors. This proposal could be short-term penny wise and long-term dollar and profit pound foolish."

Notice the absence of *but* in this front-end-loaded message.

Demonstrate Respectful Meeting Behaviors

Be on time for meetings.
Prepare ahead of time for the discussion.
Stay focused on *what* is being discussed, not *who* is saying it.
Avoid any offensive or disrespectful language or references.
Keep your temper (nobody else wants it).
Listen much more than you talk.
Talk in proportion to the number of participants at the meeting.

Communication Assessment

1. Do you communicate effectively in meetings? *yes* ☐ *no* ☐
2. Do you understand your role in a presentation-of-information meeting? *yes* ☐ *no* ☐
3. Do you listen effectively? *yes* ☐ *no* ☐
4. Do you refrain from disrupting the information flow? *yes* ☐ *no* ☐
5. Do you avoid postmeeting peer venting? *yes* ☐ *no* ☐
6. Do you avoid dominating the discussions in meetings? *yes* ☐ *no* ☐
7. Do you encourage others to participate? *yes* ☐ *no* ☐
8. Do you display zero tolerance for criticisms of others' statements? *yes* ☐ *no* ☐
9. Do you contribute to the creation of multiple options? *yes* ☐ *no* ☐
10. Do you understand the level of authority in team decision-making meetings? *yes* ☐ *no* ☐
11. Do you refrain from always trying to win? *yes* ☐ *no* ☐
12. Do you avoid malicious compliance? *yes* ☐ *no* ☐
13. Do you avoid contributing to topic digression? *yes* ☐ *no* ☐
14. Are you successful at controlling your negative reactions in team meeting discussions? *yes* ☐ *no* ☐
15. Do you avoid the pattern of consistently delivering negative messages? *yes* ☐ *no* ☐

Any *no*-responses offer opportunities for growth and development.

Your Guide to Leading Effective Meetings

All STPs are finding more and more opportunities to lead all different types of meetings. Your challenge to lead may be based on your formal position, topic expertise, being selected in the absence of the traditional leader, or taking your turn in the normal pattern of rotation. You may lead by choice or be drafted for the task. Either way, when you are the meeting leader, consider these ideas to increase your communication effectiveness.

Have a Meeting Objective

Why is the meeting being held and what is the intended outcome? Is this a meeting to present information, focus discussion, generate a team or group decision, or respond to a crisis? Do the people involved know the objective and purpose of your meeting?

Poorly communicated objectives result in a high number of people being unprepared. It is difficult to prepare if you are unaware of your responsibility. If you do not have a clearly stated objective, the overall meeting will be seen as an unwise use of time.

Have a Specific Agenda

Meetings do not run themselves. An agenda must be established listing the discussion topics and the approximate time to be spent on each. If you want individuals to present information or facilitate a discussion, you must notify them in advance to allow them time to prepare.

SPEC

Never meet just to meet. Always have a specific purpose/objective.

Do not allow changes to your agenda at meeting time. Some people attempt to introduce additional topics for discussion without giving others the time to prepare and think through the issue. If an important issue is raised, you are better off scheduling another meeting than to allow your agenda to be disrupted.

Adhere to Your Timelines

Start your meeting on time and respect the priorities and time demands of the participants by ending on time. Do not allow your meetings to take on a life of their own. Do not delay the start of your meeting to accommodate latecomers or allow the meeting to run too long, hindering people from getting back to their work on a timely basis.

If people are late to your meeting:

- Never stop the meeting to summarize the discussion to that point. (This forces the people who were on time to actually sit through the meeting twice!)

- Never delay the start of a meeting waiting for the person who is late. (This sends the message to everyone who was on time that their time is less valuable than the person who is late.) Ask the latecomer to meet with you later to cover what they missed.

How long should an effective meeting last? The reality is, people remember the first ten minutes and the last ten minutes of a meeting. If you want to do a great job of communicating in a meeting environment, schedule twenty-minute meetings! Meetings should never exceed one hour. Attention spans are short and people become anxious to return to their other pressing duties. Concentration begins to wane after sixty minutes, and if there are going to be inappropriate flare-ups of temper or intense disagreements, they will probably begin after the sixty-first minute.

Deal Effectively with Dominators

We discussed the importance of your not becoming a meeting dominator. It is equally important for you to deal with dominating behavior in others when you are leading a meeting. You must take decisive action to ensure balanced participation by everyone in attendance.

The best way to deal with dominators is to acknowledge their contribution, compliment them on their intellect and creativity, and ask for their understanding and cooperation in allowing others to participate as well.

An effective communication technique for dealing with dominators is this:

> "Sean, those are excellent comments and I really appreciate your creativity. I would also like to hear from others who may have some additional ideas."
>
> *or*
>
> "Thanks for your idea, Lauren. I'd like to hear from some others before you expound on that or flesh it out for us."
>
> *or*
>
> "Before we entertain follow-up comments, let's hear from everyone at least once."

If you do not successfully deal with dominators during your meetings, you diminish the overall effectiveness of the group. You will receive only a very narrow range of ideas and input, and frequently they are the same ideas rephrased in new terms. You become bogged down with old wine in new bottles. You also deny the group the benefit of receiving the creativity, ideas, and experience of all participants. The group may begin to fracture with people choosing up sides, and you will have to deal with escalating contentious interpersonal issues. Some people will probably avoid attending your meetings because they are tired of hearing the same old ideas and they resent not being allowed to participate.

SPEC

One of the most important things you do as a meeting facilitator is to effectively deal with the dominators.

Confront People Who Engage in Disruptive Behaviors Privately

If you are leading a meeting and someone becomes disruptive, avoid any public confrontation. Generally people who challenge your information are playing to the crowd, at least to some degree. They want an audience. If you engage in a public confrontation, they will win most every time. While you attempt to address the issue and establish commonality and co-operation, they are intent on drawing attention to themselves, being provocative, or disrupting the entire atmosphere of the meeting. They have a stake in causing a stir and they are not constrained by any desire to maintain professionalism, dignity, or respect. Even if you are successful at reasoning with them, it is highly unlikely they will change their position. It becomes very difficult for them to agree or back down in any way in front of the group. Once they have staked out a position, they will defend it regardless of how irrational or inconsistent it may be. They perceive they will lose face by giving in.

In the meeting, counteract their disruptive behavior by using these statements:

"Your points are very interesting, and it's obvious you have some passion about this. Let's get together as soon as this meeting is concluded and finish our discussion."

or

"I can see you have great interest in this topic and have given your
ideas a great amount of thought. I'd like to meet with you as soon
as we adjourn to have an in-depth focused discussion."

SPEC

*When someone becomes disruptive,
delay the discussion and your interaction with them until the meeting
has concluded.*

A note of caution: If you have occasion to deal with individuals whose
comments become personal or clearly demonstrate a lack of respect for
you, other participants, or people who are not in attendance, you must deal
with this circumstance immediately and openly. It is not appropriate to
wait until after the meeting. Even if you were to deal with it effectively
when the meeting is over, the others in attendance do not realize that you
have addressed the disrupter and his comments. They assume that you
were intimidated or unable or unwilling to deal with the problem, and the
negative behavior has gone unchallenged. Your refusal to deal with the incident may be perceived by others as giving it your stamp of approval.

When these unfortunate circumstances occur, immediately call for a
short break and request to talk privately with the disrupter. This indicates
to all participants that you are dealing with the issue and maintaining your
professionalism by doing so in private and not subjecting the group to wit-
nessing a heated exchange. Everyone knows you are dealing with the issue
and they are probably glad they don't have to witness the event.

If an unacceptable disruption occurs, respond by saying:

"I'm not at all happy with the direction our meeting is taking. I'd like
to call for a short ten-minute break, and, Michael, I would like to
talk with you privately."

or

"I think some inappropriate statements have been made. Let's take a
short break and then we will reconvene and continue with our
agenda. Allison, I'd like to talk with you for a moment."

This response is appropriate when anyone makes negative comments
that clearly communicate a lack of respect for others. These include:

- Personal criticisms of others (especially those who are not there to defend themselves)
- Inappropriate language
- Ridicule
- Prejudicial statements of any kind, referring to race, gender, religious, cultural, or age issues
- Threats
- Nonverbal gestures indicating anger or hostility
- Taunting

If there is a group of individuals who band together to cause disruption, offer to meet with them collectively when the meeting is over. Once again, avoid confrontation in front of the entire group. After you have met with the disruptive contingent, it is probably a wise idea to have a follow-up conversation with each one individually. Contentious positions encouraged by others frequently lessen in intensity when the person is confronted privately. Divide and conquer is very effective.

Diffusing a Hostile Meeting

Occasionally you may be presenting information or leading a discussion with a group that is entirely opposed to your message. This is an extremely difficult circumstance for even the most skilled meeting facilitator. As a scientific and technical professional, you may experience this situation with a greater frequency and intensity than other professionals, especially if you are presenting controversial information of espousing unpopular positions.

It is difficult and probably unwise to attempt to reason objectively with a group that is obviously predetermined to be antagonistic toward your information. No matter how well you deliver your message or how valid and important your information may be, a mob-oriented feeding frenzy is likely to occur. The group is intent on attacking you and your message, not processing what you have to say. Any attempt on your part to reason with them will only be rejected and probably escalate their negative emotions. You will end up being put on the defensive and possibly losing control of the entire meeting.

When faced with this difficult situation, it is best to abandon the delivery of your information and attempt to identify the issues that are motivating the group in their opposition. Be flexible and begin to defuse the situation by asking them to help you understand their issues. It is extremely important to make sure the discussion is conducted in a professional and dignified manner and respect is maintained at all times. Be careful that comments do not in any way become personal.

"I would like to hear the specific issues of disagreement. It's very important that we stay focused on problems and not people. Even in the face of disagreement, we will treat each other respectfully."

Record the issues that are raised by using a flip chart, overhead projector, or other visual aid. Be sure to limit your comments or commitments to investigating the issues only. Do not offer any guarantees of actions on your part. Though you are willing to listen and perhaps act as an advocate and investigate the circumstances, you are not willing to be put in the position of taking responsibility for correcting the issues that are raised. It is extremely important to avoid any personal identification with those issues. Do not allow your negative emotions to become engaged. If you lose it and become defensive or accusatory, not only have you lost that battle, you have probably lost the war!

After the group has identified the roots of their opposition, adjourn the meeting and agree to. . .

> . . . conduct a follow-up meeting as soon as possible to discuss the issues further (within seventy-two hours or three working days is recommended).
>
> . . . meet with each individual to discuss the issues further (again, divide and conquer).

SPEC

The ability to defuse a volatile situation involving a group is an extremely valuable skill.

Scientific and technical professionals who cultivate this communication ability increase their value to the organization and themselves.

Conclude with a Meeting Summary

The last portion of any successful meeting consists of conducting a summary and review of the discussion and any agreements reached. This is best achieved by a two-tiered method:

1. Your general summary of the critical points of information that were discussed and the specific identification of responsibilities and accountabilities
2. An effective feedback exercise inviting the group to identify their understanding of the information and commitments

This can be done orally or in writing. Consider selecting a volunteer, sometimes called a clerk, to facilitate the meeting review. Using a flip chart, the clerk leads the group in summarizing the critical information and commitments that were discussed. It is best not to allow the group members to review their notes or any handouts that may have been provided. Ask them to recall from memory. You will quickly be able to determine by observing their summary whether or not there was a successful communication. You will also be able to assess the likelihood of effective follow-up. The more specific the summary, the better. If their summary is incomplete, present the missing information again.

SPEC

It is important to establish specific responsibilities and accountabilities before the meeting ends.

Assign Accountability for Follow-up.

One of the biggest problems STPs face in collective environments is the inconsistency of postmeeting follow-ups. How many times have you heard people say that meetings are a waste of time and nothing ever gets done? The primary reason is that no individual responsibility is clearly assigned, accepted, and communicated to others. If you make a statement such as "This is an important issue and we really need to follow-up on it," the group will probably agree with you, yet nothing will be done. Why? Because personal responsibility was not assigned, and everyone (including you) will assume that somebody else is going to do it. When nobody is responsible, nobody does anything!

To establish responsibility and accountability there are four questions that must get detailed answers:

What is going to be done?
When is it going to be done?
Who is going to do it?
How will you and/or the group know it has been done?

Having specific answers to these follow-up questions will ensure that your meetings will generate concrete results. Do not move from one topic to another or conclude the meeting until these questions have been clearly answered.

Communication Assessment

1. Do you lead meetings effectively? *yes* ☐ *no* ☐
2. Do you ever fail to establish a meeting objective? *yes* ☐ *no* ☐
3. Do you always have a specific meeting plan? *yes* ☐ *no* ☐
4. Do you start meetings late or allow them to run too long?
   yes ☐ *no* ☐
5. Do you ensure that meeting discussions do not become personal or disrespectful? *yes* ☐ *no* ☐
6. Do you confront meeting disrupters publicly? *yes* ☐ *no* ☐
7. Do you neutralize the negative impact disrupters have on your meetings? *yes* ☐ *no* ☐
8. Do dominators tend to unduly influence your meetings?
   yes ☐ *no* ☐
9. Do you always identify commitments for postmeeting follow-up?
   yes ☐ *no* ☐
10. Do you leave some meetings wondering whether your message was delivered effectively? *yes* ☐ *no* ☐
11. Do you conduct postmeeting summaries?
    yes ☐ *no* ☐
12. Are you frequently disappointed that postmeeting commitments are not always kept? *yes* ☐ *no* ☐

Any *yes*-responses to the even-numbered questions and *no*-responses to the odd-numbered questions are opportunities for growth and development.

12

Communication Skills
for Managers

As with all managers, those in the scientific and technical professions face monumental challenges in today's organizational environment. Some of these challenges are similar to those faced by their counterparts in other functions and professions, and many are unique to STPs, due to the tasks and people they influence. Leading people in a scientific and technological environment is far different than ever before in our economic history.

The Realities of Management for STPs

If you are an STP who manages others or you aspire to a management position, you need to be aware of a number of factors. There are some management issues within the scientific and technical community that are unique to that environment.

The Pathway to Promotion

The vast majority of men and women who are elevated to leadership positions are promoted because of their exceptional technical abilities. They have been very good at what they do, and their exceptional individual performance earns them promotion and they become responsible for leading others. Their intellect, experience, and proven record of achievement earn them upward movement.

In some circumstances, people are moved into leadership positions because of longevity. They get promoted because they have been around the longest. This is undoubtedly the least efficient way to select managers. Fortunately, this pattern is becoming more rare. Promotions should never be awarded solely on the basis of selecting the person who has lived and breathed the longest! Obviously, longevity has no correlation to exceptional technical or leadership abilities.

Others achieve promotion in scientific and technical environments through internal politics. They are elevated because they are politically connected to the organization's internal power structure. Though this is a less-than-ideal basis for choosing leaders, those selected through this process at least have an effective internal network of support in place.

Regardless of how the selection is made, management ability or leadership potential is rarely considered. Technical proficiency, longevity, or political connections do not necessarily equate to effective management skills. Those of you who do achieve leadership positions quickly discover that your talent and individual productivity no longer determine your success. Success is judged by your ability to get the job done with and through other people. No longer is your personal productivity of paramount importance. Now, it is your skill in increasing the personal productivity of *others* that counts most. For many of you who become managers this is a rude awakening, especially when you realize that not everyone shares your levels of skill, abilities, and willingness. Scientific and technical professionals who become managers discover they are required to use skills that have previously been undeveloped and untrained. There is much more to managing than just telling people what to do!

Lack of Training

Once you have been promoted, the problem is compounded because it is all too common in scientific and technical environments for managers not to receive the appropriate leadership training necessary to do their jobs. Just as communication and interrelational skill development is not readily available for scientific and technical professionals during their education years, effective management growth and development curriculums are glaring omissions from most organizational training offerings. You are called upon to get the job done with and through others with little or no training. Your responsibility and accountability are high, whereas preparation, training, and ongoing development are nonexistent to low. Apparently, you are expected to have been born with the necessary skills.

Scientific and technical managers are put at great disadvantage because of the absence of skill development. Your typical training consists of someone telling you "We are behind you one hundred percent . . . just go do it!"

Reactive Micromanaging

Many managers in all functions and professions fall prey to the temptation to micromanage, yet it is especially prevalent in the scientific and technical community. In the absence of leadership training, you revert back to behaviors of trying to do it all yourself. This is especially true when stress and pressure escalate. The tendency to try to control more and keep your finger in every pie can become overwhelming. Most STPs chafe under micromanagers, and it ranks among the top complaints they have about the people who manage them. Typical comments are these:

"They just will not leave me alone to do my job."
"She wants everything done her way."

Highly autocratic, authoritarian micromanaging management styles are becoming more counterproductive and obsolete with each passing day. If you have ever been managed by a micromanager you have firsthand experience of the frustration and damage that result.

Poor communication skills contribute to the creation of micromanaged environments. When effective communication exists in all directions, the need for a close, controlling management style decreases significantly.

To effectively meet your challenges as a manager, you must assume personal responsibility for your own training. In many cases, the organization may subsidize your training efforts, and even if it does not, it is in your best long-term interest to invest in yourself and your career. Fund your own growth and development if necessary. Those of you who are willing to pursue the enhancement of your management and leadership skills will receive benefits beyond your own enhanced leadership performance. You will quickly leave your management peers in the dust and will have the golden opportunity to move upward at an accelerated pace. Unfortunately, it is often the case that many scientific and technical managers do not take the initiative to pursue training on their own. When they do, they choose further technical development, pursuing topics of personal interest and comfort. Many do not realize the importance of or are not willing to pursue the development of their own management and leadership skills. Frankly, their loss can be your gain.

Communication and Motivation

The challenge of managing other scientific and technical professionals is further complicated by the issue of motivation. The typical management style in many organizations has in the past been fear or implied threat. Most STPs are not motivated by fear or threat. If their manager somehow threatens their job, most scientific and technical professionals will respond in one of two ways. Those who are the most creative and productive will seek an environment more conducive to job satisfaction. They will simply move on. Talented people are very confident in making elective job changes and most do not hesitate to seek new opportunities if it is in their best interest.

Those who feel that their options are limited react by rebelling and significantly lowering their productivity. They escalate their resistance by reducing their support of the overall organizational goals. Today's scientific and technical professionals are not motivated by fear or a desire to please their managers. They are motivated primarily by personal gain, what they derive from their job. It is not what you could take away from them that counts; it is what they get from their job that really matters. Though individuals define their gain, or job satisfaction, differently, there are some issues of commonality. Your ability to communicate effectively to determine the issues of gain is an important aspect of your job as a manager. Your skills contribute to creating a motivational environment, increasing job satisfaction factors and ensuring that people are happy and highly productive in what they do.

SPEC

 Scientific and technical professionals derive motivation and job satisfaction from many traditional factors such as enjoying what they do, upward mobility, and adequate compensation.

There are other significant motivational factors that you can influence:

Enhance the Perception of Meaningful and Challenging Work.

STPs want to make a difference. They do not want to feel that their efforts are being applied to busywork or in pursuit of activities that do not have a meaningful impact on the organization, its customer base, or their particular area of interest. To successfully manage the staff, it is important for you to continuously communicate and reinforce the importance and value of what they do. One of the best techniques for doing this is to connect STPs to the outcome of their activities. In other words, help them to understand the big picture of what they are accomplishing as opposed to the limited view of their individual function. For example:

- *A chemist conducting tests in a pharmaceutical lab is working to create drug therapies to cure disease or ease pain.* The limited view is conducting tests; the expanded big picture is curing disease or easing pain.
- *A software designer is creating programs to give businesses the capability for greater efficiency and profitability.* The limited view is creating software programs; the expanded big picture is increasing efficiency and profitability for a greater number of businesses.
- *A design engineer is perfecting a safety device to reduce injuries and deaths from industrial accidents.* The limited view is working on a safety device; the expanded big picture is saving lives and protecting families from tragedy.

The more clearly you can communicate the value of the staff's efforts and the vital role they are playing in the achievement of an ultimate goal, the more you stimulate productivity, creativity, and job satisfaction. Challenge yourself to discover new ways to connect the staff to the positive real-world outcomes.

- Walk them through the entire process, allowing them to see what happens after they have finished their individual contributions.
- Conduct on-site customer visits to observe their product or service in its final application.
- Solicit and communicate customer comments or testimonials to stress the satisfaction created by their efforts.

Give Away How-Decisions

In Chapter 10 we discussed the important issues for STPs who are communicating change. These issues are of even greater significance for STPs who are managers. It is extremely beneficial for scientific and technical professionals, who take great pride in and ownership of what they do, to be allowed to determine *how* they are going to achieve their goals or successfully accomplish their tasks. If you want the people you influence to take pride in their work, experience increased job satisfaction, and be more productive, allow them as much latitude in determining their own approach as possible. STPs take pride in their expertise and intellectual capabilities. Let them use these capabilities to figure out how to achieve the organization's goals.

SPEC

STPs are too bright and creative to be denied input into how-decisions.

When delegating responsibility and asking people to come up with their own methods, use the same communications as you do when managing change:

"Here is *what* we are going to do."
"This is *why* we are doing it."
"This is *when* it must be accomplished."
"*How* do you think we can make it happen?"

Though you will not always be able to involve all people in these decisions, especially in areas concerning law, policy, or compliance issues, there are many opportunities to involve them that you may be currently ignoring.

Can you identify a minimum of five current circumstances where you could let go of *how*-decisions?

Provide Appropriate Feedback

When people offer input such as suggestions or ideas, it is of critical importance that you provide timely feedback on the results of their recommendations. While they are willing to be forthcoming with their information and recommendations, many managers do not process this input appropriately. The flow of input dries up quickly and a tremendous amount of valuable creativity can be lost if this information stream is not managed correctly.

SPEC

An effective manager will provide appropriate feedback within forty-eight to seventy-two hours of a recommendation being offered.

"Chris, I thought about the ideas that we discussed a few days ago and I really believe they have merit. We are going to begin to institute them within the next two weeks."

or

"Rich, I've been thinking about the discussion we had a few days ago and how much I really appreciate your ideas. I really don't think we will be able to implement them, here's why . . . "

or

"Michele, I've thought about the recommendations you made on Tuesday. I don't know right now whether we will be able to implement them, and I am continuing to follow-up and find out. As soon as I have an answer, I will let you know."

It is not necessary that you always agree with their input or implement every idea that is generated. The important thing is to honor their effort and intellect by investing your time to provide meaningful feedback to your employees. This communication technique ensures that employees realize their ideas are valued and makes them aware of the outcome of their efforts.

In the absence of this timely feedback, most STPs will assume that their ideas or recommendations were not valued and their frustration will probably lead them to refrain from offering suggestions and input in the future. Rejection, even if only implied, does not encourage future involvement or effort. In the absence of feedback, most people will assume something negative. Even if they do not like your response, it is important to communicate the value of their input by providing appropriate feedback. Doing so sends a message of professional respect, acknowledges the depth of their contribution, and affirms your relationship.

Use Positive Recognition

The most effective communication tool for managers is the use of positive recognition. Unfortunately, most do not use this tool to anywhere near its greatest potential. Today most STPs feel they are underpaid, overworked, and underrecognized. In far too many scientific and technical environments, positive recognition has degenerated into mere silence. People are not told when they are doing a good job, and the implied message is "You receive your paycheck on a timely basis and I am leaving you alone to do your work. What more do you want? If there's a problem, I will let you know. No news is good news."

The fact is, this is not enough. No news is *not* good news when it comes to positive recognition. Everyone wants positive recognition. In the case of STPs, they are willing to work hard to receive it and they *refuse* to ask for it. They are not about to come begging for positive reinforcement. You need to be aware of the efforts and accomplishments of people and provide acknowledgment for the unique contribution they make to overall success. Silence, or the mere absence of criticism, is not sufficient. You must clearly communicate to people when they are doing a good job. Failing to do so escalates resentment and lowers job satisfaction and motivation. Positive recognition incurs no cost, takes little investment of your time, and yields tremendous benefits.

Formal recognition is very important and you should pursue and encourage it for everyone. Many STPs do receive formal recognition for their efforts. They are given awards for achievement and receive testimonials from the people they serve and perhaps receive the recognition that comes with publication of their work.

Effective informal recognition is the element that is lacking in most scientific and technical environments. Informal recognition is looking someone in the eye and thanking them for their efforts and achievements. It is the proverbial pat on the back, or "Atta girl." Undoubtedly you are not receiving the positive recognition you deserve and neither are you giving to others that which they are due. Few things motivate a person more than receiving positive words of recognition.

Guidelines for Giving Informal Recognition.   There are four guidelines for offering informal recognition to people. Incorporate all of these into your messages of positive feedback.

Recognition Must Be Specific. Generalized praise or acknowledgment is perceived to be insincere. Saying to someone, "You're doing a good job, keep up the good work" is a rather hollow endorsement. People do not react positively when they receive such comments. At best, their response is neutral or "ho hum" and they may actually feel resentment or anger because someone thinks they can be conned into working harder by such empty encouragement.

SPEC

Specific recognition honors the recipient for being a unique individual and making a very valuable contribution with his or her efforts.

A more effective alternative is this: "You did an excellent job in solving that problem this morning. You really assessed the circumstance well, diagnosed the root cause, and identified the best option to solve the problem satisfactorily. You really did a good job and I appreciate your efforts."

Always make positive feedback specific. It communicates your awareness of the person as an individual making a unique contribution. All STPs want to be acknowledged for their individual contribution. They want to know they are appreciated and valued.

Communicate Positive Recognition Privately. While formal recognition is delivered publicly for others to witness, informal recognition should be delivered in private one-to-one communications. Offering positive informal recognition publicly may embarrass the person receiving it, and may create animosity in those whose performance is not being recognized. Public informal praising also presents the risk of offering positive recognition to one for achievements duplicated by many. For example, you may recognize one person for her excellent problem-solving effort while there are others who have achieved similar results and were not recognized. The truth is, you may not be aware of everyone's accomplishments. You do not have total knowledge of the everyday, ongoing, minute-to-minute efforts and achievements of all your people. Public praise of individuals runs the risk of creating perceptions of favoritism, which is a significant factor of demotivation.

Go to the person's office or work space, invite him to your office, or meet in a neutral area out of the sight and hearing of others. Communicate your sincere appreciation of his efforts.

SPEC

 *Always give positive informal recognition in private.*

CASE STUDY 7

Lisa is a manager in the IT department of a major retail organization. She requires a monthly report from all her people that includes a status update on their current projects. In a staff meeting she publicly recognized one of her programmers, Coles, for the quality of her most recent report. "Coles, your monthly report was the best I have ever seen. You were very concise in your analysis, all of your projects are ahead of schedule, and your recommendations were very thought provoking. I wish everyone did as good a job in their reporting."

Among the problems Lisa has created with this misuse of recognition are these:

- She has publicly recognized one and publicly criticized the rest of her group.
- She offered no examples of why Coles' analysis and recommendations were exceptional. The rest of the group has no benchmark or reference upon with to judge their reporting and efforts for improvement.
- Coles has now been enthroned as "teacher's pet" and may experience varying degrees of chiding, ridicule, or resentment from her peers.
- The rest of the group is probably thinking "What about me? My reporting isn't bad! Why isn't she saying anything about me?"

Communicate Positive Recognition in Writing. Whenever possible, offer specific positive recognition in writing as well as orally. It does not have to be formal—a handwritten note can be very effective. Putting positive recognition in writing adds both importance and permanency to the communication. Written recognition is tangible proof of acknowledged value.

Real-World Commentary

Frank is a vice president of a company that designs, sells, and services highly sophisticated medical diagnostic equipment. He recounted this experience:

> When I was a regional manager in our medical services division, I managed a number of people who worked in regional offices around the country. My people provided regular maintenance and emergency response service to our client medical facilities. Our people had to have strong electrical and IT knowledge. They also had to have a medical background to effectively do their jobs. Though I visited all of the offices regularly, we communicated primarily by phone, e-mail, and fax. Whenever someone achieved a significant accomplishment or I became aware of an effort that was really above and beyond in serving our clients, I would send a letter thanking him for his efforts. On one of my regional visits I was invited to the home of one of our service specialists for dinner. When she gave me the house tour, I noticed that all of the letters of recognition I had sent to her over the past five years were framed and mounted on the wall in her family room. I realized at that moment how powerful those letters really were and what a great impact they had on people.

SPEC

Positive recognition in writing is something that can be shared with others and its impact lasts for an extended period of time.

It is also an effective strategy to provide copies of recognition letters to other managers, especially those higher up in the organization. Not only does it make them aware of your efforts in recognizing people, it also gives them the opportunity to add their comments and forward them back to the person being recognized. Imagine the impact of getting a note from your boss's boss congratulating you on an achievement!

Focus Positive Recognition on the Quality of Work. In some professions, people prefer to receive feedback about themselves personally. For many, it is very rewarding to know that their managers and peers like them and they are recognized as having exceptionally high quality of character, honesty, and positive intentions. These are also important for STPs, yet they strongly prefer to be recognized for the *quality of their work*. This includes their professional achievements, and their adherence to high standards of ethics. Because they have such a strong identification with what they do, praising their work is tantamount to praising them individually. Though they will never object to recognition focused on them personally, they place much greater value on comments that recognize the quality and importance of their work. Recognizing them for exceptional quality of contribution is more meaningful than honoring them as exemplary individuals. Praise them for their efforts, preparation, thoroughness, and attention to detail. STPs are proud of what they do; let them know you are too!

Communicating Deadlines

Deadlines and time pressures are anathema to STPs. They are driven to produce exceptional quality and they see deadlines as robbing them of the time necessary to produce their best work. Many STPs will abuse deadlines if they are not strictly enforced. As a manager, you must not only communicate the importance of compliance with the established timelines for a project, you must also announce very specific deadlines for beginnings, formal updates, and conclusions. Typically, they will not like the establishment of deadlines and you will probably have some of your most significant conflict with them over issues of timeliness. No matter how uncomfortable it may be, clearly communicate the time parameters and hold them accountable for compliance. If you don't, they will take advantage of you. If you are unclear in communicating deadlines, you provide the built-in excuse of "Sorry, I didn't understand."

As a scientific and technical manager, you will receive the deadline performance that you are willing to tolerate. If you tolerate delays and missed deadlines, you will experience high incidence of delays and missed deadlines.

SPEC

If people realize the failure to meet deadlines is a serious problem, they will comply with your time demands.

Most STPs resent deadlines. They perceive that time pressures consistently deny them the opportunity to perform to their greatest capability. They are driven to achieve at an exceptional rate, and unfortunately, the time pressures of today's workplace environment restricts their ability to do so. In this regard, you must selectively identify circumstances and opportunities when deadlines can be relaxed and timelines can be extended to allow the pursuit and achievement of exceptional quality. Though you do not have the luxury of doing so with every task, it is important to realize the necessity of doing so occasionally. Never allowing STPs to have optimum time for achievement has a cumulative effect. Each situation builds on another, and at some point piled-up deadlines become the straw that broke the camel's back. Break the interconnectedness of these time squeezes by selecting the best opportunities to lower the time pressure and encourage the pursuit of exceptional quality. Even though your options and influence may be limited, this is a valuable strategy in managing today's STP. Time is a management tool that can be used to your advantage or disadvantage.

Delegate to STPs' Strengths

All of the people you manage have unique strengths and individual weaknesses. Part of your role as a manager is to identify these strengths and determine how to use them to the individual's and the organization's best advantage. Identify what people do exceptionally well and seek opportunities to allow them to do more of it! This increases productivity and overall efficiency. It is in the people's best interest because it allows them to build their confidence, take pride in their achievements, and further practice and develop their most valued skills. By delegating to their strengths, you help to provide the building blocks of success.

Delegating to people's strengths does not imply that their weaknesses should be overlooked, ignored, or underdeveloped. Work with them to increase their skills in any areas of need through the provision of training, guidance, and opportunity. Challenge their weaknesses and reinforce their strengths.

Communicate Closure

Many scientific and technical managers find themselves having to deal with employees' resentment stemming from issues or experiences in the past. Some people perceive they have been mistreated by the organization, individuals, or perhaps even past managers. Others may have received abusive treatment in past jobs with different organizations and they bring with them a cynicism or fear that their past negative experiences could be duplicated working for you.

Employees may have experienced downsizing, restructuring, rightsizing, or whatever the current euphemism may be for reducing jobs and disrupting people's lives. The scars and resentment from such experiences run very deep. It is difficult to position people for future achievement if they are bogged down in issues of the past. Among the people you currently manage may be some who have personal resentment toward you because you were promoted or hired and they were denied the position. They think they should have your job! All of these negative emotions, whether based in legitimate experience or self-serving rationalizations of past circumstances, converge to add to the complexity of your task of getting the job done with and through others.

SPEC

Helping others to achieve closure increases productivity, improves morale, and enhances the overall work environment.

Getting them to do it is not easy. Many people choose to continually feed the flames of past resentment. Doing so allows them to blame others for bad events and it also provides justification for current mediocrity. Today's reduced effort is the result of yesterday's perceptions of mistreatment. "It's not my fault that I don't work as hard or achieve as much as others. Look at what this organization has done to me over the years. I've learned that it just doesn't pay to work so hard. Around here, nobody cares." This type of an attitude not only hinders the individual's achievement, it quickly spreads to others and impacts the entire team, group, or department. Employees with such seething resentments quickly spread their negativity to others.

Effective Communication Model for Achieving Closure. Leading others to closure is a difficult yet achievable task. The following is a model with specific language to help you negotiate the process. This model incorporates many of the communication techniques discussed in the previous chapters.

1. Listen to the person's issues of resentment.
   "Obviously there have been some negative events in the past. May I ask what they are?"

2. Restate the content of the message without duplicating the emotion.
   "My understanding is you were denied promotion or taken off an important project/a bonus was withheld. . . . Am I correct?"

3. Acknowledge the past and emphasize the future.
   "I'm sure your emotion is justified. I really do not know how to fix what happened. I do not know how to change the past. I would like to ensure that nothing like that happens in the future. What can we do to make sure it never happens again?"

   Once you have had this discussion, the individual may want to continue to rehash his issues. His emotions are so tied up in the past, he is anxious to discuss his perceptions over and over. In a relatively short period of time, he may approach you and want to have a similar discussion. If he does, go to the next step.

4. Point out the similarity of the discussion.
   "Is this the same topic we discussed last week? If so, I really do not know what to do about that. We have already acknowledged there is nothing that can be done to repair what has already happened. I don't think it's in either of our best interest to continue to rehash it."

5. Reestablish future focus.
   "Once again, I will be happy to discuss how we can avoid future problems. I just do not want to continue to dwell on the past."

An additional technique for helping to achieve closure: "How can I help in getting past this? What can we do to acknowledge what happened, put it behind us, and move on? Is there any way I can help gain closure on this issue?"

Given the pace of today's workplace and the issues and events that are escalating resentment, the challenge of helping others achieve closure continues to intensify. Probably STPs do not experience more incidents of past-based negativity and resentment than others, and they certainly do not experience any less. Because of their intense personal identification with their work, many of the bad events they experience become personal and their reactions are very intense. If you have people who appear unwilling or unable to seek closure, it may be appropriate to recommend getting help from an outside source. Counseling may be available through the healthcare provider, faith affiliation, or your employee assistance program. You cannot compel them to pursue this avenue of assistance, yet it is certainly appropriate to recommend and encourage it. Some people are so consumed by past events they need help in finding some form of reconciliation.

Communication Assessment

1. Do you effectively communicate to people how important and meaningful their work is?   *yes* ☐   *no* ☐
2. Do you ignore opportunities to include staff in decisions of *how* things are to be accomplished?   *yes* ☐   *no* ☐
3. Do you provide timely feedback (within 72 hours) on people's ideas and recommendations?   *yes* ☐   *no* ☐
4. Do you fail to give people the positive recognition they deserve?
   yes ☐   *no* ☐
5. Is the informal recognition you offer. . .

   . . . specific?   *yes* ☐   *no* ☐

   . . . offered in private?   *yes* ☐   *no* ☐

   . . . frequently put in writing?   *yes* ☐   *no* ☐

   . . . focused on quality of work?   *yes* ☐   *no* ☐
6. Do you refrain from communicating deadlines and timelines to people?   *yes* ☐   *no* ☐
7. Do you delegate to people's strengths?   *yes* ☐   *no* ☐
8. Have you ignored or been ineffective in communicating through closure with people?   *yes* ☐   *no* ☐

Any *no*-responses to the odd-numbered questions (1, 3, 5, 7) or *yes*-responses to even-numbered questions (2, 4, 6, 8) identify opportunities for growth and development.

Coaching Skills

Confronting an employee about issues of poor performance or disruptive behavior and helping them to correct their weaknesses is a challenge for any manager. Most managers in the scientific and technical community are not trained in coaching skills, and coaching skills are 100 percent communication skills. Some are reluctant to address these issues with employees for fear of getting a negative reaction. Even if you have been trained to successfully confront and coach employees, it is not a skill most of you enjoy using, nor do you have the opportunity to perfect your skills through practice. These are not circumstances you face every day, and it is difficult to maintain these skills when you only have occasional opportunities to apply them.

The first stage of confronting and coaching employees for correction is to accurately diagnose the root cause of their performance or behavior problem. Before you can communicate the appropriate corrective action or change you want them to make, you must accurately determine the reasons for the problem. Many managers react to problems without first considering the root cause. In fact, it is much easier to tell employees what they are doing wrong than to explain what you want them to do differently.

My book *The Bad Attitude Survival Guide* offers eight corrective actions available to managers:[1]

Increased communication
Training
Relocation of the employee
Removal of barriers
Allocation of resources
Increasing employees' control over their environment
Implementation of the discipline process
Termination

How do you determine which corrective action is appropriate? Use the following questions as guides:

Guidelines for Assessing Corrective Action

1. Does the employee understand the expectations, standards, and objectives for which she is being held accountable?
   yes ☐   no ☐
   If the answer is no, increased communication is probably the appropriate corrective action.

2. Can the employee accurately restate the expectations, standards, and objectives in her own words?   yes ☐   no ☐
   If the answer is no, increased communication is probably the appropriate corrective action.

3. Does evidence or proof exist that the employee has received specific training to meet the requirements of the job as set forth in the job description?   yes ☐   no ☐
   If the answer is no, implementation of training is probably the appropriate corrective action.

4. Can the employee summarize, articulate, or demonstrate the specific steps, guidelines, or procedures necessary to achieve success in the assigned tasks?   yes ☐   no ☐
   If the answer is no, implementation of additional training is probably the appropriate correction action.

5. Does the employee demonstrate the ability to do the job for which she was hired and assigned?   yes ☐   no ☐
   If the answer is no, relocation of the employee to another position is probably the appropriate corrective action.

6. Does the employee question the standards, expectations, and objectives, or express doubts about their validity?   yes ☐   no ☐
   If the answer is yes, implementation of additional training is probably the appropriate corrective action.

7. Does the employee face legitimate barriers in successfully discharging her duties?   yes ☐   no ☐
   If the answer is yes, it is your role as a manager to remove those barriers.

8. Does the employee legitimately face a lack of resources to successfully perform the duties assigned to her?   yes ☐   no ☐

If the answer is yes, *it is your job as the manager to obtain the necessary resources.*

9. Is the employee frequently taken away from normal duties to assist in projects, solve problems, or address crises? yes ☐ no ☐
   If the answer is yes, *increasing the employee's control over his or her environment may be the appropriate corrective action.*

10. Does the employee refuse to meet the expectations, standards, and objectives of the job description duties? yes ☐ no ☐
    If the answer is yes, *implementing the disciplinary process is the appropriate corrective action.*

11. Have all previous attempts to address poor performance and/or disruptive behaviors failed? yes ☐ no ☐
    If the answer is yes *and you have documentable evidence meeting the requirements of your existing organizational policies and procedures, then termination is probably the appropriate corrective action.*

Ten-Step Coaching Model for Scientific and Technical Managers. Once the corrective action has been identified, it is appropriate to communicate your concerns and recommendations to the employee. When you do so, follow this communication model.

1. Communicate your verifiable observations.
   "Here is what I perceive is happening."
   "Our standard of performance is . . . and this is what I believe the current level of performance is."

2. Request and listen to the response.
   "What are your perceptions?"
   "I'd like to hear your thoughts."

3. With the employee, summarize all responses.
   "Let's summarize our perceptions."
   "Let's see if we can agree on our individual perceptions."

4. Seek the employee's recommendation for corrective action.
   "How do you think we can best deal with this problem?"
   "In your opinion, what is the best way to correct this?"

5. State your recommendation for specific corrective action.
"Here's what I think needs to be done differently."
"Here's what I think will fix the problem."

6. Negotiate the commitment.
"What action can we agree on?"
"What agreement can we reach to best accomplish this change?"

7. Identify the method of measuring improvement.
"How will we know if we are being successful?"
"What will we do to measure our correction of the problem?"

8. Assign follow-up responsibility.
"Let's agree on who will be responsible for tracking our success."

9. Summarize the agreements.
"Let's be sure we both understand what is going to happen."
"Let's summarize our agreement to avoid any misunderstanding."

10. State your optimistic view.
"I feel very confident this problem will be corrected."
"There's no doubt we will be successful in bringing about this change."

In summary, the most important thing for you to remember is that your communication effectiveness as a manager has tremendous impact on the people you lead. With your communications you have the opportunity to enhance their productivity and motivation, increase the satisfaction they derive from their job, and in many cases, have a significant impact on their future success.

Ineffective management communication has a negative effect on many issues, including turnover, productivity, absenteeism, and escalations of negativity. Typically, when STPs assess their current and past managers, they give higher ratings to those they consider to be excellent communicators. You have probably had the experience in the past of working for someone who did not communicate effectively. You know firsthand the frustrations inherent in that experience! Be sure to assess your skills, continue to strengthen the areas you do well, and dedicate yourself to overcoming any communication weaknesses. The results will have an impact on your career and on others'.

13

Mastering Organizational Politics

"Politics" is considered to be a bad word by many scientific and technical professionals. Many take pride in their refusal to engage in or play organizational politics. They may perceive this as taking a high road position, yet it is not necessarily a strategy that enhances their careers. The bottom line is, politics makes the world go round. If you choose to remain aloof from organizational politics, do not expect the same positive benefits that accrue to those who understand the issues and cultivate good relationships. By refusing to participate, many of you literally make yourselves political prisoners. The results are generally problematic: access to organizational resources can be diminished and barriers to performance may remain in place for you while they are removed for others.

In the past, you were not called upon to be politically astute. It was not a necessary skill. Today, lack of political acumen is a luxury you cannot afford. Failing to master internal political circumstances can result in having less access or influence and increases the likelihood of being excluded from the main focus of organizational activity. If you want to find yourself on the outside looking in, refrain from internal political involvement. You do not have to like it; you just have to understand it!

One of the reasons you may find yourself at a political disadvantage is that you may not know how to engage in political activity. People in other functions and professions may be more politically astute by their very nature. You are often at a disadvantage because you work independently or in environments somewhat removed from mainstream activity, observations, and discussions. In truth, you and many other scientific and technical professionals just may not know what is really going on in the rest of the organization.

Organizational politics has many different definitions. Some have positive connotations, others are dripping with acrimony. Organizational politics is not "sucking up to the boss." The three cornerstones of internal politics are these:

Being held in high esteem by others
Developing a keen sensitivity to the shifting organizational priorities
    and issues
Building effective relationships

You will have to make a dedicated effort to develop your political awareness and expertise. This is not about learning to be manipulative or Machiavellian. It is about learning to be more influential and competitive in increasingly complex internal political environments. Your communication skills will play a huge role in your ability to develop enhanced political savvy.

Before we continue, complete the following assessment to determine your political strengths and weaknesses.

Communication Assessment
1. Do other departments, teams, or groups appear to have greater access to and influence on organizational leadership than yours?
   yes ☐   *no* ☐
2. Do other individual STPs appear to have greater access to and influence on organizational leadership than you do?
   yes ☐   *no* ☐
3. Do others consistently receive important information before you do? *yes* ☐   *no* ☐
4. Do others appear to consistently receive more resources—including funding, time, support, and staffing—to complete their projects and tasks than you do?   *yes* ☐   *no* ☐
5. Do other STPs appear to be on a faster, more direct career path than you?   *yes* ☐   *no* ☐
6. Can you cite specific examples where others have greater success in garnering support for their ideas or projects?   yes ☐   no ☐
7. Do you frequently feel as though you are at a political disadvantage?   *yes* ☐   *no* ☐

Any *yes*-responses indicate a need to increase your internal political effectiveness. If you answered *no* to all of the questions, either you do not need to read this chapter or you may need an objective second opinion.

The following are a collection of thoughts, ideas, and recommendations to enhance your access, influence, and overall success.

Increasing Your Political Effectiveness

In order to master organizational politics, you need to develop three similar yet distinct basic abilities:

The subordination of self
The willingness to apply your skills in pursuit of work that is not of personal interest
The willingness to support the efforts of others

Subordination of Self

This is the ability to set aside personal desires and perceptions to pursue the goals and objectives of others. This is especially critical as you rise higher up on the organizational ladder. Those who insist on playing the role of Frank Sinatra by perpetually singing "My Way" usually find themselves politically ostracized with diminishing access and influence. It may be one of the reasons they are not promoted into management or senior technical positions. Those who have the ability to say "Whether I support this initiative or not really doesn't matter; if it's what leadership/the boss wants done, I'll give it my total support" find themselves in positions of greater political influence.

CASE STUDY 8

Norah is a research chemist in a consumer products organization. She shared this example.

One of our largest customer organizations strongly recommended that we adopt a process improvement program which they had developed internally. This company was extremely focused on increasing its internal efficiency and wanted to ensure that its suppliers, such as our organization, had this same commitment and dedication. While the customer readily admitted there were no problems with our quality or efficiency, they wanted us to embrace their program to maintain consistency and establish common methods of reporting and communication. We already had a similar program in place, which was very effective and much better than the one being recommended. In fact, changing to the customer's methods would cause us significant internal hassles. We faced the reassigning of personnel and the initiation of some policy and procedural changes, which, frankly, were not really necessary. We were also going to have to do a lot of cumbersome retraining. The hassles were just not going to be worth it. I saw no compelling reason to change our current methods and was personally not in favor of disrupting our system to make meaningless or frivolous adjustments.

I also quickly realized it was very important for both the director of our department and the plant manager to enthusiastically support the customer's wishes. The pending change was obviously political and not necessarily intended to increase our efficiency or enhance our quality. Pressure was coming down from the highest levels to keep the customer happy and further strengthen our relationship. When I realized that the decision and changes were political and not technology- or quality-driven, I was willing to support the change. Some of my peers were not and they made their non-support very clear. They continued to challenge the procedural necessity of the changes we were being told to make, and from their point of view, they were right. They just weren't able to get past their narrow interpretation and see the overall bigger picture. While adopting the changes was a short-term hassle, implementing the changes led to some positive long-term benefits for the customer, our leadership, and, frankly, for me. While making the changes was not going to improve our quality, they certainly weren't going to hurt it either. I sure was not going to be the one standing in the way of making this customer happy, and those who did not support the changes paid a price.

Subordination of self requires flexibility and a willingness to apply one's own efforts and activities to accomplishing the overall greater goals and the important priorities of the moment. Political issues and circumstances tend to be acute: they develop quickly, reach a high intensity for a short period, and suddenly shift or diminish rapidly as the focus moves to other priorities. The pace and unpredictability of political developments run counter to the controlled orderliness preferred by most STPs. Politics is not hard science nor is it driven by the exactness of technology. Developing and maintaining a keen awareness of what the current issues are requires constant vigilance, and many STPs are unwilling to maintain such vigilance. Being without a clear political line of sight puts you at a great disadvantage. Is it a price you are willing to pay?

Pursuit and Support of Work
That Is Not of Personal Interest

Closely aligned with subordination of self, is the willingness to pursue goals and undertake initiatives and tasks that are not necessarily personal choices or favorites. The bottom line is making yourself pursue the work even when you do not want to do it! Many of you vigorously pursue the things you want to do and delegate or procrastinate on the things you do not. Mastering internal politics requires the ability and willingness to balance personal likes and preferences with overall internal organizational interests.

SPEC

You do not have to like it; you do have to make yourself do it!

The true internal political test is that others should never know whether you truly support, like, or have great interest in what you are doing. Your behaviors and communications should never betray your true perception.

Petulant messages such as "I'm only doing this because I have to" do not enhance your political influence. Pouting has low payoff! Maintain your professionalism regardless of your personal thoughts.

Supporting the Efforts of Others

Supporting others in their efforts to achieve success and never blaming, scapegoating, or publicly holding others responsible for problems is an important part of developing strong internal political relationships. Avoid creating in others the perception of achieving personal success at the expense of them, and never be seen as taking credit for the success of others.

When people realize that you always help to portray them in their best light and you do not expose them to criticism to protect or enhance yourself, you become a highly sought out collaborator. People are anxious to work closely with you when you consistently prove that you are willing to share credit for achievements with them and never take credit for their individual work or ideas. Developing internal relationships based on consistent projection of this attitude positions you to seek their efforts and support when you need help from them. If you have built effective relationships, you have an established account from which to draw. If you have not established the relationships, or have somehow been unresponsive or perhaps predatory in the past, people will understandably avoid interaction with you whenever possible.

SPEC

- *Always make others look good.*
- *Never make anyone look bad.*
- *Never take credit for the efforts and accomplishments of others.*

What are the communication tools and techniques you can implement to build successful internal political relationships?

Developing Your Political Tools

In the pursuit of participating in organizational politics, there are a number of skills and behaviors clearly rooted in communication that you can implement to enhance your personal effectiveness.

Invest the Time to Build Effective Internal Relationships

To increase your internal political effectiveness, you will have to make an investment of your time:

- Use breakfast and lunch opportunities for formal or informal contacts and discussions.
- Dedicate time after work to cultivate appropriate important relationships.
- Plan occasional weekend time to support organizational activities.
- Be willing to inconvenience yourself to assist others.

All these activities require the investment of one of your most precious and limited personal assets—your time.

You must also take the time to increase your internal networking exposure. Seek opportunities to meet people in other organizational areas, especially those with whom you do not routinely come into contact. This will require you to extend yourself and to make some sacrifices of time. Get involved in activities not related to your work. Increase your visibility! Whether it is the United Way Campaign or other opportunities for community outreach, dedicate your time to participate. If the organization holds a social function, be sure to attend. Let people see not only that you have great skill in the laboratory, you can also whip up a pretty good barbecue sauce. Not only are you a computer whiz, you also know your way around a baseball diamond. Be willing to use your organizational skills to organize the children's games at the company picnic. There are many opportunities to make personal connections with others within your organization. The higher up the organizational ladder you go, the more meaningful your willingness to participate becomes. Everyone expects the staff to do it, and when leadership or senior people are willing to involve themselves, it sends a huge positive message. *Get involved!*

Extend your professional expertise to addressing organizational issues and solving problems. If a cross-functional problem-solving team is forming, whether it is addressing issues of scientific or technical importance or not, communicate your willingness to participate. With your intellect you can make a valuable contribution, regardless of the topic. As often as possible, offer to use your knowledge and expertise to the advantage of others.

SPEC

It's impossible to meet or communicate with too many people.

When people outside the organization visit your facility, volunteer to conduct their tour, or at least to lead the portion that involves your area or function. There are many ways for you to increase your visibility and network of contacts if you are willing to do so.

The greater your visibility and the more people you have access to, the more career and professional success you will enjoy.

Relate to Others as Individuals

One of the most meaningful efforts you can make is to demonstrate an appropriate personal interest in the people around you. This includes those in your intimate work group and others with whom you have ongoing interaction or whose support you depend upon, either now or in the future. Along with learning about their professional interests and being responsive to their workplace issues, discover and demonstrate appropriate interest in their personal lives as well. Inquiring about family, nonwork activities, and personal interests and achievements is one of the strongest building blocks of relationships. You do not build relationships with others by telling them all about yourself. You do build relationships by allowing others to tell you about themselves. People like people who listen to them. If you want to be likable, be a good listener!

SPEC

Your ability and willingness to listen is your most effective relationship-building communication skill.

There is a distinct line between creating appropriate relationships and becoming too close to the people with whom you work, and there are risks associated with crossing the line. The main problem is the hazards of having to ultimately manage people who have become your "buddies." Do not become so involved with people's personal lives that it causes unwanted problems. Do develop appropriate relationships.[1]

If you read an article that may be of interest to someone, copy it and forward it on. If someone is having a family event, inquire as to how it went. If someone's children are active, ask about their games, plays, recitals, etc. It is important to demonstrate to people that you see them as unique human beings and not merely as one-dimensional performers of a particular function. It is also important to acknowledge that they have personal lives separate and distinct from their professional or organizational pursuits.

Be Responsive to Internal Communications

When requests are made—for information or opinions or assistance of some kind—respond as quickly as possible. Though some of these may be administrative, and are probably a hassle to complete, and are of low priority to you, they are important to someone. Never end up on the list of people who ignore communications by not responding. Do not make others have to chase you for your response. If opinions are sought, provide yours. If a coworker needs information, supply it as quickly as possible or tell them where it can be found. Always be the first to reply, not the last. Be conspicuous by your promptness.

Never Become the Bottleneck

When others are dependent upon you, be responsive. Do not allow any delay or inactivity on your part to cause someone else to have a performance problem. If someone needs your input, approval, or verification, provide it expediently. If work has been transferred to you for interim activity and then it is to be passed on to others, be sure you complete your work in a timely manner. When others are positioned to receive your work and then add their quality or effort, always be sure to support them by performing within the timelines. This includes the submission of paperwork as required. Never put yourself in the position of being blamed for the failures of others. Becoming a bottleneck is a fairly common occurrence for STPs and it increases their negative visibility. Always maintain a consistent flow of activity.

To avoid becoming a bottleneck, you must accurately communicate deadline capability and avoid procrastination. As we have discussed numerous times throughout this book, when others are dependent upon you it is of critical importance that specific timelines and commitments be clearly communicated. You must know exactly when your response is needed. Avoid terms like "right away" or "ASAP" (which for many people means *a*fter *s*ome *a*ppropriate *p*eriod).

Identify specific deadlines. If they cannot be met, the time to communicate that reality is when the task is first assigned, never at the time of failed deadline. Do not wait to hear the agonizing thud of failure to begin explaining yourself or justifying your actions. If you cannot meet the deadline, tell your team members or your boss upfront when they can expect completion. Never say, "I can't have it for you by five o'clock today." It would be appropriate to say, "Five o'clock today is not possible, I can have it for you by ten tomorrow morning." Give them the factual information they need to make their own effective decisions. They may choose to wait for you to complete the task, or find some other alternatives. Do not commit to five and then have to apologize for your unkept agreement.

SPEC

Identify timelines and make early corrections to avoid facing performance failure issues for yourself and others.

If you find that you have committed to a deadline that you cannot meet, it is extremely important to notify people as quickly as possible. If it cannot be done by five, let them know by three. The earlier you involve others in the problem, the more time you allow them to adjust and react. Early communication positions you to become their partner in strategizing for alternatives. Though it is never a comfortable circumstance to inform someone of your inability to keep a commitment, the timing of your notification can lessen the impact. Many STPs hesitate to give early notification to avoid the discomfort of communicating bad news. This is usually an unwise tactic. Unfortunately, priorities shift, other pressures intensity, and current activities take more time than expected. Commitments cannot always be kept. Avoid these circumstances as much as humanly possible and communicate effectively when they do occur.

Never allow missed deadlines to be the result of your procrastination. While others are generally willing to accept occasional unavoidable missed deadlines, they are hard-pressed to accept stark procrastination or outright failure or refusal to perform. Avoid even the appearance of procrastination at all costs.

Building effective relationships hinges upon keeping agreements. People need to know that you can be counted on to deliver. You enhance your political effectiveness if people know that your commitments made are commitments kept.

Avoid Venting

At any given time there may be significant reasons to be unhappy, and regularly occurring events may contribute to your frustration; nevertheless, take great care not to become known as a venter, whiner, or complainer. This means developing the skill of "noncommunication": possessing the wisdom of silence! Never say anything to anyone that you would not be comfortable reading in the weekly newsletter! You never know when your critical comments may come back to haunt you.

Many times venting is done at the expense of others. Do you frequently take someone else's name in vain? One of the most disrespectful things that you can do is to talk about someone when they are not there to defend themselves. If you have ever been in the circumstance of discovering that others have been critical of you in your absence and you were unable to give your side of the story, you know the pain and anger generated by such an experience. If you feel compelled to vent about events or other people, take your critical communication elsewhere! There is nothing more common in today's workplace than a whining complainer. Elevate yourself above the crowd by refusing to participate.

SPEC

Venting or whining is unacceptable.

Venting is a manifestation of the desire to be heard without any accountability. It is problem identification without the commitment to problem solution.

Unless there is a reasonable solution at the conclusion of the communication, venting and critical comments are a waste of time and can come back to get you. If you are identifying a problem and seeking a solution, it then can become a productive conversation. If you are merely seeking agreement or affirmation of your critical negative comments about events or other people, it is unfair, unproductive—and, frankly, immature.

Avoiding critical comments directed toward those above you in the organization is particularly crucial. Though their decisions or actions may seem foolish, remember that they may have access to information and data unavailable to others. Always avoid negative criticisms. Political damage can be done if your statements fall on the wrong ears. You may be called upon to provide tomorrow's leadership for today's venting partner. Always be careful with emotion-driven critical information.

Avoid Cliques or Negative Entanglements

It is very normal to develop a set of especially strong internal friendships. Be careful not to become aligned with a particular group, especially one that acts like a clique, excluding others. Never put yourself in a situation of "us-against-them." Always position yourself to be a supporter of all, antagonist to none, and open to everyone. Your internal activities and support of others should not depend on whether you like them or their being part of your group. Offer enthusiastic support to everyone who can benefit from your expertise and do not limit your allegiance or activities to a specific group. Deny no one access to your knowledge and experience.

No doubt there is some merit to hitching your wagon to a rising internal political star. Closely aligning yourself to someone above you, who appears to be one of the favored few and positioned to move rapidly upward within the organization, can be beneficial. This is a strategy practiced by many and has both upsides and downsides. Though advantageous for some, this can be a hazardous or counterproductive strategy for STPs. You are much better off broadening, not limiting, your alignments. Be aware that if you choose this alignment strategy, it could have a negative result. If the rising star suddenly crashes and burns, you could find yourself buried somewhere in the ashes.

Avoid Perpetuating Conflict

Workplace conflicts will undoubtedly occur, and though many are based on professional disagreements, others will be rooted in interpersonal issues. Regardless of the cause, always be willing to take the initiative to resolve the conflict. Position yourself to be the one willing to take a risk, reach out, and seek interactive resolution. Unfortunately, it is all too common for STPs to withhold any resolution overtures and blame or hold other parties responsible for resolution failure. This is primarily due to a lack of training and skills in the area of conflict resolution, and perhaps an occasional desire to be unyielding. Many people equate attempts to resolve as caving in, when in reality it is a mature attempt to move forward.

Effective communication is always the key to conflict resolution. To successfully resolve conflict, you can use many of the skills discussed throughout this book. In particular, you must effectively:

- Listen to the issues and perceptions of others
- Communicate assertively, not aggressively, avoiding any *you*-based messages
- Separate opinion or emotion from fact
- Avoid negative nonverbal communication
- Implement successful feedback techniques (having people check for understanding in their own words)

Effective Conflict Resolution Model.   There are many effective models for conflict resolution. Some are better than others, and there is no such thing as a bad model. The worst model is better than none at all. This is an effective model; use it until you find something that may suit you better.

1. Confront assertively: "I think there's a problem and I'm sure that we can work it out."
2. State the problem. . .
   . . . assertively.
   . . . respectfully.
   . . . unemotionally.
   . . . supported by facts and data.
3. Confirm your communication by means of a summary: "I want to be sure I have communicated effectively. Help check me out. Summarize my statements."
4. Seek the other person's point of view: "Help me understand how you see the situation."
5. Offer summary: "This is what I heard. Am I correct?"
6. Summarize points of agreement and discord: "These are the points on which we seem to agree [list as many as possible] and these appear to be the few points of contention [minimize as much as possible, avoid distortion]."
7. Offer options and brainstorm agreements: "What works best for both of us?" or "What outcomes can satisfy both of us?"

8. Identify the best option: "This appears to be the best option. Are we in agreement?" *or* "This option looks best to me. What are your thoughts?"

9. Negotiate responsibilities.
   Who is going to do what?
   How will we know it's done?
   What future communication may be necessary?

10. Celebrate your resolution: "I'm really glad we were able to work this out. Thanks for your help and openness."

SPEC

Always allow some time for postreso-lution reconsideration.

Encourage everyone to consider the resolution proposal and reconvene (no longer than twenty-four hours later) to ratify the agreement and review areas of responsibility. It is always a good idea to allow time for reconsideration. Not only does this encourage a quicker resolution because everyone realizes they will have additional time to consider it, you also avoid the possibility of people feeling trapped by resolution commitments they may become uncomfortable with later. Resolution remorse is very common. The resolutions to minor conflicts require little or no time for reconsideration; resolution commitments for significant conflicts can be given up to twenty-four hours for reconsideration. If anyone involved is not ultimately comfortable with the resolution agreements, identify the points of disagreement and negotiate acceptable alternatives. Do not try to enforce unacceptable resolution agreements. Once ratified, resolution agreements are cast in stone!

Do Not Hold Grudges

Many STPs embrace the philosophy of "I don't get mad, I get even." Obviously, this attitude is counterproductive. Be willing to give up the issues of the past and move on. It is important for others to understand that you have the ability to overcome past issues of disagreement and move forward without seeking to extract revenge.

SPEC

Learn from the past—do not continue to live in it. Do not position yourself to be a revenge seeker just waiting for the opportunity to extract your pound of flesh.

Let bygones be bygones. Communicate to those around you that you realize that not everything can go your way and you are above becoming mired in negative thoughts about past events. Communicate maturity to others by focusing your efforts and behaviors on current and future issues.

The most common behaviors that show someone holds a grudge are these:

- Failure to interact (ignoring people perceived to be responsible for past problems)
- Subtly withholding support
- Treating others with lack of dignity or respect

STPs who are seeking revenge do not overtly sabotage someone else's efforts. Theirs is a more subtle response, taking the form of a covert withholding of support. They do not take an action to ensure someone fails, they fail to do something that would contribute to success. The behaviors are of omission, not commission.

Demonstrate Your Ability to Maintain Confidentiality

It is important to be able to keep secrets. Becoming known as someone who allows confidential information to leak or who is willing to selectively share inside information becomes a huge political liability. The ability to maintain confidentiality is highly valued. Although some others may be unhappy when you do not divulge confidential information, it is always in your best interest not to do so. You can state: "I'm not at liberty to share this information. As soon as I can I will. I'll make sure that you and everybody involved hears it as quickly as possible."

Confidentiality applies to both organizational and personal information. Never betray personal confidences and always maintain control of any critical organizational information with which you are entrusted. Make everyone aware that you are trustworthy by consistently maintaining confidentiality. Trust is something that is earned and then extended. It cannot be commanded or requested. When others tell you how trustworthy they are, it is best to be skeptical. When others *show* you how trustworthy they are, you can take great confidence in establishing a mutually trusting relationship. Be guided by this strategy in building your political relationships.

Avoid Any Abrasive or Abusive Conduct

Abrasive or abusive conduct is defined as anything offensive to an individual or group of people, including the following:

- Humor at the expense of others
- Verbal or nonverbal acts of intimidation
- Temper tantrums
- Inappropriate language
- Behaviors that could be construed as harassment

Always keep in mind that offense or harassment is in the eyes of the receivers. As with communication, it is not what you intend that counts, it is what others perceive, how your behavior looks and feels to them. Avoid all communication or behavior that has the potential to be interpreted as abusive or abrasive. It's not about crossing the line of acceptability; it's about not even *approaching* the line!

If others demonstrate such conduct, distance yourself from any indication of agreement and never participate by *adding on*. When spontaneous, humorous statements or observations are made that could be considered abrasive or abusive, be sure to identify your awareness of its inappropriate nature: "Although that may have been funny, and I laughed too, we still must realize that such comments or jokes are not appropriate for the work-place. Let's be sure we avoid those in the future."

One of the most ugly components of abusive or abrasive conduct in to-day's workplace centers around individuals taunting each other. While good-natured teasing and banter are a part of many healthy relationships, there is a boundary that can be crossed when such activity becomes continual or abusive taunting. Never allow or participate in any demonstrations of taunting in your environment, and clearly communicate your displeasure and rejection of the behavior in others. When someone indicates that teasing has gone too far or an area of sensitivity has been broached, immediately back off and encourage others to do so.

Apologize Appropriately

When you have occasion to apologize to someone for your comments or behavior, and everyone experiences those circumstances, do so with maturity and clarity. The failure to make apologies in the workplace does great damage to the person owed the apology and also to the transgressor. We are uncomfortable with apologies and do not know how to extend or receive them. Because of our discomfort, most apologies, unfortunately, go unspoken. Some are miscommunicated in statements of implied blame: "I am sorry you reacted that way; it's not what I intended."

Five-Step Model for Apology.   If you are guilty of inadvertent abrasive or abusive conduct or an apology is appropriate for any reason, use the following five-step communication model.

1. Apologize as soon as possible.
Offer the apology as quickly as possible. Do not allow the circumstance to fester. If necessary, allow a maximum of ninety minutes for emotions to cool and never allow an apology to go unoffered for any longer period of time. Timely apologies avoid any extended damage from the negative incident or comment, and the quicker they are offered, the easier they are to complete.

2. Be very specific.
Do not offer generalized apologies; they contain tremendous potential for misunderstanding. For example, perhaps during a disagreement with a peer you used some inappropriate language. Do not offer a generalized apology such as "Michele, I would like to apologize for what happened this

morning." Michele may perceive that you are apologizing for your entire disagreement, when in fact, you are apologizing only for the use of inappropriate language. If she accepts the general apology, she is likely to have a subsequent intense negative reaction when she discovers that the disagreement still exists! Be very specific with your apology: "Michele, I would like to apologize for the language that I used during our discussion. Although we disagree, it was wrong of me to talk that way." This makes it very clear that you are apologizing for being disrespectful, not for the disagreement.

3. Identify your personal reaction.
Tell them how your behavior makes you feel.

"Michele, I'm not proud of myself when I act that way."
or
"I realize talking that way is offensive to you and it certainly doesn't enhance my argument."
or
"I feel very badly when I treat others with disrespect."

This communicates that your behavior or comments had a negative impact on you as well as on them. It also emphasizes your complete understanding of what actually happened. You are clearly communicating that the problem is not their reaction, it was with your statements or behavior and you are taking responsibility for what happened.

4. Offer a mutually affirming statement.
Commit to avoiding future problems because it is in the best interest of both of you to do so.

"I'm better than that and I will not allow that to happen again. We won't have a repeat of this in the future."
or
"Our working together demands that we both behave maturely, and I promise that this will not happen again."
or
"We need to treat each other with respect and I promise that I will not repeat any similar statements in the future."

5. Thank the other person for his or her understanding.

These are effective workplace apologies that are helpful in your personal life as well.

"I appreciate your understanding."

or

"Thank-you very much for excusing my behavior."

or

"I'm sure we'll both be able to put this behind us, and I thank you very much for your understanding."

Communication Assessment

1. Do you consistently balance your interests and goals with those of the overall organization?   *yes* ☐   *no* ☐

2. Do you avoid or procrastinate on tasks or activities you do not like to do?   *yes* ☐   *no* ☐

3. Do you invest the time to build successful workplace relationships?   *yes* ☐   *no* ☐

4. Do you avoid participating in organizational events?   *yes* ☐   *no* ☐

5. Do you demonstrate an appropriate personal interest in the people you work closely with and those most important to your overall success?   *yes* ☐   *no* ☐

6. Do you hesitate to become involved in cross-functional problem-solving efforts in areas outside of your current responsibilities?   *yes* ☐   *no* ☐

7. Do you respond on a timely basis to all internal communication?   *yes* ☐   *no* ☐

8. Are you ever perceived to be a bottleneck or to be slowing down the success or momentum of others?   *yes* ☐   *no* ☐

9. Do you avoid venting or being critical of others?   *yes* ☐   *no* ☐

10. Are you aligned with any organizational cliques?   *yes* ☐   *no* ☐

11. Do you attempt to resolve conflicts quickly?   *yes* ☐   *no* ☐

12. Do you tend to hold grudges?   *yes* ☐   *no* ☐

13. Do you always maintain confidentiality?   *yes* ☐   *no* ☐

14. Do you engage in abrasive or abusive conduct?   *yes* ☐   *no* ☐

15. Do you personally avoid excessive teasing or taunting and intervene when others may be doing so?   *yes* ☐   *no* ☐

Any *no*-responses to the odd-numbered questions (1,3,5,7,9,11,13,15) or *yes*-responses to the even-numbered questions (2,4,6,8,10,12,14) indicate opportunities for growth and development.

Mastering organizational politics is not just "sucking up" or "brown-nosing" (there are many such disparaging terms). It is facing the reality that politics matter and internal relationships are a significant contributor to personal and professional success. Communication lies at the heart of developing and maintaining these important relationships.

14

In Closing

In 1802, with the help of Robert R. Livingston, Robert Fulton launched a small steam-driven paddleboat. Before that time—since the dawn of creation—humans had never traveled faster than the speed of the fastest horse or the fleetest ship under sail. In 1807, Fulton's ship, the *Clermont*, traveled from New York City to Albany, New York, in the remarkable time of thirty-two hours. Prior to that passage, this same journey took four days by sailing sloop. The voyage of the *Clermont* may well have been the most defining moment in the early Industrial Revolution and it gave birth to a period of unparalleled contributions by scientific and technical professionals to humankind's quality of life. Look how far we have come in two hundred years. It is a mind-boggling experience just to compare today's scientific and technological achievements with those of a mere twenty years ago, let alone comparing our current era with the entire scope of known history.

Is there an end to our scientific and technological capabilities? Who knows? If there is, we certainly are not yet close to approaching it. We are still in the embryonic stages of discovery and are nowhere near to reaching our full potential. As a scientific and technical professional, you must be dedicated to continuing to grow in your ability to communicate with the people around you if you are to reach your full potential and maximize your capabilities. Effective communication skills enhance your professional endeavors and also impact the quality of your personal life. Do not undermine your capabilities or diminish your overall success by clinging to poor communication methods. You are too good to allow yourself to be hindered by the inability or unwillingness to become an increasingly effective communicator. Communication is an acquired skill, so you do not have to settle for ineffectiveness or mediocrity.

To help you in your pursuit of communication effectiveness, we have discussed numerous topics:

- The six critical communication realities that you face in your professional endeavors.
- The importance of building the bridges of effective communication between the content and intent of your message and the emotional impact on and accurate comprehension by the receiver.
- Ways to influence how others receive your communication. We focused on influencing the recipient's ability and willingness to absorb your information and enhancing the accuracy of his or her comprehension.
- The critical skills of giving and receiving criticism successfully.
- Increasing the efficiency of your communication with your boss and other people above you in the organizational hierarchy.
- Effective techniques for communicating your critical technical information to nontechnical people.
- The challenges of effective listening, and the tools for increasing your listening abilities.
- Strategies to deal more effectively with customers and those who provide funding and resources for your activities.
- The specific skills of communicating successfully in environments of change.
- Increasing your success when communicating in meetings and team environments.
- The special challenges and effective communication strategies for scientific and technical managers.
- Techniques for increasing your communication effectiveness while you master the internal politics of your organization

All of this information is critical to your future success and development as a scientific and technical professional. Learning the skills and adapting the techniques and strategies outlined in this book will not be easy. To do so, it will be necessary for you to overcome your lifetime communication patterns and also to establish new methods and create new communication habits in their place. You will not be perfect the first time you try to implement any of this information. Do not burden yourself with such unrealistic expectations. If you do, failure and frustration will set in rapidly.

In fact, some people give up the quest for increased communication effectiveness rather quickly. They see the challenge of changing their communication patterns as intimidating or undoable, and revert back to their previous behaviors almost immediately. Even if this happens to you, having read this book you will at least have a better understanding of why communication problems exist and where they come from, and you will have a greater ability to diagnose the problems when they occur. You will now also have the knowledge to identify the communication errors of others and neutralize their impact on you—they will no longer have the ability to trigger your negative reaction to their advantage. If nothing else, you will exercise increased control over your communication experiences.

Are you willing to take the risks associated with change—risk temporary failure on your way to success—and persevere and diligently practice the techniques contained in this book? If so, you will experience personal growth and a relative explosion of communication effectiveness. The key elements in that growth will be *repetition . . . repetition . . . repetition.* The choice is yours. Either the willingness is there . . . or it isn't. Only the person whose face you see in the mirror can provide the answer to that question.

Test Your Communication Commitment

Please take the time to thoughtfully respond to the following assessment. By doing so you will begin to develop your personal action plan to transfer the information gained from the assessment into tangible results. Completing this exercise will yield your blueprint for success. Here you have the opportunity to tell yourself what you are willing to *commit* yourself to doing differently. Are you ready to make such a life- and success-enhancing commitment?

- List the three most important things you learned from this book.
    1._____
    2._____
    3._____
- List two positive things you are no longer doing that were previously a part of your routine communication skills. Perhaps they have been either forgotten or, for whatever reason, have ceased to be a part of your inventory of communication skills.
    1._____
    2._____

- List five of your most significant communication challenges. Be as detailed as possible, identifying specific individuals and typical predictable circumstances and areas of disagreement.
    1._____
    2._____
    3._____
    4._____
    5._____

- For each of the five challenges identified in Question 3, directly above, list two specific strategies for change you can make in your communication efforts to successfully avoid future problems or miscommunications.

Challenge #1
Strategy 1 _____
_____
_____

Strategy 2 _____
_____
_____

Challenge #2
Strategy 1 _____
_____

Strategy 2 _____
_____
_____

Challenge #3
Strategy 1 _____
_____

Strategy 2 _____
_____
_____

Challenge #4
Strategy 1 _____
_____
_____

Strategy 2 _____

_____

_____

Challenge #5
Strategy 1 _____

_____

Strategy 2 _____

_____

_____

- List three provocative communication patterns in others that tend
  to trigger negative responses in you. Be as specific as possible.
    1._____
    2._____
    3._____
- List ten specific things you will do to avoid allowing yourself to
  react with negative emotion to the provocative circumstances you
  listed in Question 5, above.
    1._____
    2._____
    3._____
    4._____
    5._____
    6._____
    7._____
    8._____
    9._____
    10._____
- List three specific things you will do differently to communicate
  more effectively with your boss.
    1._____
    2._____
    3._____
- List five specific techniques you will implement to increase your
  listening effectiveness.
    1._____
    2._____
    3._____
    4._____
    5._____

- List three people who would benefit from getting a copy of this book as a gift.
  1._____
  2._____
  3._____

NOTES

chapter 1

1. *U.S.A. Today*, Oct. 28, 1999, page 28A.
2. CNN Interactive, October 2, 1999, Associated Press, "Mars Probe Mishap Shows Metric System Still Tripping Up Americans."

chapter 4

1. Harry E. Chambers, *Getting Promoted: Real Strategies for Advancing Your Career* (Cambridge, Mass.: Perseus Publishing, 1999).

chapter 7

1. Sally Scobey, *Focused Listening Skills*, Career Track Audio Presentation (CareerTrack Publications, 1996).
2. Ibid.

chapter 10

1. Harry E. Chambers, *The Bad Attitude Survival Guide: Essential Tools for Managers* (Cambridge, Mass.: Perseus Publishing, 1998), page 257.

chapter 12

1. For more information on corrective actions available to managers, see Harry E. Chambers, *The Bad Attitude Survival Guide: Essential Tools for Managers* (Cambridge, Mass.: Perseus Publishing, 1998).

chapter 13

1. You can find out more about this issue in Harry E. Chambers, *Getting Promoted: Real Strategies for Advancing Your Career* (Cambridge, Mass.: Perseus Books, 1999), pages 152–154.

INDEX

ABOUT THE AUTHOR

Harry E. Chambers, president of the Atlanta-based training and consulting group Trinity Solutions, Inc., is an internationally known performance improvement specialist, working with organizations that are committed to improving the productivity of their managers and staff. He specializes in leadership development, diagnosing and correcting performance problems, increasing communication effectiveness, and dealing with people who demonstrate bad attitudes and negativity.

With a reputation for providing content-rich programs that focus on delivering real-world strategies and techniques, he has earned a client list that includes United Technologies, the Marriott Corporation, *Inc.* Magazine, the Make-A-Wish Foundation, and the International Brotherhood of Electrical Workers.

He, his wife Christine, and son Patrick live in the Atlanta suburb of Peachtree City and a cabin in the north Georgia mountains.

For more information, please contact Harry E. Chambers and Trinity Solutions, Inc., at 1–800–368–1201.

E-mail: trinitysol@aol.com

Web: www.trinitysol.com